UNITED TILL I DIE

First edition

B. MacInnes

D1438474

Published by:

Bruce MacInnes
8 Camberwell Drive, Ashton-under-Lyne,
Lancashire OL7 9SW

Photo section set between pp. 128-129

Arthur H. Stockwell Ltd., bear no responsibility
for the accuracy of events recorded in this book.

ISBN 0 9539890 0 3
Printed in Great Britain by
Arthur H. Stockwell Ltd.
Elms Court   Ilfracombe
Devon

Dedication:

This book is dedicated to my three children, Robert, Natalie and Alex, with all my love and affection.

Preface

The author wishes to state that this is an accurate account of his life as a Manchester United supporter. Any errors or inaccuracies are due to slight lapses in memory due to the passage of time. No books were used to check the results or events in this book. All persons, friends and acquaintances mentioned, are those that I have met up with during those years. Some have knowledge of being mentioned in this book, and there is no intentional disrespect to anyone whatsoever, and no offence is intended when describing incidents that have occurred.

Bruce MacInnes.

United Till I Die

My first chapter details how I became involved in following the greatest club in the world, through the eyes of a Manchester United fanatic.

Here I was a fourteen-year-old average schoolboy footballer who had dreams of playing for Manchester United like every schoolboy player. My idol at this time was the great Denis Law. I was sent to see the headmaster, Mr Heaton, at Saint Damian's Roman Catholic School in Ashton-under-Lyne, Lancashire, for drawing him saluting with his trademark arm in the air, scoring another great goal for the Reds. A painful experience this was, as I received two of the strap; it hurt, but who cared! In my eyes Law was God!

I remember United winning the European Cup in 1968; I was ten years old, my older brother Wallace another Red was twelve years old. We could not watch the match as we had no television but my dad knew someone who said we could all go round to watch the game. The emotions we experienced that night still excite me to this day. Manchester United were crowned Champions of Europe. The following week Dad bought me my first pair of football boots; they were Bobby Charlton specials, with a big rounded toe; nothing like the 'Predator', the like of which David Beckham wears today. Dad's motto was please concentrate on your school work Bruce, football should come second. 'Not in my eyes' I thought!

I left school at fifteen. I remember it was Easter and I had an apprenticeship to start as a pipe-fitter/welder at Clayton Aniline in the September. On the Saturday, Manchester United were playing at Southampton. Dad had said to Wallace and I that we could not travel that far to watch a football match, so Wallace had an idea. We decided to ask Dad if we could go camping on the fields near to our house, which would give us time to go to the game by train. Dad agreed we could go camping along with our friend, Alan Caine, who now followed Leeds United of all clubs! So the three of us caught the bus to Piccadilly to catch the Football Special down to Southampton to watch the great Manchester United without telling Mum and Dad. The train was full of men wearing the latest fashion; Dr Martens boots, Manchester United scarves round their heads and on both wrists. Little did we realise what was in store for us; United lost the game 2-1; United fans entered the Southampton end before the game, along with the three of us. It was not an all-ticket game, so we just followed the flow from the train station and paid entry into the ground. There seemed to be United fans all over the place; there were two pitch invasions but eventually after the police brought in police dogs, everything was back in order. When the final whistle went, we walked back to the train station, which was about two miles away; all we saw were United fans fighting everywhere. Even then I thought that these fans were not used to seeing their team lose but this seems to be something else which we now call football hooliganism.

The early 1970s was a time when the kids used to go out in gangs, and towns used to fight with each other's gangs. Haircuts were closely cropped, now known as skinheads, and fighting was commonplace. Everywhere we went, we were known as the 'Ashton Mob'. We used to fight with local gangs from Denton, Droylsden and Stalybridge. We were feared at United matches; only the Salford mob stood a chance against us. There were between sixty and seventy of us. At every home game we would meet at Ashton Bus Station then catch the bus to Guide Bridge Station where we would meet the Gorton mob. From here we would catch the train to Piccadilly, where we would then catch another train to Old Trafford. The reason we caught the train is that nobody ever paid, as the guards were always heavily outnumbered by ourselves and so we could all barge past without having our tickets checked. By doing this, we could then use the tickets again as long as they were not clicked. We could do this every week, which we did for seasons on end, until British Rail changed their system, but by then we were going to matches by car and coach.

The local pictures in the 1970s brought out a film called 'Clockwork Orange'; it portrayed violence by gangs and the leader, Alex, the role made famous by the actor Malcolm McDowell, was a hero to most youngsters. I was fifteen when I watched the film at the ABC in Ashton. I had to dress and act like an eighteen-year-old to get into the cinema. After watching the film I thought I was 'Alex the Leader'. We were soon wearing his clothes to copy him. He wore a bowler hat, a white granddad shirt, black vest, white skinners, black Dr Martens boots, a walking stick, make-up, false eyelashes and braces.

I will always remember our most hated team, Leeds United, were playing Wolves at Maine Road in an FA Cup semifinal on a Saturday afternoon. Manchester United had a normal league game at Old Trafford and everyone planned to attack the Leeds crew at Victoria Station after the United match. About 500 lads made their way to Piccadilly to meet the Leeds boys but the police had a heavy presence in the town centre and escorted all the Leeds fans back to their trains. I remember seeing about fifty of their boys all wearing the trademark Clockwork Orange gear and I must say it scared me a little. As it was, United fans ended up fighting with Wolves fans at the station as they were singing the dreaded Munich song; this always caused trouble at the time. The police soon restored everything back to order, then we made the trip back to Ashton talking about our escapades.

United at that time had the best following of all the teams. The violence used to follow them from ground to ground. United fans used to come from all regions. London and Birmingham used to have a lot of our fans. There was not many all-ticket matches in those days and as long as you got to the ground early you had no problem getting in. United were still a big attraction at that time, having just won the European Cup. They still had a great team. Sir Matt Busby had retired; Georgie Best, Denis Law and Bobby Charlton were still idols, even though the latter two were getting on in years.

I remember going to Derby one Boxing Day; we always seemed to play Derby away on that day. It was at their old ground the Baseball Ground, which was only small; United used to take about 5,000 away fans there and always took their end, which was called the Pop Side. The problem was getting out of the ground, as there was always a mad rush to get a seat back on the train. How someone was not killed I will never know. The trick at the time was to gang round the programme sellers then steal all their programmes because at the time United used to accept away programmes, which you could use to get a Cup Final ticket if they ever got there. United lost at Derby, the fans wrecked the train back to Manchester. One trick was to take out all the light bulbs from the train then throw them at opposing fans when the train stopped at various stations. So the journey back was always in complete darkness.

The Ashton mob had a great following, like I said. At home matches we used to stand on the left side of the Stretford End, singing and chanting "We are the left side, e-i-adeo we're Ashton-under-Lyne." The Salford mob were also on the left side and it is from this area of the Stretford End where all the great United songs used to be sung with all our hearts. When we got back to Ashton, we all went to our local pub, which was called the Railway, where we would all talk about the game and how we were going to get to the next match. We also all played for the Sunday pub team, which was in the Ashton Sunday League, but United always came first. I remember one day we were playing at West Ham away and decided to all travel down on a Friday night after the pubs were shut by minibus; so about twenty of us set off to West Ham arriving in London in the early hours of the morning. On the Sunday we had an important cup game against the Ace of Spades from Oldham,

10

so we decided to have a game of football in the morning outside Buckingham Palace on Hyde Park corner until the pubs opened. We then went to a pub near Carnaby Street where we all got drunk; by the time we got to West Ham at about 2 p.m. the gates were about to close. Only Glen Auctolonie and Paul Greenwood got in out of twenty lads who had set off on a Friday night. What a laugh!

Glen was a lovable rogue, who has since sadly died at the age of forty-three by mixing drink and drugs. He was a great Red and is still sadly missed at United matches. Because two people had got into the match, we waited for them. West Ham away was another ground where there was always trouble and that day was no exception. Fighting all over the ground, inside and out. We lost the game 2-1 and decided to stay in London on Saturday night to see the sights. As you can imagine, the state of us, eight of us, had an important game on the Sunday morning! By the time we got back to the minibus, it was time to go straight to the game. We were beaten 4-0. I do not know why we even turned up in our condition, as we were still drunk from the weekend activities. Sunday afternoon was always spent in the pub talking about the next and past matches but the pubs closed at 2 p.m. — we were lucky enough to have a landlord that let us stay behind for a late drink.

My dream was to follow United into Europe. The older lads, including Tommy Price, who is a legend on the Stretford End and still travels with me everywhere, always used to go on about Waterford away in the European Cup. He went to the game with two Reds from Ashton; Tony Braithwaite and Eric Mitchell. Both these lads went to Stamford School in Ashton and were best mates. I can honestly say they were great Reds and very tough people. Their nicknames were Red One and Mitchy. If there was any trouble, they would always be there for you if needed. Sadly they have both passed away. Tony died first through cancer at forty-five years of age. He is buried at Hurst Cross Cemetery in Ashton. It was his wish that everyone came to the funeral in United shirts and I can say no one let him down. You could not

11

get into the church, it was a mass of red and white. Tony was buried in his United shirt; he hated Manchester City more than anything else in his life. I will always remember at the end of the mass, a local singer, Johnnie Rich, sang 'Always look on the bright side of life'. There was not a dry eye in the church. Everywhere you looked, people were in tears. Eric died a year or so later of kidney failure also aged forty-five. He is sadly missed, especially by Ray Price and myself. He came everywhere with us and worshipped United. Although he absolutely hated everyone else, Eric would never call the team even if they got hammered by anyone. Charlie, his nickname, would always say we'd beat them easy next time! It is a great pleasure to say that Eric Mitchell is probably the best United supporter I have known in over thirty years of travelling to see the Reds. His funeral was another sad day. The turnout was unbelievable, you could not get into the church. He is buried next to Tony Braithwaite, side by side in their United shirts, so they can still both reminisce about United games past and present. When United won the treble by winning the European Cup in Barcelona on Sir Matt Busby's birthday, the first thing Ray and I said was "That was for Eric and Tony. All our prayers have now been answered!"

My first City versus United derby match was in 1971 and I have not missed one since then. It was Sammy McIlroy's debut and he scored. The game ended 3-3; it was a great match. I was about thirteen years old and had travelled on Wood's double-decker bus from Ashton, which used to go to all the games. The coaches and buses at the time used to park at the back of the Kippax Street, City's end. When we got back after the game, City fans were smashing the windows of the buses and coaches. Luckily we were sat upstairs watching what was going on — same old story, fighting everywhere, Reds v Blues!!! We just ducked for cover and waited for the driver to set off back to Ashton with a severely damaged bus. United and City fans have a hatred for each other that dates back longer than I can remember. Tony always used to love these matches. His famous words to Chris Harford, one of the lads who never went for trouble, who could never hurt anybody, were "Chris, you'd better stay at the back when we all get to the ground because we meet these bastards head-on at Maine Road". The trouble always started outside City's Social Club. Both sets of fans used to wait for each other and like Tony had said, they would meet head-on. Chris never took Tony's words lightly he always stayed at the back, his words were "Any trouble and I'm off!" At the time City had a Social Club but United didn't have anything for their fans, we always tried to get into their Social Club for a drink but were always politely refused. Another year that there was a great battle at Maine Road, in which again the game ended a draw, was when we all decided to meet at the Bulls Head pub in Piccadilly for a drink, then go on to meet the Salford mob and travel to Maine Road in two Transit vans. So after about ten pints each, and all of us extremely drunk, we travelled to Maine Road; about fifty of us in two vans. As Tony had said, we met the City fans head-on but this time it was outside their pub which was called the Claremont Arms on Claremont Road. I must stress we were heavily outnumbered and had to retreat; Ray Price having been hit by a flying Newcastle Brown bottle thrown from about twenty yards. He was covered in blood but somehow got into the match to watch the game. My saddest memory at Maine Road was seeing City beat us 4-0 in the League Cup; it was a night match and our excuse was that Paddy Roache was in goal. Another sad day was the 5-1 defeat that City fans still talk about today. I was sat in the North Stand, which is City's end, with about 200 Reds but we all got moved to the Platt Lane end before the match started. It was a sad day for United, City played well and I cannot argue with the result. One derby game in the seventies, we were playing City at Maine Road. It was a night game and just before the kickoff the Ashton lads were involved in a brawl with the City supporters on the Kippax Street. They were singing the Munich 58 song, so Bish Walker ran across the road and waded straight into the Blues. Before you knew it, Eric Mitchell, Tony Braithwaite and everyone else, myself included, joined in the fight. The police arrived on the scene arresting both Bish and myself. Just at that moment, a City fan I had known for years from Ashton called David Tomasson, was walking past, he kindly came to our defence and told the police that the Blues had started all the trouble. The police, who were just about to handcuff us both and throw us into the Black Maria, relented, giving us a severe reprimand instead, so luck was on our side. The game was a boring 0-0, draw both City and United had a player sent off. Lou Macari did not appear in the second half along with City's Mick Doyle. After the game there was even more trouble on the way back to Piccadilly. This time we went to the aid of Mick Grogan whose gang from Salford were battling with Blues outside a park. Again the police arrived, so we quickly left the scene. Years later, the Stalybridge branch used to take a double-decker bus to Maine Road with over one hundred lads on board. The City fans never ever came near us again! There is something about derby games that got you going; even the build up to the derby game had you on edge. I always used to have arguments at work every week with a big Blue called Jack Delaney but deep down we still respected each other. City had a player who hated United. It was Mick Doyle, their number 4 at the time. He was living on Saint Albans Estate in Ashton-under-Lyne and lucky for me I was his paper lad! I told every Red I knew where he lived. He used to get verbally abused by all the Reds nearby. We also used to take it in turns to write MUFC on his front door in felt-tip pen!! I still see Mick Doyle to this day. He plays golf at Ashton where I sometimes play. I don't think he hates United half as much now but perhaps we gave him enough reason to, with all our antics. Even in later years, derby matches had the same effect on us. Nobody liked talking to Blues on the eve of a derby. At Clayton Aniline, where I served my apprenticeship as a pipe-fitter/welder, there was a big City following and I must say the City fans outnumbered us. At work, if City ever beat United, it was time to be off sick. It was amazing what a week off could do just to let the dust settle. Like I said before, it was life or death hanging on one result. We served our apprenticeship attending Openshaw College, which was another big Blue area. I will always remember my first day there, I was sixteen and thought how tough I was because I smoked. We were all in the classroom waiting for class to start when I lit up a cigarette.

14

Later on I think the lads said "We knew you were from Ashton when you did that!"

By this time I was attending Man United matches home and away every week without fail. My best friend at the time was a lad called Paul Maher; his nickname was Doss, although we called him Twang Eyes as well! One season we were playing a night game at Coventry so Doss and I decided to have half a day off work to travel to the game with some mates from Ashton. Before I start this story, I must tell you that Coventry has bad memories for me, as two years before, as a fourteen-year-old, I had travelled to Coventry with two school friends, Ian Walker and Terry Preece. We had booked onto Maines coaches to go from Ashton to the match and back. The game was again not all ticket. We were really looking forward to the game. We all wore silk scarves and went to the match. United won; once again we were taken with the flow and entered the Coventry end which was called the West Stand. At the end of the game on the way back to the coach, the three of us were walking back talking about the events of the game when all of a sudden I heard a noise from behind; words to the effect of "Get those Red bastards". Without a thought, we ran as fast as we could to the coach park and eventually caught up with a gang of Reds also walking back to the coach park. As we all turned round, out of breath and frightened to death, we noticed that all that noise had come from one Coventry fan on his own who looked about eighteen. He had chased us up the road for about three hundred yards but given up because we were all too quick for him. I often wonder what would of happened if he had caught up with one of us; we will never know. Would we have stayed to help the one that was caught? Only God knows the answer to that one! Now, as a sixteen-year-old, I'm going back to Coventry as a big Red with a few years' experience of attending big United games behind me. Doss and I had the afternoon off work and we travelled down to Coventry in Mick Walker's car with his brother, Bish Walker, Glen Auctolonie who I mentioned earlier, and a lad called Michael Judge nicknamed Fudgey. Now Michael was another one of those lovable rogues who looked like Paul Newman, with

15

the same cheeky smile! The problem with Michael, even at school, was that he was a very good thief. He was an altar boy at Saint Mary's Roman Catholic Church but even then he used to make extra money by taking the collection money box around the church, and then when Father Couthard let him take the collection behind the altar, he would ensure he had enough money for the lads to buy ice creams and cigarettes. Unfortunately, the last I heard of Michael, is that he had to escape the country for upsetting the wrong people. He is believed to be in America but none of the lads have heard from him in over five years, so we are beginning to fear the worst. We arrived near to Coventry's ground at about 4.30 p.m. and parked the car. We were just going into a local pub for a couple of hours, when we noticed this party going on at a house. As luck would have it, these girls asked us if we wanted to join in the party. Without hesitation, we all entered the house and enjoyed the hospitality offered! We drank the house dry. At about 7 p.m., half an hour before kickoff, I noticed that Mick and Glen had gone from the house. The girls were going mad, accusing us of pinching all their records. Needless to say who had taken them, along with other items! At this point the rest of us decided it was time to make a quick exit, which we did and headed off into the darkness to the game. This next experience will live with me forever, as it is the only time I have ever been in trouble with the police apart from when I was fined £4 by the local bus company for writing 'Bruce MUFC' in felt-tip pen on the school bus upstairs on the back seat! We met up again with Mick and Glen. All six of us entered the West Stand, Coventry's end with other United fans. Just as the teams had come onto the pitch, fighting broke out behind the goal where we were. Coventry fans were fighting some United boys we knew from Denton, so the Ashton lads all joined in, myself included; unlucky for me, the next thing I knew was three policemen escorting me out of the ground into a Black Maria. The police told me I would be appearing in Court in the morning. The other lads called at the police station after the match but were told I was being charged for threatening behaviour. United won the game 2-1 but it didn't matter to me I was scared to death. I was placed in a cell with other fans from both teams and just wanted to get home to Mum and Dad! I can honestly say this experience scared me. The policeman who charged me said if I pleaded guilty I would be let home with a caution. I felt this charge should have been drunk and disorderly but I pleaded guilty to threatening behaviour on the policeman's advice. I was the first to appear in Court the next morning after a sleepless night, and being first in Court, I didn't know whether this was good or bad. I gave my version of events and thought I did well. The three judges spent a few minutes conferring and then gave their decision; £100 fine with £10 costs for the offence, which was the maximum fine the Magistrates could give at-that time. This was a lot of money considering I was only on about £15 a week at Clayton Aniline. They were kind though, they said I could pay it at £10 a week for eleven weeks. I left the Courts in Coventry town centre in the afternoon. United had played Coventry on a Tuesday night. It was now Wednesday afternoon and I had no money at all to get home. Luckily I explained this to a policeman who said he would drop me off at Birmingham New Street Station. He also gave me some money to ring my dad; this I was not looking forward to. As you can imagine, Dad was not happy but said we will deal with it when you get home. What he had to do was drive down to Piccadilly train station and pay for my ticket back to Manchester before I could catch the next train back from Birmingham. Would you believe it, but this train was the Aston Villa special going to Manchester as they were playing Manchester City! All I can say is that I kept my mouth firmly shut the whole journey. Dad was waiting for me at the station. I knew I was in trouble; he said to me "That's it Bruce. No more football matches until you can learn to behave yourself." I can honestly say now I know how footballers feel when they are suspended. So for the next four weeks, I was banned from United matches and it was only through Mum's hard work that Dad relented and decided to let me start watching the Reds again.

This was the only time in over thirty years of watching Manchester United that I have ever been in trouble with the police but I must say there have been plenty of narrow escapes! The ban which Dad enforced, hit me very badly as I missed the next two home games, and what was worse is, Dad had said I could follow United into Europe to watch them play at St Etienne in France. I'd even paid my money to go but he would not change his mind, so I had to miss my first trip into Europe which I was looking forward to very much. The lads had all booked to go and went for three days by coach. The worst part for me was, Dad even let me go to the coach station to wave them all off! He thought 'If this doesn't teach him a lesson, then nothing will.'

At about this time, I met my girlfriend. A girl called Carol Hazlehurst, who I must say took my mind off this ban for the next month. Could I be failing in love? Is there anything more important than Manchester United? I had also just passed my driving test at the second attempt, just after my seventeenth birthday. Mum and Dad had promised to buy me a car if I passed. They kept their word and spent about £300; a lot of money in those days. They bought me a red Ford Cortina. I knew then that my days of travelling by train to games was over — the way to go now was by car. One of my first outings in my new car was to take Carol to visit Duncan Edwards' shrine at Saint Francis' Church in Dudley near Wolverhampton where he was born. Carol's father, Graham, always said to me how good he was and how sad it was that he had perished in the Munich crash due to the severity of the injuries he had sustained. I knew then that I had to pay my respects to this great man. We arrived at the church, which is in the centre of a council estate, where an old woman kindly told me where the priest lived, because the church was closed. The priest was a lovely man. He told me that many people came to visit the shrine. When we walked into the church, the sight I saw made me shiver with pride; there stood the great Duncan Edwards. Two pictures of him were inscribed in the stained-glass windows on the right; one picture showed him playing in his England shirt, the other showed him wearing the red Manchester United strip. I was very proud to be a United supporter. We both thanked the priest then made a donation to the upkeep of the church. I gave my address to the priest, who a few weeks later sent me a picture of the stained-glass windows and underneath was a prayer for Duncan. This is one of my most treasured possessions; the big man sadly died the year I was born and it is with great sadness that I never had the pleasure of seeing him play professional football for Manchester United.

Many years after I had visited Saint Francis' Church, Tommy Price visited the shrine along with his brother, Kevin Baker and Derek How. Derek is the only one of the lads who had witnessed Duncan's football ability. He once told me that he would have gone on to captain England for many years — that was how highly he rated him. They also visited the statue of Duncan in the town centre that had been opened by Bobby Charlton. I was also told that over 50,000 people attended his funeral, which speaks volumes for the man himself. When my ban was finished, I had missed two home matches and Leeds away. That was hard to take. I never wanted to miss Leeds. United hated Leeds even then. I went the season after. At that time, Leeds did not pull big crowds and United used to take over the whole ground. We used to go behind the net in an old stand made out of tin, called the Cowshed, and that's what it was like, a cowshed! The noise the United fans made was deafening. Everyone banged on the tin with the famous chant "We all fucking hate Leeds". At that time it was common practice to wear other team's scarves on your wrists as proof of the spoils of war and having a Leeds scarf was the best proof. Every Red seemed to have a Leeds scarf and I was no exception. We, stole one on the way back to the coach. The trick was to ask the man selling them how much, then just run off as fast as you could. He would not dare chase you, as he would have to leave his stall unattended. I have many fond memories of Leeds, which I will go into detail about later.

Going back to my days as an apprentice pipe-fitter, every so often we would go on a work's trip. One was arranged to go to Liverpool to Ford Halewood to see how they assembled the cars. Yes, you are right, we could not believe that lads from Liverpool actually worked! We thought they were all on the dole! We made the trip by coach. Doss and I decided to wear our silk scarves. Whilst walking around the place, we noticed a lad wearing a Liverpool shirt. He kept hiding round a corner and every so often he would squirt something from an oilcan into the air so that it would fall onto us. He thought this very funny and would then run off laughing to tell his mates. Doss decided to tell the foreman who was showing us around and when he saw the Scouser with the oilcan, he sent him off to wait for him in his office. That took the smile off his face and we all burst into fits of laughter. Back on the coach, heading home, we saw four Liverpool fans going to the match. They were calling us Munichs from the safety of their car and we were giving them the V-signs from the coach. This carried on for a few miles down the motorway when suddenly they were out of sight. After about ten minutes, we pulled into the service station for a coffee break. Would you believe it, there sat in the restaurant were the four Scousers who had been shouting abuse at us. As soon as they saw Doss and myself, along with about forty others, they made a run for it leaving all their food and drink at the table. We were going to make chase when we noticed one of them had a calliper on his leg and thought that's not fair, let them go. We thanked them for the food and drink they had left us; it saved us spending our own money!

By now Carol was always asking me when she could come to an away match with me. That Saturday, United were playing Arsenal away. There was always a great atmosphere at Arsenal and we always used to go into the front of their end, which was called the North Bank. I tried to persuade Carol not to go, but she was having none of it. So four of us travelled to Highbury to watch the game with all thoughts of going into the North Bank out of our heads, now that we had a girl with us. We entered the Clock End behind the goal and watched a boring 0-0 draw. Yes, I was right, the atmosphere was great but the football boring, hence Arsenal's nickname 'Boring, Boring Arsenal'. Disaster struck on the way back; my engine blew up due to lack of oil. Luck has it that Dad had insisted that I joined the AA, and after about three-hours' wait on the M1, we were finally towed back to Ashton. That match cost me dearly; it cost me £200 for a reconditioned engine. On the same Saturday, it was Doss (Twang Eyes) Maher's stag do. He had booked a 52-seater coach to take all the lads to a nightclub in Bolton, called Blightie's. Mick Walker and myself had paid our money to go on the trip but after what had happened to my car, we ended up missing the trip. It was a good job really, as there had been a disagreement in the club between the Droylsden lads and a gang from Bolton. All hell broke loose. The doorman became involved, and in the end, all the lads were thrown out of the club at 11 p.m., with the coach being given a police escort back to Manchester.

In the 1970s, United's ground was closed for two matches because a flick knife was thrown from the Stretford End onto the pitch against Newcastle. Liverpool had kindly offered us the use of their ground along with Stoke City. We were playing against the mighty Arsenal at Anfield on a Friday night; United won the match 3-1. United and Liverpool fans battled on the terraces and it was half and half. We cannot say we took the Kop End, it was too big, but the intense rivalry between the fans was there to see. Liverpool was the team then, and I must say, I was a little bit jealous of their football ability. The following week I had a fall out with a City supporter over Stoke City. He said he had been to Stoke but I caught him out. I knew the visitor's end at Stoke was an open end. He said it was covered. His name was Ian Black. We ended up fighting over this, but the fight was quickly broken up and both of us were sent back to our firms to explain our behaviour. Back at work I feared the worst. I thought I was going to get the sack but I got a written warning and Ian got the same. We became good friends after that and still have a good laugh about it now whenever we bump into each other.

Back into Europe after United had played St Etienne away in the EUFA Cup, the lads came back. Mick Walker and his brother Chris, started telling me all the things that had happened. The police had put the United supporters in an end behind the goal which was like the home team's end. It was like going into the Kop when Liverpool were at home. The United fans were all behind the goal when the French supporters started to throw bottles of wine and bread at them. The United supporters retaliated by throwing them back. This caused fighting to break out which carried on throughout the game. The police blamed the United fans as usual, as did the papers and media. As a result United were heavily fined and thrown out of the tournament. After lengthy discussions with the football authorities, they reversed the decision and United were let off with a fine. They were warned about their team's behaviour in the competition and were also told that they had to play the return leg away from Old Trafford, at least 200 miles away. This fixture was played at Plymouth Argyle's ground on a Wednesday night. My girlfriend's Dad, Graham Hazlehurst, another Red from the old school, who always talked about the '58 Munich team and how great they were, was employed as a long-distance lorry driver at the time, and as luck would have it, he was going to be doing a delivery in Plymouth, so Graham offered to take me if I wanted to go. I never gave it another thought. I asked my Mum to phone Clayton Aniline for me to say I was sick, then took three days off work to go to the game and help Graham at the same time. Let me tell you, a lorry driver's work is not easy. We had to load and unload at every drop we made. It was very hard work. When I had a look at what we were delivering, I could not believe it; it was toilet rolls belonging to Francis Lee! He was the forward for Manchester City who was later to become owner of the club, but at this time he had a toilet roll business in Bolton. Graham and I had a laugh about this. We also kept a few boxes to one side that you could say fell off the back of the lorry! When we got to the lorry park in Plymouth on the night of the game, I realised I had lost my shoe somewhere along the way. It must have fallen out of the lorry, as I used to take them off to let the heater warm my feet. Anyway I had to borrow Graham's slippers to go to the game in; what a sight! We ended up getting two tickets for the match, which was not a classic, but nevertheless United won the game in front of a 36,000 full house. The rest of the lads had watched the game on a big screen set up at Old Trafford, but I had now got even for missing the away leg and felt that by going down to Plymouth to the second leg, it had eased the pain at least a little.

In the 1970s, the team were struggling. The manager, Wilf McGuiness resigned. Wilf McGuiness is now a good friend of mine. I felt the team was getting old. George was becoming hard to handle. I also felt the team did not give Wilf the respect he deserved. Wilf now works at United full time on the corporate side of things and I must confess even after hearing him on about twenty occasions, his stories still manage to fill the corporate rooms with laughter. The 1970/71 Season saw United with a new manager, Frank O'Farrell, the ex-manager of Leicester City. I remember the season well. We were ten points' clear at Christmas. Everyone was saying we would win the League as there was only two points for a win in those days, but yes you're right, everyone knows it took United twenty-six years to win the League! We had a disaster after Christmas and ended up about eighth. No disrespect to Frank O'Farrell, but I felt he was too quiet to be a Manchester United manager. The next few seasons were a fight for survival. Poor old Frank had to go, and in came Tommy Docherty, the ex-Scotland boss. In his first season he saved us from relegation showing no mercy to the old players. I felt that I had to agree, it was becoming sad to watch United week in and week out struggle on the pitch. The following season United were relegated and to this day I cannot believe what happened, even though that season was another struggle. I followed United everywhere, it all hinged on the last game of the season; Manchester City at home on a warm Saturday afternoon. Can you imagine how I felt when I saw my idol, Denis Law, back heel that goal to the Scoreboard End, even though I did not agree with the way Tommy Doc treated Denis, on giving him a free transfer to Manchester City. That back heel broke my heart. Tommy Docherty still lives near to me today. I live in Glossop, Derbyshire and he lives around the corner in Charlesworth. I sometimes see him in the local pub but I can honestly say not many United fans have much respect for him. It is alleged he seems to spend most of his time slagging United off for some reason or another. I also keep in touch with Denis and his family but I will fill you in with more details in future chapters.

Back to that United v City derby; after Denis had scored, he was immediately substituted; no Lawman salute this time. The whole crowd was in silence/disbelief. 'How could Denis do this to me?' I thought. I felt like crying but then my response turned to anger and from the left side of the Stretford End where we all used to stand and sing "We'll drink a drink a drink to Denis the king" saluting our idol, we all enmassed onto the United pitch to try to get the game abandoned. The City players were quick to get off the pitch. I have never seen Mike Doyle run so fast! The City fans in the Scoreboard End ran for cover, but there was nowhere for them to hide. Fighting broke out at the Scoreboard End but no amount of fighting was going to change the result. As it happened, Birmingham won, so no matter what, United would have still been relegated. All I can say is that it was the way we were relegated that really hurt. I went home straight after the match. I felt in shock; my beloved United were out of Division One and in Division Two. What stick I took from the City fans. There was nowhere to hide. All I kept thinking was 'Don't worry Bruce, we'll be back'. Maybe getting relegated was a blessing in disguise for United fans, for it gave the Doc the chance to rebuild the team and he did just that. Firstly he replaced another idol of mine Willie Morgan with Steve Coppell; signed Gordon Hill, king of all Cockneys, from Millwall; a big centre half called Jim Holton — "6ft 2 eyes of blue, big Jim Holton's after you" from Shrewsbury and Gerry Daly from Ireland; but for me the most inspired signing was Stewart Pancho Pearson.

In the pre-season that year, I travelled to watch United play Hull away; they drew 1-1 with Pearson scoring. He ran the game. United had signed him for about £200,000 and I knew instantly he was going to be a success. To replace the Lawman before Stewart, we had tried a number of forwards. Ted McDougal who fell out with the Doc so was sold to Norwich and Wyn Davies the ex-City forward. I felt that this team the Doc was building could get us back into the First Division. Bobby Charlton had decided to hang up his boots and try management. I think it was at Preston North End. I still remember going to Chelsea away for his last match for the Reds; the ground was almost full of United supporters even in the dreaded Shed End at Chelsea. Everyone was singing "Sir Bobby Charlton". United lost the game 1-0. I still have memories of Peter Osgood falling to his knees in front of the Shed End with his hands in the air as if to say to the packed masses of red and white legions "I'm sorry for scoring that goal". That goal was shown on Match of the Day all season. His reaction took me by surprise. I later met Peter Osgood at a sportsman's dinner for my Sunday football team, Haughton Villa. He said that he could not believe the turnout Manchester United fans gave for Bobby. I replied that I could, as Bobby had never let the red shirt down.

At the start of the Division Two season, I could not wait to get my hands on the fixture list to see our fixtures. I remember the first match was an away game at Leyton Orient in London. An Ashton lad, called Keith Jones, decided to hire a 52-seater coach to go down for the game. As usual it was filled with the Ashton mob. By the time we had got to the first service station on the motorway, we had trouble with some other football fans. Another Ashton lad called Ricky Sclar ended up being charged with assault for kicking a police dog, so we now had one empty seat on the coach; but considering there were about seventy of us on board it made no difference. United had a great result at Orient winning the game 2-0. I think Willie Morgan scored. Again there was trouble in the corner near to the corner flag with United and West Ham fans who had somehow got into our end. After the game we stayed in London. Some of us decided to go to the pictures, myself included, to watch the latest film called 'The Exorcist'. People were handing out leaflets outside to say do not watch the film but we were Reds and scared of nothing! We watched the film, and it scared me to death. I could not sleep for weeks!

The Second Division has some great memories for me. I ended up going to forty out of forty-two league games. The only two I missed were one Tuesday night game away at Millwall, not many Reds went to that match I can tell you, and the other game was a 0-0 draw at Portsmouth, which again was a night game. We made a great start to the Second Division campaign not being beaten for fourteen games. We then had to travel down to Norwich where an ex-United boy, Ted McDougal scored to break a great run. I think we lost 2-0. Again United fans had taken the Norwich end, which is called The Barclay Stand. On our way back to the train station, cars were suddenly being pushed into the river alongside the ground. I saw at least two cars pushed in by two lads who I knew.

United was now like a fortress at Old Trafford — 60,000 fans all singing and shouting. They were worth at least a goal start! Red fences had been installed all around the ground. I can remember thinking 'I hope there's never a fire in here, how on earth will they get us out alive'. The Second Division was a great season for me. United's following was unbelievable. Every ground we went to, United fans would take over. The support given was truly amazing. Like I said, I only missed two games. Bish Walker and Dave Wolley went to the Millwall game which I had missed and Bish said it was a bit scary. The football special was only half full; no one really wanted to go to Millwall on a Tuesday night. United won the game with a Gerry Daly penalty. Bish said even the United fans did not celebrate when we scored so as not to give their place in the ground away to the Millwall nutters that were in the ground.

I must say that the football the Doc's team played was what can only be described as breathtaking; the team would all work for each other. One particular game at Old Trafford against Sunderland was played in front of a 60,000 crowd, with the Sunderland fans bringing down tremendous support for their team — they filled the entire Scoreboard End. The Sunderland team had just beaten Leeds in the FA Cup Final at Wembley the year before, with some great players like Ian Porterfield who scored the winner for them, also Mike Horswill and Denis Tueart who later both signed for our rivals Manchester City. What a match this turned out to be. United went behind early on but came back from nowhere to win the match 3-2. The game was voted match of the season that year and was shown on Match of the Day on the Saturday night. It was great to be able to visit different grounds and places which we had not been to before; one of these was Oxford. I decided to hitchhike to the game with a friend called John Siddall, who now works for United as one of their stewards. We set off from Ashton, down to Manchester Piccadilly on the bus, then walked it for miles to the M6 motorway where two girls gave us a lift to Sandbach. There we waited in vain for hours, as no one would give us a lift. I remember it was freezing cold so we both decided to walk down the motorway hard shoulder to the next service station where hopefully we stood a better chance of getting a lift. We walked for about ten miles when a lorry driver stopped, called us a couple of head bangers for walking on the hard shoulder as it was both illegal and dangerous and then offered us a lift. We were also informed that we were heading in the wrong direction but he said he was going to London where he would drop us off at Paddington Station, then we could catch the first train to Oxford from there. The whole escapade was a nightmare from start to finish; it cost us as much for the one-way fare from Paddington as it did for a return fare on the football special from Manchester, so we seemed to have defeated the object of saving some money.

Oxford had decided to treat the United fans with respect and they even had Manchester beer on sale at all the pubs. The train we caught from Paddington was full of Cockney Reds and we made friends with a lot of them, who I still see today at matches. We arrived in Oxford at twelve o'clock on Saturday lunch time, and met my brother Wallace along with most of the lads from Ashton; we all had a good drink in the local pubs then went to the game. United did not lose many games in the Second Division but unfortunately this was one of them. We lost 1-0. The Reds did not mind, we were still top of the league; also there wasn't any trouble at the game, which was unusual. The kind-hearted Oxford authorities had treated the United fans with respect and in return they were all quite well behaved. The problem we had was that there was no way that I intended to hitchhike all the way back to Manchester, so we ended up jumping onto the United special. Wallace and his mate, Glen Bates passed their tickets back through the gates at the station so John and I could use them again to board the train.

We had lots of laughs that season. At one away game at Nottingham Forest, we heard that the Forest fans were game for a fight and had heard on the grapevine that there was to be a mass fight on the bridge over the river. Nottingham Forest wisely decided to give United supporters the whole of their end, which was called the Trent End, in a bid to stop the violence that was planned. United ended up winning 1-0 through another Gerry Daly penalty. United had taken over the ground and filled both ends. Nottingham Forest had a reputation in the seventies of

27

having trouble with their supporters. I remember going on holiday with my parents to Mablethorpe in Lincolnshire. It was a holiday camp and there were about ten Nottingham Forest fans in the bar. They were singing 'Nottingham la, la, la' when they were drunk so my brother Wallace used to wind them up by singing United songs. I was scared to death of them as they were all skinheads but they were not after any trouble they were just letting their hair down! Another time I travelled down to Nottingham was with the Ashton mob in two Transit vans. As we approached the Trent Bridge, we saw the Mossley lads in a bit of trouble. Bish was fighting with some Forest fans. We opened the back doors to join in the fighting when the police came and were just about to arrest me when Geoff Adshead from Clayton Aniline stood up on my behalf. I was Geoff's apprentice at the Aniline and thanked him for helping me out. By now the vans had disappeared, so I went to the game with Geoff, meeting up with the lads at half-time so getting home was no problem.

United had a great time when they played Blackpool away that season. There must have been 20,000 Reds there that day and we all decided to go down for the weekend, setting off on a Friday night. I met my older brother Wallace at his bed and breakfast hotel. His friend had robbed a fruit machine. Somehow we were swapping £2 worth of ten pences for £1 notes so he could get rid of all his change. As usual United took over the entire ground. There was a 100 v 100 game of football played on the beach after the game. United won the game 3-0. I will always remember Jim McCalliog scoring a great free kick towards the masses in Blackpool's end behind the goal.

The derby match that season was against Oldham Athletic. United lost 1-0. They smashed up Oldham town centre that night but we had no complaints about the game. Oldham had a perfectly good goal disallowed that day. Towards the Rochdale Road End, which was packed with Reds, the ball hit the stanchion inside the goal between the crossbar and goal post then bounced back out onto the pitch. The ref somehow missed it. The Oldham fans were going berserk. I don't know how he missed it but it shows that they are only human after all!

One of the away games that season, where United fans got a

28

little bit of a scare, was at Sunderland. We drew 0-0. There were about 500 of us who went up on the football special. There wasn't any trouble before the game but afterwards we all had to make our own way back. We all ended up on the wrong train with all the Sunderland fans. Both teams played in red and white. Everyone was fighting on the train. It was bedlam. Eventually the police came and got the United fans off the train. We had thought it was the football special but had been wrong. I remember walking back to the train station with John Sidhall; we were both starving so we decided to call into the chip shop for something to eat. We ordered our chips when about four Sunderland fans came in and demanded our silk scarves or they would kick our heads in. As luck would have it, at the same time as all this was going on, both Tony Braithwaite and Eric Mitchell with a few of the Ashton mob came in. The Sunderland lads made a quick exit! Tony said "Hurry up Bruce." He got his chips and we walked back to the train station with the older Ashton lads.

In the 1974/75 season, United clinched the Second Division Championship away at Notts County. I was only seventeen at the time. By now, the Ashton and Stalybridge lads were taking our own coaches to away matches. At the game it was fantastic; everyone was celebrating with the song "United are back". The match ended 2-2; the atmosphere was electric. The fans got behind the team. We all congregated behind the goal. When the final whistle went, the real celebrations began. We all used to play three-card brag on the coach; I had devised a system where you knew your hand every so often, even if you were playing blind. This took months of practice to perfect but in later years won me a lot of money off United supporters. It helped to support my away excursions! On the way back from Notts County, I won £10, which was a lot of money then, with ace/king/queen and so bought the lads the first round of beer. Little did they know about my working out the sequences. You could only use this system at three-card brag, as the pack was only ever shuffled when a prial came out, which was very rare indeed.

Talking about this, takes me back to college where Doss and I, along with some other Reds, set up a thick City fan from Hayfield called Alex Huddleston, whom we used to wind up with the song "Alex can't read. Alex can't write, but he can drive a tractor!" One morning break, Doss set up the cards so that I got a prial of threes, which is unbeatable, and Alex a prial of aces. We then played out the game. None of us could believe Alex's face when he saw his hand. He thought he'd won the pools; we were all dying to laugh. Anyway I turned him blind because I felt sorry for him. He threw his hand down on the table and went for the kitty, which was about £6. I slowly turned my hand over one by one; the shock on his face was magic. I jumped up in joy, a prial of threes. He was gutted and just said "You lucky bastard. What's the odds of two prials coming out at the same time? About a million to one." It just shows you how thick those farmers were! I have not seen Alex since those college days but am told he still watches Manchester City.

Back to celebrating the Second Division Championship. When we returned, we visited all the pubs in Ashton town centre, where I drank so much that I was unconscious. The lads didn't know what to do with me but somehow took me home to my dad's in a taxi and explained the situation to them. Apparently I had hammered the whisky and to this day I haven't touched the stuff. It made me so ill that night my mum had to stay with me all night. I stopped in bed for two days afterwards recovering. United had a lot to answer for!

In the League Cup we reached the semifinal losing to Norwich, with Ted McDougall returning to haunt us after drawing 2-2 at Old Trafford. In the second leg we lost 1-0 away at Norwich and my dreams of seeing United at Wembley were in tatters, but at least we were back in Division One.

On our return to the First Division, I can only describe our football again as breathtaking. We ended up third that season. I claimed an unequal record with all the lads of going to every match, forty-two in all. I even went to all the League Cup games, even though City beat us 4-0 at Maine Road. I will not forget that game in a hurry, as on the way back home to Ashton-under-Lyne, my older brother Wallace, along with a lad called Mick

Greenwood plus myself, caught the 216 bus back from Stevenson Square in Piccadilly. We sat upstairs. When the journey started, we had some trouble with City supporters who outnumbered us. Mick Greenwood, who now lives in Australia and works as a bricklayer, was goaded into an argument. Suddenly all hell broke loose. The three of us were badly beaten up all the way back to Droylsden where the gang of City fans jumped off the bus. Wallace had recognised their leader. His name was Carl Madden. A few years later we bumped into him when we were on a night out in Ashton. Glen Auctolonie hammered him in the toilets of the Ashton Hotel pub. I remember thinking that every dog has its day! I could handle the beating up but the 4-0 defeat was hard to take. I also went to every round of the FA Cup, which took us to the final. We lost 1-0 to Southampton at Wembley, which was my first visit there; we all had a great weekend. The weekend was marred by trouble with Tottenham fans in a pub called the Cockney Pride. Chris Walker, Mick's older brother, got arrested for the trouble. I was sharing a room with Bish, his nickname. He was a lot older than me but I loved to hear him tell me all about the United matches from the sixties. Next day we were told Chris would be appearing in Court in London, so we all said we would chip in for his fine. When we arrived at the Courts we could not believe it, Bish had already been sentenced to six months in Wormwood Scrubs. He was the first football supporter to be jailed. He shared a cell with John Stonehouse the politician who had tried to fake his own death, we were all very upset, on the way out a policeman asked for Chris's brother, Michael to hand him his Cup Final ticket; a £4 standing ticket. Mick decided he would give it to the first United fan he saw from Ashton and that was Tommy Price the legend who I mentioned earlier. I still go to matches with Chris Walker and we have a laugh about it now. He had been wearing my brand-new Ben Sherman shirt, which are now back in fashion, when he had been arrested. I keep attempting to get my money back for it, but to no avail.

The return back to Division One was special under The Doc. United were playing with two wingers, Steve Coppell who replaced the great Willie Morgan and Gordon Hill the king of all Cockneys. Gordon always had great semifinal matches but never really turned it on in cup finals. It looked like United were here to stay that season. Steve Coppell was a good winger who would have gone on to play for England more times than he did. It was whilst playing for his country that ended his career. I went to the last game he played for England. Doss Maher had arranged a trip from work to go to Wembley to watch England in their World Cup qualifying match against Hungary. England won 1-0 with Paul Mariner scoring the winner. Steve Coppell was the victim of a horrendous tackle from the Hungarian full back who escaped punishment. He was replaced in the second half by the Aston Villa winger Tony Morley. Sadly Steve never recovered from that dreadful challenge but I am happy to say that he has gone on to be a successful manager. The newspapers were giving us rave reports; I must say the lads all said how could we repeat this season even though we had lost at Wembley. Whilst I was working at Clayton Aniline I became friends with a Red called Joe Sullivan. He once said to me "Bruce, whilst you are at the matches, do you ever see my brother? His name is Pete. Everybody knows him, as he always dresses up like a tramp but he never misses any of the matches." It wasn't long before I knew who he meant. Pete was nicknamed Paraffin Pete. He had the worst voice I had ever heard. Pete wherever you are, I hope you are ok, but please do not start going to the Reds again as United now have a stand for singers, only to try to get the fans behind the team, but whenever Pete started to sing everyone stopped to listen to him; once heard never forgotten!

Again United proved me wrong. The following season, 1976/77, United continued to play good attacking football. They ended up about sixth in Division One. The climax being reaching the Cup Final again against the mighty Liverpool. By now I was a regular footballer for my local Sunday team, along with my older brother Wallace. We were described by the other lads as two outstanding players; Wallace with his skills on the right wing with pace and myself with the strong tackles in central midfield, with the great desire to win at all costs. That season Cup Final tickets were proving impossible to get hold of, but like good footballers they did not fall off trees. Somehow the Ashton Sunday League, which belonged to the FA, had two tickets.

They decided to raffle them off to the teams in the league. There were three divisions in the league. Somehow the Railway's name was pulled out of the hat. The problem now was who would be the lucky winners! The team decided to have a concert night with a local singer called Johnnie Rich to raise club funds. It was decided to place all the club members' names and the committee member's names into a hat, and let Johnnie Rich pull the names out. The only stipulation was that if your name was pulled out you had to use the ticket and not give it away. I do not believe in miracles but the first name pulled out was mine; Bruce MacInnes. The second name was my brother's, Wallace. As you can imagine we went mad. Everyone was saying what a fiddle but it wasn't, it was just luck.

We went to the final again for the weekend. United won the game 2-1 with Stuart Pearson netting the first and Jimmy Case scoring the equaliser. United then got a deflection with both Lou Macari and Jimmy Greenhoff claiming the goal. We did not care who had scored. United had won the FA Cup against our great rivals Liverpool and were now back in Europe. Nothing could make me feel better after that. Not only had we beaten Liverpool in the final, but beaten our most hated rivals Leeds in the semi. I can remember both Joe Jordon and Gordon McQueen, both later to play for the Reds, saying before the game how the ground at Hillsborough was full of Reds. They were right, you could not find a Leeds fan anywhere and we had tried! As usual the Reds had taken over the ground and won 2-1.

United played in the Cup Winners Cup that following season. I have already explained why I could not travel to Saint Etienne but the next round was a remarkable game. I had booked to go on holiday to Portugal with Carol and would you believe it, United drew Oporto away in the next round whilst I was going to be there. Carol did not fancy going to the match and decided to sunbathe instead. I asked would she mind if I went to the game? "No problem" was her reply. So I caught the train and went on my own. What a big mistake that was. United got hammered 4-0. It spoilt the rest of my holiday.

The return leg was truly remarkable; United made a brave effort. They won the home leg 5-2 going out 6-5 on aggregate but for me it was lost over in Oporto. United were to get their revenge over Oporto in later years.

The 1978/79 season has bad memories for me, both as a footballer and as a United supporter. Firstly my right shoulder kept dislocating which was very painful. I saw the Manchester City orthopaedic surgeon, a Mr David Markharn, who told me I would need a putty platt operation. This was more of a rugby injury than a football one at the time. I was off work for eight weeks. My shoulder was very painful. For months I had to have intensive physiotherapy to build up the muscles in my right arm but I had no intention of quitting that season. The Railway were beaten in the final of our League Cup after a replay against a team from Gorton called the Hare and Hounds. This was a City pub; the only good thing to come out of the two games was that I received the 'man of the match' award. At the presentation evening, due to the amount of beer we had all drunk all hell broke loose. Everyone was fighting each other. I cannot remember what kicked it off that night but everyone's trophies were broken. We ended up gluing them all together the next day. It is my belief that the Blues started all this trouble as we were heavily outnumbered at the event.

United finished about ninth that season but again we got to Wembley. This time beating Liverpool in the semi after a replay. We drew at Maine Road 2-2 and I remember not wanting to go to the replay because of all the fighting at Maine Road. Mick Walker even hit a Liverpool fan wearing a crash helmet! We also had some trouble with some Liverpool fans in a Transit van. Little did they know our Wallace had nicked their van keys from the ignition while all the disturbance was going on. He later threw them into a front garden on the walk back to Piccadilly. These Scousers were now left on their own in the middle of Moss Side at 5.30 p.m. — we decided to leave them to the Cool Cats (this was the nickname of City's main firm at the time, later they were to be known as the young guvs). We decided to hire a 52-seater coach to go to the replay. Michael Walker, Wallace's best man, had arranged everything. We all had half a day's holiday from work and got drunk in a Boddingtons' pub in Ashton-under-Lyne, which was called the Seven Stars. To this day that coach is called the 'battlewagon' because everyone was very drunk. There was fighting all down the East Lanes Road. Even in the chip shop when we stopped for something to eat. When we parked up before the match Liverpool fans were waiting for us and we met them head-on. The only disappointment was that Doss Maher, 'Twang Eyes', got arrested for what I can only describe as fowl language. As usual the Liverpool police looked after their own. Doss was later charged, missed the whole game, and received a year's ban from attending football matches. 'Twang Eyes' was sadly missed the following season but had now decided to play Saturday football for the work's team. United won the game 1-0.

The Cup Final was another great event, apart from the result, as we lost 3-2, but still had a great weekend. We were 2-0 down with minutes to go then suddenly United scored two goals in a minute with Gordon McQueen and Sammy Mac both scoring. The game was looking like extra time, when the great Liam Brady went on a run, crossing for Alan Sunderland to beat Bailey with a good header. United had lost the game. I firmly believe that if the game had gone into extra time, we would have come out easy winners.

That season United had drawn a few London clubs in the FA Cup. Along with Arsenal in the final, we had also played Tottenham, Chelsea and Fulham. We travelled all the way down to Fulham on a Saturday to find out the game was postponed after we had arrived at the ground. We were all going mad, but as we were fanatics, we even travelled down to the rearranged night game which United drew 1-1. I remember walking back with the lads to the tube station at Wembley to get the train back to our hotel in London. We bumped into Pat Crerand with one of his sons. Pat later had a pub in Altrincham, which we regularly visited after games; he has become a close friend of my family and me. I still keep in touch with him and see him regularly. He is currently working for a local radio station. He attends all United matches; it is not often you hear Pat Crerand call United.

The following season United were very unlucky not to break

our twenty-six year wait to win the league. We finished the season as runners-up to Liverpool. Again I did not miss many matches that season but injury again cost me dearly. I had to have a cartilage operation on my left leg. The same orthopaedic surgeon, David Markham, performed the op; we were now becoming friends. There were many more ops to follow. I was now the captain of the Ashton Sunday Inter League team. There were also lots of semi-pro clubs wanting me to play on Saturdays for them, but United were still in my blood!

That season we lost to Tottenham in the FA Cup. After drawing in London, I can remember thinking we would win easily in the replay, but Ardiles scored a great goal to the Scoreboard End. They even had Glen Hoddle in their goal due to an injury to the goalkeeper; but that's football! The low of the season was being beaten 6-0 at Ipswich, who even missed two penalties. We went on to win the last six games of the season. Our last away game was at Leeds of all places; even City fans wanted to come to the game. I travelled down with a lad called Peter Cummings, a Blue who worked with me at Clayton Aniline, as well as two other Reds; one of them being Phil Collinge who at the time never missed a game just like me! We stopped at a pub called the Three Arrows, a Boddingtons' pub near to Heaton Park. We ended up having that much to drink that Peter filled his tank up with diesel instead of petrol. We ended up calling out the AA who could not believe what we had done. We eventually got to the game which had attracted nearly 40,000 supporters. At least 20,000 were United fans; trouble erupted all over the ground with Leeds winning 2-0. I walked back to our car after the game with the Ashton mob. Our car was parked near the coach park, when I saw down a side street, three lads kicking holes out of one lad. I said to Wallace, my older brother, "We can't let that happen." So I shouted to them "What's going on?" The reply was "Don't worry, we are Leeds fans" and they thought we were too. We gave them the same treatment they had given the lad laying on the floor. His name was George. He was covered in blood, so we cleaned him up then took him to see his friends who had run off and left him to the Leeds fans' mercy. I still see George today. He is from St Helens and is a dentist. He always remembers that day and always offers to buy me a drink.

When Wallace returned to his minibus, they tried to drive off the car park when they found out someone had taken all the wheel nuts off the wheels; the van just collapsed with the weight of twenty lads in the back. They had a long wait for the AA and said they had seen the biggest crew of United fans walking back to the train station at Leeds. The station was about three miles from the ground. Wallace said there must have been about 2,000 lads; no one would dare have a go with that crew who didn't have a police escort with them.

The 1980/81 Season saw United have a mediocre season, finishing eighth in Division One. We were still entered into the UEFA Cup for finishing as runners-up the previous season. I was now beginning to think we would never ever win the league but am glad to say that in later years I was proved wrong. My other shoulder was now dislocating at regular times. I was putting the shoulder back in myself which was very painful as well as still playing football, so another trip to David Markham was called for and the other shoulder was pinned. I now know how Bryan Robson felt. I was being called the bionic man by my mates. I also knew that after a few more years of pipe-fitting/welding I would not be able to manage and would have to find a job with lighter duties. By now I was captain of the Open Age Manchester County Football Club managed by the great Jock Haigh. Ged Coyne, Keith Hulley, Gary Fitzgerald and Gary Lowe, who were all ex-Manchester City players, played in this team with me. I believed myself to be as good as them. Later on in my football days, I developed more and more injury problems and was out of action for another year with two more cartilage operations and torn stomach muscles. Mr Markham even commented on my dedication having all these self-inflicted injuries due to semi-pro football, but as you can imagine I replied, " To me football is my life".

In the 1981/82 Season we finished third in a two-horse race. The same happened in the 1982/83 Season with the exception being we got to Wembley after beating Brighton 4-0 in a replay. I took

Carol with me to Wembley for the replay. She was now my wife; it was her first Cup Final. The season before in the UEFA Cup Valencia had beaten us 2-1 and there was lots of trouble. United fans had wrecked a bar in Spain. The police had attacked everyone in the bar with batons. It was very scary; no one was let out until the damage had been paid for. After this, I vowed never to go to Valencia again, but as you can guess, in later years we were drawn against Valencia in the European Cup.

Back to the 1982/83 Season. It was another great season for United, as we could have won the treble with a bit of luck. We ended up third in Division One, FA Cup winners against Brighton and beaten finalists by Liverpool, after extra time at Wembley in the League Cup. Some fans have never been to Wembley but to me it was becoming my second home! I still wanted United to win the league. That was my number one priority. The season following our FA Cup win against Brighton, we had a great run in the Cup Winners Cup reaching the semifinal. It was my first experience of seeing United play against truly great European teams.

That same season we played Leeds in the FA Cup semifinal at Hillsborough. A lad called Terry Harrison, a City fan, wanted to travel with us to the game. He didn't have a ticket but had a typewriter, which he had used to type out his match ticket; it was the worst forged ticket I have ever seen! All the lads were saying he had no chance of getting in with it, but to give Terry credit, he handed his ticket in then ran through as quick as he could. When the turnstile clicked, he was in!

As I mentioned earlier, United had a great run that season in the Cup Winners Cup reaching the semifinal having beaten rubbish opposition in the earlier rounds such as Dukla Prague and Spartak Varna. In the quarterfinal we drew the great Barcelona. I travelled to the game that attracted a 70,000 crowd and United were unlucky losing 2-0 with Graeme Hogg, United's centre half, scoring an own goal in the closing minutes. The return leg in Manchester a fortnight later, was a game of football played at a breathtaking pace. There seemed to be a buzz in Manchester that night. The fans had a feeling United could pull

38

this back, myself included. Up to the time of writing, I can honestly say that this was the best match I have witnessed at Old Trafford in my thirty years of watching United; nothing can compare to that night. Barcelona had all the big names; Maradona and Shuster, who had a great game. I went to the game with Doss straight from work; we went into Piccadilly for a few pints and a game of snooker then headed off to Old Trafford. We were in the Stretford End seats; the atmosphere was unbelievable that night, and the fans raised the roof when United scored first through Bryan Robson towards the Stretford End. Robson made it 2-2 on aggregate and the fans somehow willed in another goal, which came through Frank Stapleton. United won 3-0 and were through to the semifinals against Juventus. The first leg was played at Old Trafford. United were hampered by injuries and suspensions. They drew 1-1; a fair result. United lost the second leg 2-1, losing 3-2 on aggregate; again losing to a late winner scored by the Pole Bonieck. So my dreams of going to a European Final were kept on the back burner.

My younger sister, Della, had been going out with a lad called Vinnie Garmory for a few years. She had somehow kept it from Wallace and I that Vinnie was on Manchester City's books from the age of eleven. He also captained Manchester schoolboys. She was scared of us finding out and scaring Vinnie off, so she had made my dad take a vow of silence! They are now married with two children; Sean and Anthony. Vinnie progressed from captaining City's youth team, which had won the Youth Cup trophy; Della had a picture of the City team in their blue strip with Vinnie in the middle with the ball between his legs. City had some good youngsters in their team, such as Gary Owen who, in later years, lived on Hathersage Drive in Glossop, a hundred yards from myself. I became friends with Gary, and when I went into his front room, there was that same picture on the wall! He could not believe that Vinnie was my brother-in-law. They also had players like Ray Ranson, Roger Palmer and Dave Bennett, all who left City to have successful careers with other clubs. Della used to go to sleep at night looking at Vinnie's picture but Wallace and I, no matter what the time, used to turn the picture round so that when she woke up in the morning all she would see was the back of the picture. How she hated us for doing this! We became good friends with Vinnie, as he is a United supporter even though he has played for City. One Sunday morning, Vinnie did me a great favour, which could have caused serious problems for him, as he was a contract player on professional forms. That year the Sunday team Wallace and I were playing for, were having a difficult time in the league. There was only the cup to play for. We had just been beaten 6-0 by Newroyd from Oldham at home in the league and had drawn them again at home a week later in the cup. Newroyd were a top team who had a few semi-professional players. Wallace and I had told Vinnie we were short and only had ten players. Vinnie was feeling sorry for us and said that he would play for us on Sunday in the cup. When we kicked off, I could tell the Newroyd players thought they would murder us especially after the hammering they gave us the week before. Can you believe it, we played Vinnie under an assumed name and won the game 10-2! Vinnie scored four goals. Newroyd made a complaint but the league threw it out. If Vinnie's mum and dad had found out about it, I think Wallace and I would have had a lot of explaining to do! It reminded me of another game I had played when I was eleven years old and playing for a team called Ashton Albion, who were at the time the best Sunday team in the area. We were in the Levenshume League with a team called Mercer Celtic, who were managed by the chief scout at City, Big Ted Davies, who was about twenty-four stone. They all played in the red and black City away kit and beat us 19-0 in the league! This is the biggest defeat I have ever taken on a football pitch, and yes, we had to play them again the week after in the cup at our ground. Ashton Albion won 4-2 with tremendous support from our friends; all of them Reds who hated City; but to their credit they took the defeat with pride and wished us well in the final, which we went on to win 2-0. Neil Orange and Kenny Scholes scored the two goals. They both went on to have trials at Blackpool.

The 1984/85 Season, United reached Wembley yet again against Everton; winning 1-0; but the sending off of Kevin Moran took the shine off the game. I will never forget the sight in extra time of Norman Whiteside bending the ball around the Everton defenders to score and win the cup for United. Kevin Moran, whom I met in later years in Tokyo, should never have been sent off. If Everton had won the game there would have been riots and I think we stopped them winning the treble that year. Norman Whiteside now works as a physiotherapist. He also does some after-dinner speaking and you could say that he likes a drink or two! At one presentation evening Norman stayed with us the entire evening. We all got drunk. Norman ended up singing United songs on the table!

The following season, United had a friendly match against Glasgow Celtic at Parkhead. It was August 4th, my wedding anniversary. I managed to convince Carol to celebrate our anniversary up at Celtic. So along with another friend, Peter Sharp, we went up in the car. We were told that the testimonial was being played for Danny McGrain the Scotland and Celtic captain at Hampden Park. So I drove to Hampden thinking the game was not all ticket. When we got to the ground at about four o'clock, we were told it was all ticket and the match was being played at Celtic's ground, Parkhead. How lucky we were to be asked by some official of Queen of the South who used Hampden as their home ground if we wanted any tickets. So we asked for three. Their team were training on an all-weather pitch outside the ground. Their manager came over and gave Carol three tickets at no charge. He told us to enjoy the game. I think United won the game on penalties. I have been back to Celtic on numerous occasions. It always amazes me the friendship the two sides have for one another. I think it stems from the days when we played them at Old Trafford and drew 0-0 for Bobby Charlton's testimonial. On the way back from Celtic that night, if it hadn't been for Peter, I would not be writing this book, as while Carol was asleep in the back I somehow I fell asleep at the wheel. Luckily Peter, who cannot drive, was awake and moved the steering wheel whilst shouting at me to wake up. We immediately swapped drivers; then Carol drove the rest of the way home down the M6.

After United beat Everton in the Cup Final, we were back in the Cup Winners Cup, but were not allowed to participate because of the Liverpool fans' disgraceful behaviour at Heysal. On our return to Europe, we qualified for the UEFA Cup where we beat Raba Vasa in round one. In round two, we were drawn against PSV Eindhoven. I decided to run a trip for the lads, but United, who were playing the first leg away, did not want any fans travelling to the game as there had been a lot of trouble in Europe with the English fans, and so banned any fans from travelling. This did not stop the die-hard Ashton Mob. So about fifteen of us took a week off work. My brother Wallace had noticed a special offer on a Persil promotion which said free travel into Europe between certain dates; all you needed was a certain number of Persil tops to qualify. So would you believe it, we went and raided Asda. We bought three packets of Persil each, then were all bound for Eindhoven.

We caught the morning train from Manchester on the Monday to Harwich. Then caught the ferry to the Hook of Holland. There were about two hundred United supporters going over. When we got to the train station in Holland, the police were trying to keep the United supporters together and turn them back. We managed to catch a train to Amsterdam to avoid detection, which worked. We even used our Persil vouchers on the trains! On the ferry going over, the United fans were robbing everything in sight from the duty-free shop. I even saw one fan who had been asked to take a photo of this man's family run off with the camera. I also saw a friend of mine whom I used to play football with; he was with his mate who happened to be Bernard Manning's son, Young Bernard. They were playing three-card brag with some Cockney Reds and losing a lot of money. I told them to sit out because I knew the system and sat in with the Cockney Reds. Within one hour, I had Bernard's and Colin's money back for them. They were also going to the game. They ended up coming with us for the rest of the trip. Young Bernard, who is a City fan, is doing well for himself now. He has his own roller skating business and is also chairman of his local football team, Radcliffe Borough FC.

We arrived in Amsterdam about Tuesday lunch time. We

decided to book into a bed and breakfast for three days. Amsterdam opened our eyes. We could not believe what was happening — beer, drugs and girls — all legal! A lad who was with us called Paul Hands, went with five girls in the first hour. Is that a record or what!? Within two days he was skint and had to miss the game, then wait for us in Amsterdam. "Fuck the football" he said! I remember my wife's brother Alan coming with us. He was fifteen at the time and none of the grown-ups had the nerve to go with the pros, except Paul Hands. They wanted 50 gilders which is about £15 today. Alan said if we all paid for him he would go in. So we had a whip round and in he went. "No problem" he said after breakfast the next morning. We caught the train to Eindhoven that took about four hours; again we used our Persil vouchers, which had now expired yet no one dared to tell us. There was no trouble at the match because the police in their wisdom had decided to let the approx 200/300 Reds into the ground even without tickets and with no charge; they also escorted us back to the train station. The match ended up a boring 0-0 draw with United winning the second leg. We got back to Amsterdam in the early hours and some of the lads decided to go down to the red-light district again. We set off back home on the Thursday morning, arriving back in Ashton on Friday. Can you believe that fifteen lads travelled across Europe on Persil vouchers to watch United! We could, as we had done it!

In the next round, we were drawn against Dundee United with the first leg at Old Trafford. I always remember two of their players who stood out from the rest — Paul Sturrock, their forward to whom I gave 'man of the match', and the goalkeeper, Mcalpine, who had a great game making some outstanding saves. The score was 2-2. Remember, United had not been beaten in Europe at Old Trafford but this game could so easily have changed history. A fortnight later it was the return trip. I had two options; I could either go on the United special or go in the car with Tony Braithwaite, Eric Mitchell and John Clegg. I decided to travel up on the special with a few of the lads, as it meant I only needed to take half a day off work. We caught the train to Scotland at midday, arriving there a few hours before kickoff. We then decided to sample their beer which was excellent. You had to order either a pint of dark or light, but it was very cheap! I met Tony Braithwaite in the pub. He said it was a good job I had gone on the special, as they had had some trouble earlier with some Jocks when they had parked the car. Eric was in hospital. They had no idea who had attacked them and everyone was concerned for Charlie, Eric's nickname. When the police rang his wife Gillian to tell her what had happened, the sergeant said he thought that Eric was drunk, to which Gillian replied that he couldn't be as he was on kidney dialysis as he only had one kidney. The policeman replied "I can assure you Madam, this man has had a wee too many!" Thankfully Eric got home ok in the end. United went on to win the game 3-2, 5-4 on aggregate, with Mark Hughes scoring one of his specials for the Reds. It marked a great day for me, as Doss had placed a bet on for me whilst I was at the match. The horse won at 9-1 netting me £90, so it turned out to be a great day.

I will always remember that night. I think the trouble causers in the crowd were Glasgow Rangers fans who hated United because of the Catholic situation and also because Glasgow Celtic had to replay their game that same night against Rapid Vienna. Due to crowd disturbances, United let them play at Old Trafford whilst we were in Scotland. I could not believe the sight when we got back to the train station in Manchester. Celtic fans were spilled out everywhere with empty whisky bottles by their sides. I think Celtic lost the game 1-0 and were subsequently knocked out. United reached the quarterfinals that year getting beaten by Videoton; losing 5-4 on penalties.

A few years earlier, we had a pre-season friendly against Glasgow Rangers at Old Trafford; big mistake! Rangers brought down about 10,000 fans. They took over the whole ground except for the Stretford End. Before the match, there was the usual fighting everywhere. I remember catching the bus to Old Trafford from Piccadilly. It was full of Rangers fans and they hated United. I was with a younger lad called Geoff Glover. He was scared to death and started to cry, saying he wanted to go home. The Rangers fans spared us. It was the older lads they wanted. No one paid on the bus that day. All the Rangers fans were handing the bus conductor Scottish five-pound notes so that he had no change. Not a bad blag I thought!

The 1985/86 Season for me was unbelievable. I was convinced that this was the year we would win the league. We had a remarkable start, winning our first ten matches on the bounce. The opening match of the season we hammered Aston Villa 4-0. Another friend of mine at Clayton Aniline, Phil Collinge had made friends with Gary Shaw, whom he had met on holiday. Gary managed to get us tickets for the game and stayed for a drink afterwards. He was a nice lad who had just won the young player of the year award in London. We got him so drunk he stayed at Phil's house; we took him to Smokies nightclub in Ashton-under-Lyne with all the lads and introduced him to Boddies' bitter! In return when we played Villa away that same season, he introduced us to Andy Gray and John Gidman who was later to play for the Reds. They took us to a wine bar in Sutton called the Cork and Bottle; yet again we got drunk! No one sees much of Gary now. The last I heard off Phil, was that he has had lots of operations on his knee and has had to give up the game, which is sad, as he was a great player in his day.

Vinnie Garmory was released by City. I remember Della coming home very upset. Tony Book had called him into his office and said that they were prepared to let him go as they had an abundance of left-sided players. Colin Bell, Peter Barnes and Gary Owen had now overtaken Vinnie in the pecking order. Every Friday night there was a football programme on ITV called 'Kick-off'. It was introduced by Gerald Sinstad. We never missed the programme as it gave you all the latest football information. We were told that they wanted to do an interview with Vinnie. They interviewed him at City's training ground and asked him how he felt about being released after all this time. Vinnie replied no regrets whatsoever. He said he'd had the greatest time any youngster can have and had met some brilliant people in the process. The most important thing in his life now was his girlfriend Della MacInnes. Even on his passport it was stamped occupation — Pro-Footballer. Vinnie had offers from a number of lower division clubs but was disillusioned with football and had decided to sign for a semi-professional club near Ashton called Mossley, who were at the time a well-known non-league club. They had a player called Eamon O'Keefe who went on to play for Everton and Eire. Mossley even promised Vinnie a full-time job, but he started working for the Army Pay Corp. He still works for them today. He played for Mossley the year that they reached Wembley in the FA Trophy and were beaten by Dagenham 2-1. We all travelled down to that match, which again had lots of trouble attached to it between United fans and West Ham fans. North v South teams at Wembley always seems to attract trouble.

I attended forty-two out of forty-two games again that season, which was now becoming a regular thing for me. We had some great wins beating City 3-0, Arsenal 2-1 and like I said before Aston Villa 4-0. The run was ended at Luton away, where we drew 1-1. At the time Luton was a home fans only ground and for some reason they did not want away fans at their ground, but nothing was going to stop us, so we travelled down, about twenty of us in a Transit van. We met up with the Cockney Reds. So again there was about 200/300 United fans outside with no tickets, so the police let us into the game. But after United had drawn, there was a riot through Luton town centre. United fans and Cockney Reds were smashing windows for fun. It was all led by a mad United fan from London who still travels today. His name is 'Banana Bob'. His crew were feared at United matches all over the country. They always wore scarves across their faces to avoid detection.

By Christmas that year, United had amassed a massive lead. The rot set in February and March. Again we ended up fourth in a two-horse race. I had now lost all confidence of United ever winning the league. I was praying for miracles.

The 1986/87 Season was the end of Ron Atkinson's reign. United finished eleventh, which was totally unacceptable. Ron kept up United's tradition of playing entertaining, attacking football. He won the FA Cup and Charity Shield on a number of occasions, but the obsession that the United fans had of winning the league title, had continued. This convinced the Board that Ron had gone as far as he could. I still say he was a great manager with the right attitude and character to manage a big club like Manchester United. Rumours were circulating that United players like Robson, McGrath and Whiteside were drinking together too much. I know this to be true, because most afternoons I would see them going into Henry's bar in Manchester. They would stay most of the day. So whoever followed Atkinson, would have to instil some discipline into the team. United's new manager that season was Alex Ferguson, who had success with Aberdeen. I remember thinking it's easy to do it in Scotland, but could he do it in England? How wrong I turned out to be!

The following season, 1987/88, United were going for the league again. We signed Brian McClair from Celtic and played him up front. He could do nothing wrong. Everything he hit that season went in. I think he scored thirty goals; no one had done that since the Lawman's days! Denis was now on the after-dinner circuit and also doing some television work so I booked him to do an after-dinner speech at a sportsman's event for my Sunday team, which was called Haughton Villa. At the time they were one of the best Sunday teams in the Manchester area, winning most of the region's top tournaments. The sportsman's evening was held at the Masonic Hall in Ashton-under-Lyne. I had no problem selling the tickets for the event to raise club funds at £25 a ticket. Denis brought the house down with some of his stories; we remembered nearly everything he said. Meeting my boyhood idol was a dream and we became friends. I still see him. He once said to me that if I ever wanted to meet George Best, to give him a call. He did not have to wait long. My days were numbered as a welder at Clayton Aniline, as by now both my shoulders had been pinned, three cartilages removed and torn stomach muscles, one broken jaw and numerous other minor injuries had insured this; I knew I had to leave. Who was it that said 'Football is more important than life or death'? I now know he was right! Was his name the great Bill Shankly?

One of my friends, Addy Dearnley, who is another United fanatic, had just left his job as a maintenance fitter to go into insurance; no qualifications were necessary, and he started

47

working for the Pearl Assurance. Addy could get on with everybody and over the next few years made a good living out of the insurance industry. I asked him his opinion of the situation. He said it was the best thing he had ever done and urged me to have a go. Addy now runs a pub in Stalybridge called the Pineapple. It is currently the home of the Stalybridge branch, with over five hundred members; a group of fans that worship United home and away. I wish Addy all the best in his new venture. He left the insurance industry due to the changes that were happening; all reassessments and qualifications were now needed; Addy thought it was now time to move on. He is loved by everyone at United and again started going before me. You could describe him on the pitch as an old-fashioned centre forward in the Tommy Taylor mould. He describes himself as more of an Andy Cole role, but I know different having had the pleasure of playing in the same team as him. Anyway, I took Addy's advice and applied for a job as an insurance agent at Royal London. The job was easy; you had an established round and had to collect money off your clients, also to produce sales leads for your manager. The interview was unbelievable. I met the manager in Hyde, a Mr Paul Gardiner, who said he had played for West Brom with Jeff Astle and Liverpool with Tommy Smith but I had never heard of him! After about three weeks, we had a five-a-side game, I knew then that Del-Boy, as we had nicknamed him, had never kicked a ball in his life. All this was in his imagination!

I left Clayton Aniline after twelve years. My leaving do, is still talked about today. Doss Maher, Twang Eyes, arranged for the local pub near work to put a spread on and we all ended up getting very drunk. A 'Strip-a-gram' was hired by the lads. She tried to encourage me to participate but I was well gone. A few weeks later Doss showed me pictures of the same girl in *Club International*! Now I had started a new career, which turned out to be the easiest job anybody could have and for the next eight years the money was unbelievable. At Clayton Aniline, working shifts could only earn me £12,000 a year. In insurance in my first year, I earned £18,000, which was good money considering I was only working a three-day week. The commission insurance companies were paying was hard to believe; £500 for one policy was common practice. Addy was right. The amount of people I knew always asked me to help them with their insurance needs but I let my manager do the selling until I was confident enough to do it myself.

The 1988/89 Season was a struggle for United, who finished eleventh in Division One. People were having doubts about Fergie. We managed to get to the sixth round of the FA Cup, where we were beaten by Nottingham Forest at Old Trafford. In earlier rounds we had played Bournemouth away. I travelled to the game with my friend Chris Harford, who is godfather to my first son Bobby (Robert), who is named after the great Bobby Charlton. He was born on 4th March that year. When Chris and I arrived in Bournemouth, all the hotels were fully booked. They were expecting an invasion of United fans; our accents were giving us away, until Chris had a great idea. He pretended to be part of the backing group for Mick Hucknall, who is another big Red and managed to book us into a five-star hotel on the strength of Simply Red's name. Mick is related to Chris's wife Christine and I will be mentioning him later on in this book. This reminds me of one occasion when Chris, Mick and myself entered my Sunday football team's pub called the Sycamore, which is in Cockbrook on the border of Stalybridge and Ashton-under-Lyne. We all had a few drinks. I remember Mick singing his famous song, 'Money's too tight to mention' from a Pils bottle! One of our players, Ronnie Cotterill, was not present in the pub at the time, so we rang him as he is a mad Simply Red fan. Mick sang down the phone to him. To this day Ronnie does not believe it was Mick Hucknall singing but everyone in the pub at the time knows different! Ronnie is a big Red, I once bumped into him at the European Cup Winners Cup Final in Amsterdam. We were all staying in Amsterdam. When I saw him, he was with his girlfriend, who was a UK Kick Boxing Champion. They had been mugged, and even though she was trained to kill, she had frozen when they had been mugged. We all had a laugh about this and had a whip-round for them, but Ronnie did not find it funny at the time.

The 1988 Season saw England in the European Championships, along with the Republic of Ireland. England's first game was against the Irish in Stuttgart. So myself and three others decided to go on the sick from our insurance jobs at the time to follow England. Off we went again travelling from Harwich to the Hook of Holland, passing our head office in Colchester on the way to Harwich! When we boarded the ferry, 'World in Action' were doing a documentary on football violence. The ship taking us over was full of Irish supporters and the camera crew were only there to film the trouble which never occurred. We didn't have any tickets for England's game and ended up getting drunk with the Irish lads. Little did we know that we were to be on television the following Thursday. They pointed us out to be football hooligans travelling looking for trouble. As it happens we were having such a good time in Amsterdam, we ended up staying for the whole week and never got to see any of England's games at all. We even watched England's last game in a bar in Amsterdam when they played the great Holland team. One of the lads on the trip was a local Ashton lad called Stewart Wilson. He is a great lad who is friends with the ex-United player Neil Webb and the Forest assistant manager Steve Wigley. Stewart was a good semi-pro footballer. I hear that at the age of thirty-five he has caught some form of cancer. I just hope he is ok and wish him all the best for the future. Another lad on the trip was Clifford Creehan, who was another Sunday player with whom I had played alongside for years. I was later to bump into him in Rio on the Cococobana Beach, but that's another story to be told later.

In the late eighties, I remember going to watch United play Blackburn Rovers on a Friday night in the FA Cup at Ewood Park. The plan was to catch the service train from Victoria. Everybody had a half-day off work and we met at a Boddies' pub near to the train station called the Ship, where as usual everyone got very drunk! I saw a lad I knew from Tommy Price's era, who lived in Wythenshaw — his name was Geoff Lewis. Geoff was never one to back down from a fight but the only problem was that there was no one to fight at Blackburn in those days. This didn't deter Geoff. As soon as we got off the train, Geoff was arrested for fighting with the police. Tommy nicknamed him Gladice. Geoff wherever you are, I hope the Reds are still in your blood. The same fellow once helped me out of a tricky situation at Newcastle a few years earlier. I will never forget it as he saved me from a good hiding from some Geordies, as I was walking back to the train station on my own after getting split up from the Ashton mob.

The 1989/90 season found Fergie running out of time. It was said on the grapevine that if United didn't win their FA Cup game at Forest away, he would be out of a job. We had a terrible time that season with United finishing thirteenth. Only Mark Hughes, who was now our new idol, seemed to be scoring any goals. We also took a 5-1 hammering at Forest in the league but how lucky it all turned out for Alex.

By now I was living at 44, Hathersage Drive in Glossop, Derbyshire and was introduced to a young United player called Lee Martin, who had just established himself in United's first team. Lee became a good friend of my family; both families going on holiday together, along with his wife's parents and their two children, Ryan and Amelia to Tenerife; pre-season of course! When United played Forest away in the FA Cup that season, a lot of Fergie's first team were injured. Fergie had to rely on the youngsters to pull it off. They played brilliantly to beat Forest 1-0. The United supporters packed behind the goal went crazy. There was a feeling that something special was going to happen. I remember one of the lads saying to me, "Bruce, that feeling when Mark Robins scored, was better than any knock-off I've ever had!" His name was Paul Hands; yes the same man who had five knock-offs in one hour in Amsterdam.

The following round we had to travel to Hereford. Again Chris Harford and I went for the weekend, staying at a friend's pub, who was called Bob Evans. Bob was a City fan who lived in Monmouth, South Wales. I had met him whilst on holiday in Morocco but he had always wanted to see a United game. I managed to get three tickets off Lee Martin, so we took Bob to the game with us; it was a scrappy match on a muddy park. Mick Duxbury got us through with a 1-0 win and we were on our travels again this time to Newcastle. I hired a 52-seater coach. We set off stopping at a pub en route, where we drank so much we drank the pub dry. The landlord had no bitter left! There were about 8,000 United fans at Newcastle. The police had us all in the Main Stand along side the halfway line but the fans were all so drunk, myself included, that we could not even see the match never mind the Newcastle fans. United won a great game 3-2 with Danny Wallace scoring the winner. I remember the Newcastle centre forward Quinn scoring a dubious goal with his hand, against United's goalkeeper, Jim Leighton who Fergie had signed from Aberdeen. The goal stood. United survived late pressure to march on and earn them a quarterfinal game at Sheffield United. This was an away game again. All United's games in the FA Cup that year were played away, so you could not say that Fergie was having an easy time. His chosen words are right when he says that nothing is ever easy when your name is Manchester United.

We beat Sheffield United 1-0 and went on to play two thrilling games against Second Division Oldham Athletic at Maine Road. The first game ended in a 3-3 draw with end-to-end football played by both teams. The replay was again played at Maine Road; a City fan called Mark Elliot, whose dad worked at Maine Road, got us tickets free of charge. He said he would give Tommy Price and myself a lift to the game. The result went our way, United winning 2-1 with Mark Robins, an Ashton lad, scoring the winner. So again United were at Wembley. Had Fergie saved his job I thought? Mark's luck was not in on the way home. He smashed his car up costing him £300. We laughed at him as he had taken us to the game supporting Oldham. It's just what we had expected from a Blue, Tommy and I thought it served him right!

So it was another weekend in London. By now I was arranging all the trips to United games and booked the lads into the Hilton Hotel at either Kensington or Olympia. We were booking twin rooms and letting four lads stay in each room to keep the price down. They were also finding out someone else's room number then booking everything onto that room. I remember being woken up by the CID that morning at about four o'clock. They were asking for Bruce MacInnes. They had somehow got into my room which housed about eight lads. They said "Your lads have had a great time last night Mr MacInnes." They then showed me about twenty bills totalling £400, all signed by different individuals. Some had been signed Lee Sharpe, Mickey Mouse and all the old ones, so I asked him when he wanted us to vacate the rooms? He replied as soon as possible! We managed to pay our bills somehow but only after a few arguments. Apparently everyone was on champagne. It was a costly weekend. I will never forget the policeman's face when he saw how many of us had bunked down into each room.

United drew the Cup Final 3-3, after a bit of an erratic display by United's goalkeeper Jim Leighton. I faulted him at two of the goals and I must admire Alex Ferguson's decision to drop him for the replay the following Thursday. It must have been a hard decision to make but like the man he is, the decision was made. Les Sealy was put into goal. Lee Martin again got me tickets for the game, which was to be played the following Thursday. Mick Walker and I had arranged to go to one of the lad's stag do in Amsterdam that week, but we could not miss the Cup Final, so ended up going to the final instead. We went to the game, which United won 1-0 thanks to a Lee Martin goal. Can you believe that! Mick and I decided to fly to Amsterdam straight after the match to join Gary Schofield's stag do. Gary was a Blue but played for our Sunday team and Mick was the manager of our team. We arrived in Amsterdam in the early hours and met up with the rest of the lads in their hotel, where we found out that the United and City lads had been fighting each other after United had won. It was the usual story, they had had too much beer but it did not stop us having a good time, so we stayed there until the following Monday.

United were the FA Cup winners and were now in the European Cup Winners Cup. Had Lee Martin's goal saved Alex Ferguson's career? I think so, as from then on, he never looked back. I can't say the same for Lee Martin, as he suffered a bad back injury a few years later. He is now working for MUTV. I will explain more about Lee's career later on.

On the way back from Amsterdam, where drugs are legal,

someone had placed drugs into Nipper Royle's coat. Customs searched Nipper, found the drugs then searched the whole party. We were at Manchester Airport for hours. Nipper was let off with a caution but the lads nearly crucified him for the long delay. Nipper is a good Red, he does not miss many games.

The 1990/91 Season was an average season for United but all our minds were on the Cup Winners Cup. We beat Peskimunkas and Wrexham in the earlier rounds, then there was a disastrous mix up between Lee Martin and Peter Schmeichel at Old Trafford where we drew 1-1 in the quarterfinal. We now had to go to Montpellier in the South of France and either draw 2-2 or win. The outcome was never in doubt. We knew we could win. I remember having a go at Lee Martin about making me have to go to the away leg but Lee knows I would have gone anyway. This trip was arranged by a Stalybridge lad called Andy Baxter, who arranged a great day trip with a charter flight going from Manchester. About fifty lads from Stalybridge and Ashton-under-Lyne went along. The weather in the South of France was fantastic. We all made our way to the town centre to sample the local lager. Again, we all had a good drink but the police over reacted with the United fans and attacked us all in a bar with CS gas canisters. The gas entered my friend, Johnnie Red's (Redfearn), eyes, He nearly missed the match but somehow we all managed to get in. Harry Gill robbed about twenty Montpellier scarves from a stall and gave me some to give to Robert as a souvenir. It was another great game with Clayton Blackmore securing victory for United with two goals. I remember Valderamma was playing for Montpellier at the time but he did nothing in the game. Bryan Robson kept him quiet.

United beat Legia Warsaw in the semifinal. For the first time since 1968, we were in a European final, which was played on the 15th May against the great Barcelona. The game was played in Rotterdam at Feyenoord's ground. As usual, I decided to run a trip. Another trip to Amsterdam was on the cards. We booked a three-day trip staying in Amsterdam and there were about twenty lads travelling. We had to travel down to Heathrow to catch our plane. I went down with three lads from Droylsdon who I used to work with at Clayton Aniline. They were Doss Maher (Twang Eyes) who I mentioned earlier, Gordon Durward who is a sheet metal worker and a joiner called John Shorrocks. John didn't have a lot of money. For him to make this trip, cost him dearly. He had to sell all his tools, much to his wife's disgust but John never gave it a thought, the tools were sold. We travelled down to Heathrow in my black BMW. Yes insurance was doing well for me. I was now earning a lot more money a year which was good considering I was still only working three days a week. I parked my car in the airport car park. Then we made our way to the airport's departure lounge. When we reached the first bar at Heathrow, it was just a mass of red and white. United fans were everywhere, singing and dancing. Just then, the Arsenal team who were managed by two ex-Reds, George Graham and Stewart Houston, were going to catch their plane to Tokyo to play in the World Club Championships. Arsenal had pipped Liverpool to the title that season, which had gone to the last game. The look on Tony Adam's face said it all. What are all these Reds doing here? He could not believe it. I told him where we were all going and also got both George Graham and Stewart Houston to sign my passport. George Graham said that we had better win the cup. I said good luck to him, but I hated them and prayed that they would get stuffed. The love for Arsenal from United fans is non-existent dating back to when Brian McClair missed a penalty in the dying minutes of an FA Cup game at Highbury. He ballooned it over the bar and the Arsenal players took the piss. There was also the mass brawl at Old Trafford when both teams had points deducted for fighting and also the sending off of Remmy Moses, which cost him his Cup Final place. Anyway Arsenal were beaten in their game, which pleased us all!

We all met up at the hotel in Amsterdam, where there were about fifty lads from the Tameside area. Eric (Charlie) Mitchell had booked with me on this trip but had to cancel due to his kidney condition. His replacement was a lad called Buggsy; another Red from the legend Tommy Price's era in the 60s, so I let the two of them share a room. On the day of the game, the rain pissed down all day. There was a local Manchester group called James playing a concert outside the stadium in a park free of charge. The song they sang that night still stays in my mind. It was 'Sit down, sit down next to me'. We sang that song all the way through the entire game. We were all so drunk in the stadium, that we were drinking non-alcoholic beer and lager. It wasn't until about three rounds later, that we realised, only after being told by some other Reds, that it was alcohol free but no one gave a toss! United won the game with Steve Bruce scoring a header, and the great Mark Hughes scoring one of his specials from an acute angle. United were crowned Cup Winners Cup Champions. The celebrations began and went on all night. I remember feeling sorry for Lee Martin who had been taken ill with his wife Kath and had missed the game. He ended up watching the game in the team hotel. We all caught the train back to Amsterdam and hit the bright lights, ending up in a disco until the early hours with Gary Davies the DJ. I remember Gary being a DJ in Manchester at Placemates. We had a good laugh with Gary that night and he ended up dancing on the tables with us. The next day we had to be back at Schipol Airport to get our flight back to Heathrow. We arrived in good time to catch the plane home but when the four of us tried to book in Doss (Twang Eyes) had lost the flight tickets that we had entrusted him with. The lads were not happy. Doss had no idea where they were and searched everywhere. All the other lads were laughing at our predicament and carried on with their return flights. John Shorrocks and Gordon Durward, who were left behind with myself, were now giving Doss plenty of stick. We had no money left and were now stuck at Schipol Airport in Amsterdam. The airline said we could get a flight back in the morning. The only thing we could do, was wait in the airport lounge and try and keep calm. All the lads had work to go to that Friday, so Doss was getting even more stick. We all ended up getting drunk on the duty free we were supposed to be taking home and most of the night we sang all the old United songs to pass the time away. Then at about 2 a.m. a miracle occurred. Mick Hucknall the singer, and MUFC fan, entered the airport lounge. He had been to the game and said he was heading to America to write a song for the singer Diana Ross. He took pity on us and gave us a VIP card which he said we could use in one of the VIP guest rooms at the airport. We never gave it a thought. We thanked him took the pass and within minutes had entered the VIP room. No one challenged us, so we helped ourselves to the best Dom Perignon champagne, cigars and emptied the cupboard of all its stock. This would take away some of the disappointment of missing our flight. By this time, the four of us were extremely drunk. We ended up trying to get a few hours' sleep before our flight home. We awoke nursing the most awful hangovers you could imagine. We made our way over to the check-in desk. It was half an hour before our flight. Everyone was relieved. All we wanted to do was get home to see our children. Just then Doss put on his coat which he had been carrying and when he placed his hand in the sleeves the airline tickets fell onto the floor. The look on his face turned to horror. We all ended up jumping on him. He was lucky to get out alive but at least we knew the wives would believe the story as only Twang Eyes could do something like that.

In the 1990/91 Season, I had two good memories. One was going to Arsenal for a night game in the Rumbelows Cup. We ended up hammering them 6-2 with Lee Sharpe netting a hat-trick. United played brilliantly and nothing could stop them, everything they did went right. They had beaten Liverpool 3-1 in the previous round and now only Southampton stood in their way. We beat them after a replay 3-2 drawing 1-1 down at the Dell. We were now drawn against our most hated club Leeds United, in a two-legged semifinal. Semifinals always bring out the best in United fans. A lot of them think the semis have more to play for, so no one likes to miss them, myself included.

I remember the 82/83 Season when we won the FA Cup 4-0 against Brighton in a replay. As I said before, we all took our wives and girlfriends to the game. I remember catching the train back to where our coach was parked. We had all split up but had arranged to meet at a pub called The Case is Altered where all the Tameside Reds meet when United play at Wembley. It is near Kilburn, the tube station is Dollis Hill, famous for some memorable battles with both Liverpool and Aston Villa fans. We caught the tube back with our wives Carol and Pauline my brother Wallace's wife; there was a disturbance on the tube which was full of Brighton supporters and only a handful of Reds. One of the Brighton supporters was calling Bryan Robson for some reason and the Reds were having none of it. All of a sudden, a Red head-butted the Brighton fan and must have broken his nose. He was a Geordie Red and had took offence to the Brighton fan. We thought the Reds were going to get a beating and were ready to help out, but as luck had it, everyone just stayed silent and the air was calm again. When we got back to The Case is Altered, the celebrations started again. We drank until the early hours. The landlord of the pub, an Irish MUFC supporter, gave me a picture which I still treasure today. It is a picture of the 1968 European Cup team, all signed with the autographs of the players across their chests. He said "Have this Bruce. You are a better supporter than myself. I know it is going to a good home." I thanked him very much and accepted the gift.

Now in that same 1982/83 semifinal the League Cup was a two-legged game against our second most hated club Arsenal. We had drawn them at Highbury first and decided to hire a 52-seater coach. My friend Phil Collinge, a lad who I had worked with at Clayton Aniline, always went to the matches with me at that time, along with his cousin Tony, who now lives in America. They are both great Reds but it took Phil years to realise that I was a better Red than him. He hates to admit it, but if push came to shove, I think Gobby would admit it now! We both knew a lot of Reds from Ashton where I live and from Failsworth where Phil lived. We met at a Boddies' pub in Failsworth, called The Lamp Inn, and went to Highbury for the first leg. We stopped at a pub near to the ground and drank as usual, as much as we could before the game. It was a massive pub and eventually all fifty-two of us were on our knees following each other around doing the famous 'Hi ho it's off to work we go' from the film Snow White and the Seven Dwarfs. The whole pub was in stitches. It soon got to seven o'clock and it was time to go to the game. A few of the lads didn't have any tickets and were trying to get into the North Bank, Arsenal's end. I was in the Main Stand but went to the North Bank to try and get my brother-in-law Peter Hazlehurst a ticket. He ended up queuing with the Arsenal fans and after a disagreement ended up head-butting an Arsenal fan that had sussed him out as a Red, so we had to make a quick exit before we were given a good hiding by the Arsenal fans. Peter got a ticket at face value and I made him get into the ground quickly. I went to the Main Stand with the rest of the lads. The performance United gave was excellent. In the first half United went at Arsenal in true fashion and by half-time they were leading 4-0. We knew we were going to Wembley again, which was fast becoming my second home. The football could not be played at the same pace for the second half. I remember Arsenal caught us with two late goals, scored by Tony Woodcock the ex-Notts Forest forward who went on to play in Germany. For me the 'man of the match' was the England winger Steve Coppell, who scored an absolute gem to the Clock End, which was packed to the rafters with Reds. United won the game 4-2 and were eventually beaten by Liverpool at Wembley 2-1. I feel we were robbed in that final as the Liverpool keeper should have been sent off for bringing down a United player, but it wasn't to be.

United were heading for another Wembley appearance now in 1990 and only Leeds could stop us getting there. The first leg was played at Old Trafford. United won 2-1. This left an exciting second leg at Leeds with just a one goal lead. Could United do it? The performance of a left-winger called Lee Sharpe for United was brilliant; he slaughtered the Leeds full back Mel Sterland. All the lads were wondering if he could do the same at Elland Road. The away leg was played on a Sunday. The police would not allow many United fans to travel so we were given a terrible allocation of tickets. As usual my contact at United, Lee Martin, had no problem getting me tickets for the game. I must take this opportunity to thank Lee personally. He always managed to get me at least four complimentary tickets for both home and away games. When Lee was released by the club to join Glasgow Celtic, it broke my heart. I called at his house and begged him not to go but his mind was made up. Lou Macari, the new Celtic boss, had offered him a contract that was hard to refuse. Lee showed me the contract and I had to agree, although all his bonuses were geared towards Celtic beating Rangers.

I went to the second leg with my brother-in-law Peter Hazelhurst, using the two tickets Lee had got for me. Because of the dreadful allocation, most of the lads had to give the game a miss. The tickets we had were for the Captain's Lounge at Leeds costing £25.00 each, and it was a stipulation that suits were to be worn as it was in the Leeds's players' enclosure hospitality lounge. What a nightmare! United won the game 1-0 with a late Lee Sharpe goal and yes he did it again murdering their fullback Mel Sterland. Lee was given 'man of the match'. The majority of United fans were seated in the Captain's Lounge seats which were directly at the side of the Leeds end, the Spion Kop. They abused the United fans all match spitting on women, children and the elderly. I now knew why we called them scum. I felt sorry for any Red who was daft enough to wear their colours. As the whistle went, the Leeds fans ran onto the pitch to try and get at the United supporters who were all then told to get into the hospitality area as soon as possible. We had suits on and did as we were told. When we entered the hospitality lounge, we sat next to Vinnie Jones, the now famous film star. The ex-Wimbledon and Leeds player was with another Leeds player Chris Kamara. The hard men of Leeds were both injured. They told us to be very careful and to be quiet as some Leeds yobs always managed to get into the bar area. We got ourselves some sandwiches and a drink when I saw two United supporters who I know very well; they were Peter Fallon (nicknamed Strett after the Stretford End) and Kevin Littlewood a refrigeration engineer. They both entered the bar area very smartly dressed with club blazers and club ties on, but their clothes were covered in spit. I felt very sorry for them. They spotted Peter and I straight away and came over to us. I spoke to Pete and said to him "You are on your own here mate. Get the police or someone to get you to your car, because if you stay in here, you are going to get hurt." I was right. About twenty Leeds fans against two — the odds Leeds fans like. They already had them in their sights. When the police arrived, they gave Strett and Kevin an escort to their car. We stayed in the bar until the coast was clear. I could not believe that Leeds supporters would wreck their own ground but they were smashing windows just to get at the United supporters. Peter and myself then managed to walk back unharmed to the car and drove home.

United were at Wembley once again in their jinxed cup the League Cup. It was against Sheffield Wednesday which again we lost 1-0. It was the only time I have been at Wembley where the Wednesday fans had a 50/50 crowd against the biggest supporters in the land, MUFC. They sang throughout the game and got behind the team. I think United thought they would win easy but nothing is easy in football. Wednesday deserved their win and it was good to see Ron Atkinson, our old manager, win something. I always felt that he played entertaining football when he was manager at Old Trafford.

The 1991/92 Season was for me the start of all United's successes. I could tell that there were good times ahead. The team spirit was right and all the players were working for themselves. This could be United's year I thought. Could the wait for the league title be over? At Christmas, United were still near the top and had a convincing 6-3 win at Oldham Athletic away on Boxing Day with Andrei Kanchelskis beating Oldham more or less on his own. That evening we had arranged to play a team of United supporters from Norway at Ashton United's ground in a friendly; both supporters club branches took the game seriously. The Stalybridge branch came out easy winners winning 6-2, with myself netting two goals. We ended up going to the game extremely drunk, again having consumed the wine 20/20 (Mad Dog). I travelled with Eric Mitchell and Tommy Price, who did not have a ticket, Tommy was offering £200 to anyone who would sell him their ticket but no one took him seriously. I knew he was serious as he is now a millionaire. We walked down to the ground and still Tommy had no success, even at those prices the Oldham fans would not budge. A policeman on a police horse tried to move Tommy on, but Tommy was having none of it. When the horse turned round Tommy hit it so hard with his hand that the horse bolted and sent the policeman belting halfway down the road. This was the one time Tommy did a runner! Eric (Charlie) and I entered the ground. We met up with Tommy later on where we all had a laugh about it.

Towards the end of the season, United were fighting for the league but fixtures were piling up on them as well as injuries. In the FA Cup, would you believe, we drew Leeds away and won 1-0 with a Mark Hughes header to the Leeds end. Leeds were fighting for the league as well, so this was a great result for United. Again we took a 52-seater coach from Stalybridge. This time United had insisted on a fair allocation of tickets, so about 8,000 fans packed behind one goal. The march down to the United end past all the Leeds fans was awesome. We walked past their end all singing the 'We hate Leeds scum. We all fucking hate Leeds' song. They would never have had a go at this lot. The motto is "Might get done but never run". Dave Ashworth, a bricklayer friend of mine, who lives near to Lee Martin in Glossop, nearly broke ranks to have a go at the Leeds scum singing Munich '58 songs but I managed to get him back in line. It was half an hour before kickoff and Tommy wanted to go to the toilet and decided to go in a Leeds pub called The Peacock wearing his United shirt. We waited outside for him. No one would have a go at the legend Tommy Price, and at nineteen stone, I wouldn't like to take a punch off him. Anyway outside the pub were all the Leeds crew. Again Tommy sang the 'We all hate Leeds' song but no one dared to have a go at him. We entered the ground and watched United win 1-0.

In the same year in the FA Cup, Southampton beat us on penalties at Old Trafford after a 0-0 draw at the Dell. Their goalkeeper at the time, Flowers, had an outstanding game, although I think United had a perfectly good goal by Bryan Robson, which crossed the line disallowed, with the ref insisting it had not crossed the line. The TV replays afterwards proved me right.

In the same 1991/92 Season, after knocking our rivals Leeds United out of the FA Cup at Elland Road, I was shocked to find out that we had drawn them again in the Rumbelows Cup. The game was a night game at Leeds. United again were given a generous allocation of tickets. About 6,000 Reds went to the match. We had organised two coaches to travel up, and Nigel our branch organiser, had arranged for us to stop off at the same pub we had stayed at for our FA Cup game earlier in January where there had been no problems. The pub is situated about five miles from the Leeds ground. We all had a good drink before the game and the landlord who was a nice chap said it would be no problem for us to call back for a drink after the match. It was a typical English cup tie, played in a hostile atmosphere. Again United came out the winners. The local police kept us secured in the ground for thirty minutes until they had cleared the streets of all the Leeds head-bangers. They then safely escorted us back to our coaches. We then headed straight back to the pub on the outskirts of Leeds. We were welcomed back into the bar, which was a large pub, situated on a main road. One of our coaches parked in the pub car park while the other had to park a short distance away. Everyone was enjoying themselves in the pub. Half were in the vault playing pool, whilst the other half, myself included, were in the best room talking about the game and what a great win it had been. Ten minutes before last orders, a gang of about twenty lads walked into the best room. I could sense there was going to be trouble. Their leader, who was a tall fat bastard, ordered a pint from the bar but a lot of them didn't even buy a drink. This prepared me for the worst. They then started arguing with a group of Reds in the corner saying how lucky we were to win. It was plainly obvious that these lot were after trouble, so I stood up about ten yards away from them and shouted to the leader "What's the problem mate?" To which he replied "You were lucky tonight. Keep your nose out I'm not talking to you." I then replied "If we were lucky, then your lot are a bunch of shit." The lad then angrily threw his pint pot at me. Fortunately it missed my face but hit Tommy Price on his shoulder. All of a sudden all hell broke loose; there was a mass brawl in the best room. There were about another twenty Leeds fans outside trying to get into the pub but they didn't realise there was another full coach of Reds in the vault. They all rushed outside from the back entrance and chased the Leeds fans away. The group who had entered the pub took a hammering, then quickly made a dash for the door; within minutes the police had arrived. The Leeds fans had smashed all the pub windows. The licensee explained to the police that it was the Leeds fans' fault, so the police asked us to drink up then gave us an escort to the coaches. Again the Leeds fans had not done their homework. Fancy having a go at the Stalybridge branch!

In the Rumbelows Cup, United won some tough matches. We now had a semifinal against Middlesborough, playing away first on the 4th March, my son Robert's birthday. I arranged for a coach to travel up to Middlesborough for the first leg, stopping at a pub nearby in Billingham. A few friends of mine from the Royal London, where I was now working, had arranged this for us. One of them was a lad called Dave Dyson with whom I still keep in touch; we had a great time up there, especially as the beer is a lot cheaper than down here! The first leg was drawn 0-0 but fighting with the Middlesborough fans in the ground led to about six of us, myself included, being detained in the cells. Lucky for us, David Dyson said it was the Middlesborough fans' fault and with him being a 'Boro fan, the police let us all go. My opinion of it was that Eric (Charlie) would take no shit off the Middlesborough fans and we all had to steam in to sort it out.

A few weeks later, we all received letters from Middlesborough FC saying that we would not be welcome at the ground again, so we would have to be careful at Middlesborough in future. Everything was OK on the way home, apart from an argument amongst ourselves. Paul Price, Tommy's brother and Addy Dearnley, had a fall out. Paul ended up biting Addy's finger nearly to the bone. Tommy and I restored order and we continued home without further incident!

The return leg was won by United 2-1. We did the same for the Middlesborough fans as they had for us and ended up drinking them under the table on Boddies' bitter! United were at Wembley again. This time against Brian Clough's Nottingham Forest, who had a great reputation in this tournament, but United were flying and feared no one. Lee Martin again provided us with tickets; the Kensington Hilton was again booked for the weekend. The seats Lee had got us were up in the Olympic Gallery at a cost of £100 face value. The views were fantastic, although the atmosphere up there in the gods is not the same. United won the game through a Brian McClair goal, and at last we were crowned Rumbelows Cup Winners, the wait was worth it, but not as much as winning our first league title. The match was not a classic.

Throughout the match there was a lot of fighting between United and Forest fans. Thousands of United fans had somehow got into the Forest end. We were later told that the main culprit was the Forest manager Brian Clough but I don't think any action was taken due to his bad health.

April that year, was a disaster for United. They had to play four games in eight days, which I still say played into Leeds' hands. It was a total disgrace to the FA who should never have let this kind of situation arise, especially to my team Manchester United. We drew away 1-1 at Luton and should have easily won the game on 18th April. We then threw away our slight advantage over Leeds by losing 2-1 at home to Nottingham Forest. As an ex-player myself, I could see the tiredness in the players' legs. I couldn't stand the things that were happening but what hurt the most was travelling down to West Ham on 22nd April for a night game. United's support was tremendous. West Ham were already relegated. I saw all the lads at the game. Banana Bob's lot from London were there, along with O'Neil's lot from Manchester. These are the real boys. There were about 150 of them all wearing black balaclavas. The West Ham lot stayed well away. We all went boozing in a pub near to the ground that is owned by a friend of mine; a big Red from London called Cockney Mick. The pub is called The Prince Alfred all the United and West Ham fans meet up there after the game to have a pint together. This match was different. West Ham played as if their mothers' lives depended on it and won the match 1-0. I could feel the league drifting away from us. We all went back to Mick's pub where we all drowned our sorrows. To make matters worse, West Ham fans attacked Mick's pub, throwing CS gas canisters through the windows. When we went out to confront them they had all vanished, they had even let our coach tyres down. We didn't mind the delay, as it meant we could stay in the pub until the AA came to rescue us!

We now had to win our last game away at Liverpool. The West Ham fans had been singing, 'You lost the league at West Ham'. I could not bear to hear the Liverpool fans singing the same thing. Could it be possible that United would lose, thus giving the league to Leeds who had the great Eric Cantona playing for them. My worst fears turned out to be right. Liverpool played as West Ham had, as if their mothers' lives depended on it, and beat us 2-0. All I could think of is why does every team and their fans in the whole country hate United? Leeds won the league by four points, so knocking them out of both cups that season didn't help our cause at all. United's last game was at Old Trafford against Spurs, which United won 3-1. The only good thing to come from that game, was that it was Gary Lineker's last game.

United won the European Super Cup Final at Old Trafford against Red Star Belgrade. The final was reduced to one match due to the Civil War in Yugoslavia. In defence of the Cup Winners Cup, after beating a Greek team in the first round, we were drawn against Athletico Madrid, playing the first leg away in Madrid. I decided to travel to the game with a friend of mine from Stalybridge called Nigel Roberts (Nidge). We travelled in style going with British Airways direct to Madrid. I drove us down to Heathrow in my car. When we boarded the flight, which was Club Class, I was lucky enough to be seated next to my idol Denis Law, the King, who was going over to do some TV work. Denis signed my passport and we became friends, so when we arrived in Madrid, Denis got us accommodation in his hotel for three nights. He was not happy, as there was a problem with Athletico's chairman and the TV rights, so the game was not shown, and Denis had wasted his time travelling all the way to Madrid before finding this out. Lee had got me tickets for the game. United were awful, they were hammered 3-0, with Athletico's forward Futre running the show up front and the German Schuster in rnidfield. United were complaining that two of the goals were offside, but I think Gary Pallister had a nightmare of a game and Athletico took full advantage.

We spent three days around Madrid's Grand-Via and took a trip around Real Madrid's San Bernabou Stadium. I remember thinking how I wish I could see United play there; as it happens only time would tell. The game at Old Trafford was drawn 1-1. That was the end of United's defence of the Cup

Winner's Cup. United were out. What could have the been the treble, ended with United only winning the Rumbelows Cup that season. I still knew better things were around the corner.

The 1992/93 Season kicked off badly for United with them losing their first two games. The first 2-1 away to Sheffield United who had a new chairman, Michael McDonald who lived near to me in Glossop. Mick always got tickets for me if United played at Sheffield as well as players' lounge tickets. I used to meet Mick every Friday evening for a few pints in the Lowes Arms in Denton; he made his money from scrap metal. There was talk that he was going to buy Manchester City, but nothing came of it. He was a keen City fan but never went. We called these people True Blues. In the next game we lost 3-0 against Everton at Old Trafford. Our local bookmaker, a Blue, was offering odds at 8 to 1 for United to win the league. So £200 of my money was placed on United to win. I knew I had a good bet.

The turning point for me, was the away trip to Southampton for a night game where Dion Dublin scored a late winner for the Reds. I travelled down to this game in a Transit van with the Macclesfield Reds. My brother Wallace drove the van. It was another very long journey, but it was definitely the turning point. United won the next five games on the trot. Torpeado Moscow knocked us out of the UEFA Cup on penalties. Aston Villa knocked us out of the League Cup and Sheffield United knocked us out of the FA Cup with Steve Bruce missing a late penalty. So United were out early of all the cups, they could now concentrate on the league title after a twenty-six year wait.

This season, Addy Dearnley was celebrating his fortieth birthday and booked an executive day at Old Trafford for the Norwich game. About twenty of us paid £100 each for a great day. United won 1-0. We had a free bar all day and took full advantage to get our money's worth. After the game Eric Cantona and Gary Gillespie were introduced to us. Eric was kissed fully on the lips by Tommy Price, who had won the signed match ball for getting the score right, along with the nearest time of the goal as well. I will never forget the look of shock on Eric's face;

he just couldn't believe it. We all had a great time. Eventually, at about 7 p.m., United's Head of Security, Ned Kelly, had to ask us all to leave. We were singing all the old songs in the bar. Wilf McGuiness entertained us with all the old stories and Paddy Crerand ended up singing with us all in the bar. What a great day it was, I will never forget it.

I knew then that we were going to win the league this year. The most expensive seats we paid for were at Chelsea, where we had to pay £25 to sit in their Main Stand; I thought it was a disgrace. United drew 1-1. In January we went down to QPR away, where United won 3-1. The seats we had were right behind the goal. Tommy Price and myself found ourselves sitting next to Dani Behr, the TV presenter, who at the time was rumoured to be dating Ryan Giggs. Tommy kept kissing her fully on the lips every time United scored. She could not get away. All the lads were laughing. He nearly crushed her slight frame to death. Tommy weighs in at about nineteen stone!

On sixth March that season, we played Liverpool away, winning 2-1. Again we had a run in with the Liverpool fans at the Shankly Gates. Ray Price, Tommy's brother, was arrested. The police were kicking lumps out of him in the police van. It was only when he pretended to have a heart condition that the Liverpool police stopped hitting him, charged him and let him go quickly. This all happened about an hour before kickoff. On his release, he jumped straight into a taxi and came to the Liverpool ground to watch the game. He was bailed to appear in a Liverpool Court on 5th April, which was the same day that United had a night game at Norwich. I took Ray to Liverpool in the morning for his Court case, where he was fined £100 and banned from United matches for the remainder of the season. This never deterred Ray. We drove straight from the Liverpool Courts to Manchester Airport where, through Lee Martin, we had booked two seats to travel with the United team to Norwich. United won 3-1, killing them off quickly with three early goals. This ended Norwich's hopes of winning the league. United fans were singing the dreaded song 'We're going to win the league, so now you're going to believe us'. It was a long day but it was worth it!

That season also saw Tommy Price get arrested at Blackburn where we drew 0-0. Before the game started, Tommy ran onto the pitch to talk to his idol Peter Schmeichel and to also try and pinch his towel whilst he was there. Peter did not find this funny and the police eventually arrested Tommy. After the game all the lads on the 52-seater coach waited for Tommy, but he had already been cautioned and paid for a taxi back from Blackburn, thus beating us all home. Back at his workshop the following morning, I went to visit Tom. He used to have a team picture of United on his wall behind his desk but he was that angry at what Peter Schmeichel had said, that he had blacked him out of the picture with a felt-tipped pen. I could not help but laugh at Tommy. He's United daft just like myself!

The Sheffield Wednesday game at Old Trafford that season was again unbelievable. Lee Martin had again come up trumps and managed to get me some players' lounge tickets. I always used to take my son Robert with me into the players' lounge after the game, where Lee would get all the United autographs for him. We left dead on ninety minutes to walk around to the players' lounge, United were losing 1-0. I must admit I thought they were going to lose but the ref played about eight minutes extra. Trevor Francis their manager was going ballistic. United somehow scored two late goals to the Stretford End, both of them headers scored by Steve Bruce.

The next big decider for me was the night game at Crystal Palace. Again Lee booked two seats on the United plane. Ray Price and myself travelled to the match with the players. When we arrived near to the ground, we saw the Stalybridge branch's coach outside a pub, so we asked the Supporters Club Chairman, Barry Moorhouse, if we could get off the coach and have a drink with the lads. Barry was not very happy about this but anyway we jumped off the coach at the traffic lights and went into the pub. The match was a classic; United won 2-0 with goals from Ince and Hughes. Our problems began after the match, as we couldn't find the coach to take us back to the airport. We had to pay £60 for a taxi. We arrived with minutes to spare before the plane was due to fly back with the team to Manchester. We were the last two to board. Barry was not amused with us, but with

United winning, he managed to force a smile. When we took our seats, the whole plane started clapping; even the great Bobby Charlton clapped us on board. It was with a bit of sarcasm! That evening our rivals Blackburn were beaten by Aston Villa, so it looked like we were at last going to win the league. Tonight United had played in their green and yellow quartered strip. The kit manager, Norman Davies, let Lee have the reserve strip which they always carried with them. Lee got all the players to sign the shirts and let me have the whole set. I had them all framed. Tommy and myself had half the team each. They are still my most prized possessions.

United were at last crowned Champions at Old Trafford against Blackburn Rovers, and the atmosphere that day on a sunny afternoon was fantastic. There were flags and banners everywhere. The relief on the supporters' faces could be seen everywhere. It was a very emotional day. It still sends a shiver down my spine when I think about it. Gary Pallister managed to score a free kick, thus ensuring that every United outfield player had scored that season. The lap of honour was great. The face of Sir Matt Busby, in his seat smiling, will live with me forever. At last United were crowned Premier League Champions.

The last away game of the season was at Wimbledon where there were over 20,000 United fans. It was spoilt by the antics of a few head-bangers who invaded the pitch and so spoiled the celebrations. United were unable to do the customary lap of honour with the trophy. We had again booked into the Kensington Hilton and stayed for the weekend. The celebrations went on until the early hours. Back in Ashton, on Sunday night, we had a brilliant time; thousands were singing and dancing in the streets which the police had closed to traffic and just let people carry on celebrating until the early hours of Monday morning. United were now back in the European cup

The 1993/94 Season kicked off with a great 2-0 win at Norwich. Tommy and I drove down in my car, with Tommy doing the driving. We made it back somehow in under three hours on a Sunday, which isn't bad considering the distance to Norwich.

Also this season we lost 1-0 at Chelsea with the great Eric Cantona nearly scoring from the halfway line with the ball hitting the bar. David Beckham eventually did this feat a few years later, but Eric had tried it first at Chelsea. United beat Arsenal 1-0 at Old Trafford, with a great free kick from Eric to the Scoreboard End. It was looking like United were a force to be reckoned with. The derby game at Maine Road was a classic. United were losing 2-0 to City at half-time. I still had the feeling we could win the game. I was sat just behind the United bench with Tommy. In the second half, United soon drew level with two quick goals from Eric Cantona to the Platt Lane End before Roy Keane grabbed a late winner for the Reds. The game is shown on TV replays and is on videos all over the country. It shows Tommy and I celebrating with the United bench and Alex Ferguson. After the game we had tickets for the Joe Mercer Suite in the Main Stand. Tommy was so excited, that he started singing the 'If I die in the Kippax Street' song in front of all the Blues, but they were so sick, they could not believe what had happened, 2-0 up; 3-2 down, they were in shock. We had parked our coach on the Kippax Street and on our return three of the lads had been arrested for various offences. I saw one City fan that I knew from Denton called Steve Jackson, a die-hard Blue. He must have been a head-banger as he had a blue City shirt on. He stopped our coach and asked for Bruce MacInnes. I was sat in the middle of the coach. He walked down the coach with his blue shirt on. When he reached me he said "Well played," shook my hand, walked off the coach and disappeared. Now that must have taken a lot of bottle!

A classic game that season was at Liverpool on 4th January. It was a night game Tommy and I bought two tickets from a United tout called Martin for the Main Stand. We knew we had to keep our mouths shut, which I knew would be very difficult for Tommy. We went to our seats which were at the very back of the stand. We were sat with the ugliest looking Liverpool supporters I have ever seen. The smell in the air was cannabis. I knew we had to behave ourselves. The game was another classic. United went 3-0 up in the first half; all the goals were scored to the United end. Liverpool regrouped and came at United in the second half scoring three goals to make it 3-3. Nigel Clough scored two and Razor Ruddock scored the Liverpool equalizer — so we came away with a draw.

United were now playing some great football. People were now talking about the double or even the treble, which years ago was unheard of. A new ground that we went to that season was Swindon away; Eric Cantona was having a bad time with the referees. He was dismissed for stamping. United drew 2-2. One Swindon fan punched Mark Hughes in the face when he tried to take a quick throw down the touchline. This made the United fans furious and after the game there were running battles between the United and Swindon fans. On the way back our coach stopped at a lovely pub in the countryside; it was a glorious day and there was an off-licence by the side of the pub. Everyone was drinking outside the place. It was overrun with United fans; hundreds of them. The off-licence only had one young girl working the till, with no cameras to watch for stealing. I could not believe it, the United fans stole everything they could get their hands on, from crates of beer to bottles of champagne and loaded up the coach; so needless to say everyone got drunk for free all the way home!

The next away game, Eric was sent off again. This time I thought the decision was very harsh. It was at Arsenal and they had him sent off, in my opinion, the way only Arsenal can do, by conning the referee. Throughout the 1993/94 Season, United maintained their form and again kept their Championship, although we had a 2-0 defeat at Blackburn where Alan Shearer scored both goals. We gave Shearer a lot of abuse throughout the entire game, singing 'There's only one greedy bastard' but Shearer got his revenge. Walking back to the car after the game, we found ourselves surrounded by Blackburn fans. Eric Mitchell (Charlie), had decided to sing the Shearer song again and all the Blackburn fans were singing 'There's only one Alan Shearer'. Anyway, Charlie head-butted one of them and it was a free for all in the middle of the road. We were outnumbered about five to one but we did not care, no one would have left Eric to get hammered. Ray Price and myself steamed in. We thought we were going to get killed. Just then Stevie Cope from Dane Bank approached with about ten Reds and helped us out. We all walked back in a group with a police escort. When I saw Steve later, I thanked him for helping us out.

In the FA Cup, United won 1-0 at Sheffield United with a Mark Hughes goal to the Sheffield end. The football United played before the goal was superb. Every player was involved in the build up and the movement was great. Again the team was playing for each other. I began to think the treble could be possible, especially after we beat Norwich away 2-0, then Wimbledon away 3-0. We now had a home game against Charlton who brought great support to Old Trafford. Just before half-time, Peter Schmeichel was dismissed. The Charlton fans thought they would win, but United took off Paul Parker and put Sealy in goal. United played great football and won the game 3-1. Again they were drawn against Oldham Athletic in the semifinal. For some strange reason, the FA decided on Wembley for the game. This upset both sets of fans as we had to travel two hundred miles, but that's the FA for you.

The semi was not a classic. Neil Poyton, the ex-Everton fullback, gave Oldham the lead in extra time. I thought United were going out, so I phoned my mum. She said to pray to Saint Jude, which I did, and with seconds remaining, Mark Hughes scored one of his trademark volleys to equalize. It was a cracking goal. The replay was to be played at Maine Road. United won the game easily 4-1. Andrei Kanchelskis ran the show, running the Oldham defence ragged. He always saved his best performances for Oldham Athletic; we were now at Wembley again. The final was to be between Manchester United and Chelsea. We hammered them 4-0 with two Eric Cantona penalties. The Chelsea fans were furious and there was lots of trouble after the game. It was pouring down with rain as I walked back to the tube with Tommy and Ray Price and Eric. I begged Eric to keep his mouth shut as there were plenty of Chelsea fans around and to my astonishment he did! We were stood on the platform with all the Chelsea fans. All the United fans were on the other side when a lad called Gary Wright from Droylsden spotted us and shouted over "Hi Bruce". He threw a can of lager over, which I opened straight away. We started to drink it. I can only say that we got away lightly. The Chelsea fans were still in shock!

I didn't arrange a weekend trip for the Chelsea game, as my wife Carol, was pregnant with our third child. She was already one week overdue. She didn't want me to miss the game, so I drove down with Tommy Price, armed with a mobile phone. I must have had twenty calls from people winding me up to say Carol was having the baby and could I get to the hospital! As luck would have it, she had the baby the next day. It was a boy and what better name to give him than Alex Ryan MacInnes, naming him after what for me is the greatest United manager of all time.

This was the year United won the double. In the League Cup, which was now called the Coca-Cola Cup we played Stoke City away, losing 2-1 in the first leg. As you can imagine there was a lot of trouble at Stoke. To give Stoke their due, they brought a good crew to Old Trafford for the second leg; about 8,000 of them. Again there was trouble after the game. United won 2-0. We then had to play Leicester at home, who we beat 5-1, then Everton away who we beat 2-0. I went to this game without a ticket but I managed to buy one outside the ground. I had to sit in Everton's end, which is called the Gladice Street, and try to keep my mouth shut! We then drew at Old Trafford with Portsmouth winning the replay 1-0. Again there was trouble after the game. Pompey's fans wanted to have a go at United's crew, but all that happened was a few minor skirmishes, nothing to write home about. I went to this game with Derek Howarth from Denton, who is a friend of Mick Hucknall. We drove down in Derek's car and it was another long trip. Derek does not miss many matches. He also has two brothers; one called Simon, who is a plumber and still travels with me today; and Lil — no one knows where he is. Lil and Mick Hucknall grew up together. I remember going to football with Lil in the 70s. He was United mad, like the rest of his family. We were playing Cardiff City away in the league. There was trouble with Cardiff's crew. They had put the United fans in an end like the Kippax Street at City. It was half United fans and half Cardiff fans. They were singing Munich '5 8 and we were singing Aberfan, the scene of a mining disaster in the sixties. Both sets were attacking each other. The trouble continued onto the streets afterwards. Lil was photographed kicking a Cardiff fan on the street with his jet-black hair and white pants. This was printed in *Shoot* magazine which was big in those days and also on the back page of the *News of the World*. It seemed like the whole world was after Lil Howarth. Wherever you are Lil, look after yourself. Mick Hucknall still asks after you whenever I see him.

After beating Portsmouth, we had an easy semifinal against Sheffield Wednesday — winning 5-1 on aggregate. We now had to face Aston Villa in the final. Again I arranged a 52-seater coach for the final. This time staying at the Olympia Hilton in London we had a great weekend, but the Villa fans were only after trouble. That weekend, everywhere we went in London, Villa fans were causing trouble. I was now getting sick of it. It was at the time when all-day drinking had just come into force. The timing of the game did not help matters. That Saturday night, I had arranged to meet my brother-in-law, Alan Hazlehurst, who worked as a fireman at London's Earls Court Olympia for years. Alan took us around all the pubs in Shepherd's Bush. Again Villa fans were everywhere. You would have thought they had never been to Wembley before. Come to think of it, I don't know whether they had been. Anyway we entered one big pub; about thirty of us. Tommy Price heard some fans singing. There was about fifty of them. He thought they were singing 'Glory, glory Man United' and started to sing the song along with them. They were in fact singing 'Who the fuck are Man United' to the same tune. They were Villa fans not United fans as Tommy had thought. All the Villa fans stopped singing but Tommy continued as if nothing had happened. There was deadly silence only Tommy's voice could be heard. My heart was in my mouth. I said to Tommy "Keep it quiet. We are outnumbered here." One of their boys said to me "You had better get him out of here for his own safety." So rather than spoil a good weekend, we all finished our drinks then went off to the Hammersmith Palais. Alan had arranged it with the doorman for us all to get in free, by telling them we were all firemen from Manchester on an outing. He flashed his card, so we all went in without any problem. What a great night that was!

The next morning after breakfast, we heard that Villa fans had again attacked United fans. This time at a pub called the Punch and Judy in Covent Garden. We all got onto our coach. I said to the lads "Let's get to the Case is Altered in Kilburn, where we know all the Tameside Reds will be. We all had a good drink before the game, without seeing many Villa fans, but on the tube station at Dollis Hill there were over 100 of them standing on the platform without making any effort to get on the train. We knew that they were only after trouble. All the United fans, with their girlfriends or children, were being intimidated by this gang. We knew how to deal with this, so about fifty of us went over the bridge and came down the other end. The fifty ran at the Villa fans who were now stuck in the middle. There followed a mass brawl that lasted about twenty minutes. Just then a tube arrived and the Villa fans scrambled onto it. They got what they deserved. I was sick of having to move away from them. They did not think they would meet a crew of United fans like the Tameside Reds, but they were in for a shock. I ended up breaking my hand and had to have it put into plaster the next day. United lost the game 3-1, in a scrappy match; but what a tremendous season it was; two out of three can't be bad. I felt sorry for Lee Martin, who was now in Celtic's first team at fullback. I was thinking how much money he could have made if he had signed that one-year contract to stay at United. He would have been in the players' pool for both cups and for winning the league. Also he would have had European Cup games under his belt, because of the stupid ruling that FIFA had about English and home-grown players. Lee would have made a hell of a lot more money if he had stayed.

That season, in the derby game against City at Old Trafford, United won 2-0. I was sat in the Main Stand next to Paul Hands. At half-time we went to the toilets, where there was an argument going on between some Reds and Blues. Upon closer inspection, it was Coronation Street's Curly Watts, who was rumoured to be a reformed alcoholic and also a big City fan. He was wearing a City scarf, big blue City specs, with windscreen washers on them! He was saying how crap United were and making a complete and utter fool of himself. Paul said to him "You had better shut your mouth Curly or else you will get a slap no matter who you are." Knowing Handsy as I do, with nearly twenty-five of his forty-two years having been spent in prison or borstals, he was not joking. Curly made the right decision by shutting his mouth. He then tried to walk away, falling about drunk. We could not help but feel sorry for him.

I would now like to go back to a friend of mine who was another United supporter from Ashton-under-Lyne; his name was David Andrews. One pre-season, we were playing Blackpool away on a night game. I had arranged for about twenty of us to go to the game in a Transit van. We picked up in Middleton at the Old Albion pub another gang of Reds. This was a Boddies' pub and we set off with Phil Collinge with whom I worked with at Clayton Aniline. We parked up in Blackpool town centre, then went for a drink. We told all the lads to be back at the van at midnight as we were all split up. Another lad who had come with us, was an ex-Crystal Palace and Man City player called Gary Lowe. Before going back to the van after the game, Gary and I called into a chip shop to get something to eat, when we were approached by two lads who asked Gary where he was from. I noticed that the two lads had knives hidden underneath their chips. I told Gary to run for it. The two lads gave chase but they had no chance of catching us. Gary had played under Terry Venables at Crystal Palace as well as Malcolm Allison at Maine Road, so we were both quite fit. We made it back to the van where most of the lads were waiting for us. We quickly explained the situation to them. When the two lads appeared, they did not know what to do. All the lads jumped out of the van. It was like the Alamo. These two lads were finished and took a good beating. 'Serves them right' I thought. The only problem we had now was that the car park was locked until the morning. Most of the lads had work to go to the next day. This was when we needed Dave Andrews. He said he would save us, so off he went into the night! About an hour later, he reappeared, this time carrying a large box which I thought were tools. In fact he had been breaking into cars to find a hacksaw. What he had actually found in one car, were lots of dirty mags and sex aids of all descriptions! The lads knew that they would be kept occupied now throughout the night. As luck would have it, four lads in a car asked us what the problem was? They were carrying a hacksaw and they even sawed through the chain for us. We were away leaving the car park locks on the floor. By the time we had dropped all the lads off, then returned the van, Phil Collinge and myself had to start work. Clayton Aniline didn't get much work out of us that day.

David became mentally ill and was diagnosed as a schizophrenic. He unfortunately hanged himself at a young age. He is still remembered as a good Man United fan. My thoughts are still with you today David. Gary Lowe drifted from pro football to non-league football. Gary was a gifted footballer. Some say he was the best footballer to come from Ashton-under-Lyne, but that is a matter of opinion. He went to Hong Kong to play for Hong Kong Rangers with the great Bobby Moore coaching them. He decided to rent his house out to one of the Hereford team, Joe Laidlaw, whilst he was playing abroad. When he returned, he had a problem. Joe had not been paying any rent into Gary's bank. He was now squatting in his flat. Gary asked me to go down to Hereford to help him sort it out diplomatically. I said I would. We drove down midweek and to my astonishment Joe would not let Gary into his own flat. He had acquired a big Alsatian dog. I told Gary that he was on his own with this one. Months later it was all settled. I think the Hereford chairman had to step in. I still see Gary, but not as often. He now manages a non-league team called Curzon Ashton FC.

Back to the Season of 1993/94. In the European Cup, United were drawn away to play Kispest Honved; the Hungarian champions. I decided to run a trip to Budapest, staying for one night in the capital by luxury coach. The cost worked out at £115, including match tickets. We also had tee shirts printed with the slogan 'Stalybridge Supporters Club on Tour'. So fifty lads took the week off work. Then we set off on a 2,000 mile round trip, that only the lads who travelled can describe. We travelled overland on a Sunday night, sleeping rough on the coach. Our first stop was at a bar in Austria. The owner thought it was his birthday. Fifty lads asking if he was open! He was just about to close, but when I vouched that everyone would pay up, he was persuaded to stay open for us. We drank until the early hours. By then everyone was very drunk. When it was time to pay up, the owner started asking all the lads how much they had drunk expecting them to be honest and to pay for everything that they had consumed. Not one of them admitted to having more than two pints of lager. After being there for four hours, we must have drunk the bar dry. The poor owner let us all go so as not to cause any trouble. We all slept right through to the next stop of a very long journey. Everywhere we stopped in different countries, no one had any currency, so again by the time it came to paying everyone was just buying the cheapest thing, such as a cup of tea or coffee! When we arrived at the hotel on the morning of the game, no one could believe how cheap but beautiful Budapest was; pints of beer were about twenty pence. About twenty of us decided to charter a boat, then went in style down the river, which splits Buda from Pest, drinking for next to nothing all day. United won the game 3-2, letting Honved back into the game with two late strikes. Keane scored two goals with Eric Cantona getting one. The return journey was a laugh; all the way back as soon as any one had closed their eyes to get some sleep someone would steal their drinks! We arrived back at the Star Pub in Ashton on Friday night. I had arranged for a friend called David Moffett to pick me up, then take me home to Glossop, so that I could have a few beers. We had travelled over 2,000 miles without incident, then Moff drove his car 300 yards from the pub to take me home and smashed his car straight into the back of a taxi at the roundabout. Only Moff could do something like that! We beat Honved 2-1 at Old Trafford and were then drawn against Galatasaray in the next round.

This was to be an experience I never want to repeat. It is the only time in my life that I can say I am glad to be coloured. At the time of writing this book I would like to take this opportunity to express my sadness at the loss of two Leeds United fans who were brutally murdered at their club's game in Galatasaray. I am not a lover of Leeds, but no football game is worth losing your life for. The first leg was played at Old Trafford, and to give Galatasaray their due, they came at us with the final score ending up 3-3; Eric Cantona saving our blushes. United had the game sewn up. It was only a lack of concentration that changed the events. Within minutes we were 3-2 down and could easily have lost our unbeaten European record at Old Trafford. I also have to admit that the Galatasaray fans got behind their team. They sang throughout the entire game. For the second leg I decided to travel with Ray and Tommy Price, Pete (Strett) Fallon, Charlie Orr, Cockney Mick from the Prince Alfred pub in West Ham and Derek Howarth; seven of us in total. We had also decided to travel in and out with United for safety reasons. We arrived in Turkey at about 11 a.m. — on our arrival, we were all asked to queue in single file and to have our passports ready. There were hundreds of Galatasaray supporters with banners saying welcome to hell and English pigs, etc., etc., waiting for us at the airport. At passport control, we were told that we each had to hand over a five pound note to the policeman. Then the other policeman would stamp your passport and let you through. It was a very disturbing situation which was taking hours to complete. I knew it was bad when Tommy handed his new five pound note to the wrong policeman. The policeman took the money then in full view of everyone put it straight into his pocket. The next policeman said to Tommy "Five pounds please" to which Tommy replied "I have already given it to him at the side of you." The policeman was having none of it and poor Tommy had to pay another five pounds, then was sent to the back of the queue for daring to speak out of turn.

After about three hours waiting, we were taken out of the airport and hustled onto our coaches. To be fair to United, they had told us to be inside the ground in plenty of time but none of us took any notice. When we got into the town centre, there were rumours flying about that about two hundred United supporters had been deported the night before for various disturbances, with some of them being arrested. They had all booked with, yes you've guessed it, U/F Tours the same firm which we had nearly booked with, so our luck was in so far. Tommy Price and myself were shown on BBC 1 News at the airport — which is another claim to fame! All seven of us tried to stay together but the situation was getting worse. Istanbul has a population of ten million and is a law unto itself. I just knew problems were going to occur. We got to the ground four hours before kickoff. Tommy and Ray Price had decided to go in early as they are both white with blond hair and blue eyes. Tommy had a United sweatshirt on with a big Red Devil on the front, and so felt that they had nowhere to hide. The rest of us decided to go for a drink in a nearby bar, which turned out to be a big mistake. Within seconds we were surrounded by hundreds of Galatasaray fans. We quickly decided to try and get into the ground. Again we were made to queue at the ground in pairs. It is hard to describe the situation. Apparently, the ground had been full since 1 p.m.; all their fans get together and sing to create an atmosphere. The police had their own sets of keys to the ground. They were letting all of their friends in free into an area exclusively for United supporters. Hundreds of United fans didn't get into the ground. For me, a bit of magic got me in. An eagle eyed policeman saw me queuing up with the United supporters thinking I was a Galatasaray fan he beckoned me to approach him. He then opened a side door with a key. Now I was in the ground. All the other fans were locked outside, even though they had genuine tickets for the game. The atmosphere in the ground, I cannot compare with anything. The singing and dancing was like something out of Zulu. One end would chant to the other who would then get the other side going. Then they would end up singing together. The intimidation was unbelievable. Only five out of our seven got into the ground, with Strett and Charlie Orr being locked out and deciding to make their way back to the airport, which was probably the safest place to be. In the ground you had to sit or stand where you could. Derek Howarth had his head split open;

F

someone threw a spark plug, which hit him; it could have killed him. These people were both maniacs and fanatics. I was wearing the smallest United badge you could imagine but I took it off and threw it away. I wanted to get out of this alive. I daren't even imagine what would have happened if United had got through, but as it was, the game ended a 0-0 draw which meant the Turks would go through on the away goal ruling. Nothing was over yet, as Eric Cantona was sent off, the Turkish police attacked both him and Bryan Robson with batons in the tunnel after the game. I knew at the time the FIFA ruling about English players did not help, but I found it strange that Alex Ferguson had not played Mark Hughes. I could find no explanation for that, but who am I to question Fergie's tactics? When the final whistle went, the sky was lit up bright red with fireworks. The noise was deafening. Guns were being shot into the air. Even machine guns were used. Everyone was sounding their horns. The celebrations went on for days. United were out, I knew that these European nights were what it was all about. I also knew that there would be many more European games to follow.

When we arrived home, United blamed the Turks for everything. They were right. It was a long way to go to be treated like that. I said then that the Turks were corrupt. They should have been booted out of the tournament.

At about the same time, Sir Matt Busby died. He had seen the empire he had built, win many things at last, including the League and Cup double. How I wished we could have won the European Cup for him too, but that was still a far-off dream. Although only time would tell. A few weeks before the great man's death, we went to Old Trafford for another birthday celebration. Ray Price, having consumed a lot of alcohol, was trying to find the toilet, when he quickly turned with me right behind him. This resulted in him knocking this old gentleman over accidentally in the old stand; to our horror the man flat out on the floor was Sir Matt Busby himself. All the United security were around Ray saying "Do you know who that is? What have you done?" All Ray could see was Sir Matt stretched out on the floor. He was hysterical; apologising profusely. I said to him "Come on, we had better get in our seats quick." I hoped everything would be ok for Sir Matt. Two weeks later he died. We still rib Ray about this, but on a serious note it was nothing to do with this, it was a complete accident on Ray's part. Sir Matt's funeral went past Old Trafford; Manchester was in mourning for a great person and human being; Blues and Reds joining together for once. Tommy and I bought a bouquet of red and white roses with the message "Thanks for the memories". For Sir Matt, we drove to Old Trafford where people were now gathering to pay their respects, laying flowers and scarves at the old Scoreboard End. We lay our tribute in the middle of them all. By the following day thousands of tributes were there. I was told months later, that a documentary had been made which had shown our flowers in a close up. The programme was shown all over the world.

The following Saturday, United were playing Everton at Old Trafford. I would like to thank the Everton supporters for honouring the one minute silence for the great man. I cannot say the same for the Leeds fans who were at Blackburn. They booed throughout the one minute's silence. I can still remember the look of disgust on both Gordon Strachan and Howard Wilkinson's faces today. I cannot understand the depths some football supporters will go to in their hatred of other clubs. The respect people have for Sir Matt Busby and football, will stay with me until my dying days. I still remember him trying to pick up my eldest son Robert. I hope and pray that Robert will remember that day. I always mention it to him; in years to come he will be able to tell his friends that he met Sir Matt Busby.

The following pre-season, United arranged a friendly at Celtic Park playing Glasgow Celtic. Lee Martin, who was the Stalybridge Supporters Club President, arranged tickets for me. So off we all went up to Glasgow. We arrived at about 11 a.m. We decided to take in the stadium tour, where we bumped into Lou Macari. He signed autographs and chatted to us all for a while. I will always remember there was a replica of the European Cup, which was not in a glass case. Tommy Price picked it up then tried to put it on his head! We met all the Celtic supporters in the Celtic Club where we all sang songs together. These two sets of fans are, in my eyes, the best supporters on earth and their loyalty to each other is something to be proud of.

The Charity Shield that year was between United and Arsenal at Wembley. We went down to Mick's pub, the Prince Alfred, as Mick had said, that if United ever won the double, he would let us celebrate for free! Mick kept his word — we never spent a penny. A full weekend on the piss. He even laid on some entertainment for us. We all slept anywhere in the bar. There were two full coachloads and the place was heaving. On the Friday night, I went down to the East End with John Redfern and Dale Ellis to the Blind Beggar Pub, which is famous for the Kray twins' killing of Jack The Hat McVitie. We had a great night. Then went back in a taxi to the Prince Alfred. The actual match was a dull event, so we left a few minutes early to get out of the mad rush. I thought the trophy would be shared. It was only when we got back to the Prince Alfred that we heard United had won 5-4 on penalties. The FA had decided that it had to be settled. 'Thanks for telling me' I thought. United were now the undisputed team of the nineties and I was thinking more about the European Cup adventures. Also the money we were spending on Manchester United was madness. New strips for the kids were costing me a fortune. I would like to take this opportunity to say that no matter how much money I have spent on Manchester United, my three children Robert, Natalie and Alex, have never suffered in any way. They have always been my number one priority as anyone who knows me will tell you.

The 94/95 Season was a disaster for me. I still travelled everywhere watching United, but I was becoming disillusioned with my job as an insurance man, so I decided to leave Royal London after nine great years, after having a fall out with my boss. I was approached by the United Friendly to go and work for them. The insurance industry was going through a difficult period; first with the pension scandals and then with the retraining; so that all insurance personnel were now regulated under the same umbrella, the PIA. This also meant being qualified by examination in giving advice. I felt it was the right move, even though some companies took it to the extreme. I also thought the timing was right to move into something else as a backup. A friend of mine who lived around the corner in Glossop, Derbyshire, suggested a nightclub venture. He said that with all our contacts, we could make some real money for our pension. His name was Keith Gratrix. At the time, he had an accountancy business in Hazel Grove, Stockport. I thought about it very seriously and decided to give it a go. The club which was up for sale was called Dollars in the centre of Glossop. It was the only place with a 2 a.m. licence. After Keith had looked at the books, I decided to go into partnership in the entertainment business. A chain of events made it very easy for me to decide to give insurance a break, as I was stopped for drink driving and banned for twelve months. This would have made it very difficult to keep my contacts, with no car. I decided to manage the club full time. I moved into the nightclub, which we had purchased off a Mr Keith Lowry, who is a well-known name in Manchester circles. I had no knowledge of the industry at all, but after a few months' training, I soon became familiar with the pub game. Keith who is not so keen on football but likes Manchester United, never stood in my way for any ideas I had about the running of the club and left it all to me. I decided I wanted a grand opening, to do something which would put Glossop on the club scene, so I phoned a friend of mine who owns a windows company in Denton called Malburn Windows. His name is Stewart Kenyon; I knew he was a City fan, related to Mick Hucknall and also a good friend of my idol Denis Law. He asked me if I would like to go round to Denis Law's house one Saturday morning, for a chat, which I accepted without hesitation. Whilst we were there, I met Denis and his family. Stewart told Denis how I was in the process of purchasing Dollars nightclub and asked him if he would like to attend the opening night with his family. Denis said it would be a pleasure and like the gentleman he is, asked if there was anything else I would like him to do. I cheekily asked if he could bring Georgie

Best and his wife Alex. He surprised me by saying to leave it with him. I told him that I knew Paddy Crerand, along with his wife, and also John Aston and his wife would be there. For those of you who cannot remember the 1968 European Cup team, John played on the wing and won the 'man of the match' by destroying the Benfica fullback. Paddy Crerand was a great footballer, who we had signed from Glasgow Celtic. Denis rang me the following week as he had promised, to tell me that Georgie would be delighted to come to the opening with his wife Alex, so I rang John and Paddy, who also said that they would attend.

Everything was arranged for a Thursday evening, for the grand opening of Dollars. We had five hundred tickets printed and the whole town was talking about the event for weeks before. The buffet that evening can only be described as world class. It is still talked about today. The Stalybridge branch brought two full coaches; the Macclesfield branch one coach. Alan Platt, the Manchester United Master of Ceremonies, also attended. It was an enjoyable evening for everyone who attended. People still talk to me about that night today. It's not very often you can get four of the '68 European Cup team there on one day, but I managed it! We had arranged to meet everyone at the Midland Hotel in Piccadilly, Manchester, then drive them all to Dollars in two Jaguars which we had hired for the day. My partner Keith and I arrived early. I must say that I was nervous when George's agent Phil Hughes rang from London to say George had missed his train. My first thought was that if he could let some football managers down then why not Bruce MacInnes! Phil Hughes reassured my worst nightmares and said George would be on the next train up from London. At the time of writing, George is recovering in hospital from what everyone knows is a liver condition caused by drink. I wish him a speedy recovery and would like to thank him for the memories. A few years earlier, my wife Carol and her sister-in-law met him in his bar in London. When he heard their northern accents, he bought them both a drink saying that northern girls were the best and it was always good to hear a northern voice! Now George was coming to the opening of my own nightclub. I am now in the process of opening another bar in Tenerife, which I intend to call Besties, after the genius himself, who I still say is one of the greatest players I have ever had the pleasure to both watch and meet.

We were all having a drink in the Midland Hotel's bar; some of the stories Denis and Paddy were telling, were hard to believe. It's right what they say about footballers, they are the best people to meet, as they really know how to enjoy themselves. I remember Paddy telling me how his house had been burgled and his European Cup winner's medal had been stolen. The last he had heard, was that someone had bought it in Glasgow. Things like this should not happen. How can anybody try to make money out of someone else's success? After an hour, George arrived with Alex, who went straight to her room to get changed. George was already dressed very smart and was ready for the occasion. We spent another hour in the bar listening to George telling us about some of the things that have happened in his lifetime. I felt very sorry for him, but like George said, he was very lucky to have been brought up as a footballer and given the chance. He said he wouldn't change a thing. His memories are all he has left. The only thing he has left of his football memorabilia, is his first pair of football boots his father bought him at eleven years old. All the rest has either been stolen or sold. He said that he hoped that his first wife Angie, with whom he has a son called Callum, has all his football medals, including the European Cup winner's medal stored in a safe place on behalf of Callum. We could have listened to George all night. He is truly a lovable character.

The evening went great, with all the players having their photos taken and signing autographs throughout the night. I even remember having a dance with Alex, who is a beautiful lady with long blonde hair. She truly adores George and loves him very much. She also told me that her parents didn't live far from the club in Buxton, Derbyshire. The papers did a big spread all about the opening night. George had a great deal to drink. He was drinking wine which was not a big seller in the club. I remember having to send one of the girls to the off licence to get some more! I knew George was enjoying himself

87

and why not! So now everyone knew where Dollars was and also who the new owners were.

The 1994/95 Season, we all felt could not possibly be as good as the year before both for football and enjoyment but nothing surprises you about MUFC. We had a good start to the season. Our first defeat was at Leeds in September losing 2-1. Further defeats at Ipswich 3-2, Sheffield Wednesday 1-0, followed by six straight wins in October and November, put us in a commanding position. Included in these wins was a 5-0 hammering of Manchester City at Old Trafford. This made amends for that 5-1 hammering at Maine Road a few years earlier. Who says what goes around comes around? Andrei Kanchelskis had another stormer, scoring a hat trick, but there were rumours circulating Old Trafford that he was on his way out due to a fall out with Fergie. Gambling debts were also mentioned as well as links with the Russian Mafia. Kanchelskis was a great winger for United, who I said would be hard to replace, but another youngster called David Beckham was emerging.

Our nearest rivals that season were Blackburn Rovers who, under Kenny Dalglish's guidance and Jack Walker's money, were to fight us all the way. We had already beaten Blackburn away 4-2 in a classic match. Although I felt sorry for Henning Berg, who was sent off. He later signed for United along with David May another ex-Blackburn player, who has now accumulated a lot more medals than Alan Shearer. Just before Christmas, we lost 2-1 at Old Trafford to Nottingham Forest, then had a good run, doing the double over Manchester City 3-0 at Maine Road; 8-0 on aggregate — not bad eh! Two defeats on Merseyside, 1-0 at Everton and 2-0 at Liverpool, helped Blackburn Rovers keep up the pace but the match of the season for me was the 9-0 hammering of Ipswich Town. This avenged the 6-0 hammering we took at the hands of Ipswich at Portman Road in the late 70s. Everything United tried that day, paid dividends. Andy Cole scored five. I must say that I was surprised Kevin Keegan sold us Andy Cole for Gary Gillespie, our winger, plus cash. Again rumours were flying around about young Gillespie's drinking and gambling but no one can argue about Alex's judgement in the transfer market. This season everyone was saying the league could go to the last match of the season. How right they were, it did. With Blackburn at Liverpool, United had to win at West Ham. We thought Liverpool would lose on purpose for Kenny Dalglish and also because we knew Liverpool fans hated United, but I must hold my hands up, I still cannot believe it but Liverpool beat Blackburn at Anfield with United drawing at West Ham. The support United had at West Ham that Saturday afternoon, was unbelievable. Over 10,000 Reds were there. We had the whole of the Bobby Moore Stand. The Reds never stopped singing, but it was not to be. We missed a number of good chances; the West Ham goalkeeper played well. Our rivals Blackburn Rovers won the title by one point; that's football for you! What annoys me is that we beat Blackburn both games that season and only lost six games, but still ended runners-up.

In the FA Cup, United beat Sheffield United away 2-0, then Wrexham 5-2, Leeds at Old Trafford 3-1, QPR at Old Trafford 2-0 then Crystal Palace after a replay. I have bad memories of Crystal Palace, firstly in the FA Cup Final replay, where I thought Palace tried to kick United off the park before losing to a Lee Martin late winner and also because of the Eric Cantona incident which everyone knows about where Eric kung fued a Palace fan! For me the semifinal was spoilt by the death of a Palace supporter killed by a coach, which crushed him as he tried to get away from both sets of fans that had clashed before the match. United were again at Wembley, this time against Everton, who we had beaten before. But this time we lost 1-0 in a scrappy match. Let's not take anything away from Everton, they worked hard and closed us down. I would just like to add at this point, that since Manchester United have played at Wembley in Cup Finals since 1968, I have only missed two, including the Charity Shields. I am very proud of this record, which has been thirty-two years in the making.

In the Coca-Cola Cup, United were beaten by Newcastle after taking care of Port Vale the round before. United were not taking this tournament seriously. Alex Ferguson still seems to treat this cup as a chance to look at the youngsters. I can't say I blame

Alex, as it is a long hard season, especially when you think how many games are played by the first team. By now most of the lads weren't interested in going to the Coca-Cola games. I had been to well over 1,000 United matches, if you take into account the pre-season friendlies. I was averaging over forty games a season, which I don't think is bad by any one's standards.

The European Cup was now my dream. I wanted to see United win that one trophy which had started it all off for me. That year, 1994/95, in the European Cup we were drawn against Gothenburg beating them 4-2 at Old Trafford. My mate the bricklayer David Ashworth from Glossop, had taken a job in Germany to earn some extra money; he had also split from his wife and had decided it was time to go abroad to start over again. Dave rang to tell me to meet him in a bar called the Dubliner, an Irish bar in Gothenburg, as he was going over with a group of brickies for a week in Sweden. I had never been to Sweden before, but had been told it was very expensive, so we took our own bottles of spirits with us. I had Bacardi, Tommy Price Whisky, Ray Price Vodka; Sammy Gilbey who is another Red from Ashton-under-Lyne who went to the Waterford away game with Tommy didn't take anything, as he is very careful with his money! He will only spend if he has to, but is nevertheless a good MUFC fan. He is always the heart and soul of any trips and always has the lads in stitches with his jokes and tales of United in the 60s. The format of the European Cup was different back then; now it is in the format of a league. United were in a group with Gothenburg, Galatasaray and Barcelona. By the time we played Gothenburg in November United needed to win to have a chance of going through. We ended up losing 3-1 with Jesper Blomqvist, who now plays for United having a great game. He gave United's defence a torrid time, especially David May who had a nightmare game at full back. When we entered the Dubliner, it was packed with United fans; hundreds of them. We searched everywhere for Ashworth but could not see him. Just then, Tommy looked over to his left and there was my mate Ashey dancing on the tables singing all the old United songs. When it was time to leave, Ray was in a panic as he had lost his match ticket. One of Ashey's mates had some spares but was asking £120 a ticket. Ray was having none of it. We were going to hammer the lad and take the ticket off him. David Ashworth even offered to pay for the ticket when they got back to Germany but the brickie still wouldn't have it. After a while the brickie came up and offered the ticket to Ray, who in turn told him to stick it up his arse and had better fuck off. Ray Price is a tough lad. This lad was getting very close to a good hiding. I diffused the situation by getting the lads outside. We all said we would chip in to get Ray a ticket from a tout near to the ground. As luck would have it, I bumped into two friends of mine from Gorton, Martin and his brother Skip, Martin makes his living from MUFC. I have no problem with that, as he is a good Red but the lad that Ashey knew, was just trying to cash in on another person's misfortune. Martin gave Ray a ticket for face value and we all went to the game. Like I said United lost 3-0 but at least I had seen Ashey who went back to Germany. His last words to me were "Take care Bruce and I'll see you in Barcelona."

United's next game in the European Cup was away to Galatasaray, where they drew 0-0. I have to admit that after the problems we encountered the year before, I said to the lads "Count me out of this one." No way was I having any of that again but Tommy Price and Sammy Gilbey still went. Tommy said that the atmosphere was not as good second time around but the circumstances surrounding this match were different. Even so, the Galatasaray fans had their own band which played throughout the game. Talk about intimidation. How does FIFA let teams like that get away with it? I will always remember the problems Peter Schmeichel encountered when he tried to escort one of their supporters off the pitch at Old Trafford. He was slaughtered by the press. The way they went on, you would have thought he had a death sentence hanging over him. Anyway United drew 0-0 away, so it looked like they were beginning to learn tactics on how the Europeans played. Then followed an exciting 2-2 draw at Old Trafford, against Barcelona in October. Two weeks later was the crunch match in Barcelona.

I was now working as a sales team leader for United Friendly Assurance in Stockport on Wellington Road. They knew nothing about my outside activities in the nightclub, and to be fair to them, even helped me out with a driver when I lost my licence. David Ashworth rang from Germany to tell me that he was going over, but Carol told him that I had a lot of insurance exams to get through, so wouldn't be going. I remember all the lads booking for the trip from the Stalybridge branch. About forty of them were going but my mind was made up, I'll give this one a miss and concentrate on my insurance exams. I remember going into the office very early on the morning of the game, where I started to do some revision. All of a sudden, I rang my wife Carol to tell her that I had to go to the game. Something was telling me I had to be there. She asked how I was going to get there, to which I replied that I didn't know but was going to Manchester Airport to find out. She was great about it as usual. She said "I'll see you whenever" and off I went to the airport. I parked my car at the airport in the Hilton Hotel car park. United supporters were everywhere. I went straight over to Barry Moorhouse, the United Supporters Club Chairman who works long hours for Manchester United's travelling supporters arranging all the trips. I explained my situation to him. He in turn said " Bruce all you can do is wait and see if anybody fails to turn up." So I waited just on chance. Again I prayed to Saint Jude the patron saint for hopeless causes. There were two more people who had the same idea as me, but I was first in the queue. Their names were Billie McFee and his daughter Samantha. I still see these two at matches all over the world. Anyway, as luck would have it, some people could not make it, so all three of us were allowed to travel to the Nou-camp.

There were 10,000 United supporters who made that trip to Barcelona; the cancellation was on the same plane as the Stalybridge branch. Luck was definitely on my side. I sat next to my best friend Ray Price. The match tickets were handed out on the plane. We all ended up going down to the famous Ramblers in Barcelona, where we enjoyed the day. I was thinking how I was going to meet up with Ashey and whether he had decided to travel.

There were over 100,000 people at the match. United fans had the worst view imaginable on the third tier and we were told to sit anywhere. I turned round to sit in the gangway, as there were no seats empty. To my surprise, who was at my side, but yes David Ashworth. He had again made the trip from Germany, paid £100 for his ticket outside the ground. Over 100,000 people in the stadium and I had to bump into Ashey! We watched the game. United were hammered 4-0. They were outclassed in every department, so I had no complaints. David returned to Germany, but by the sound of what he was saying, I knew it wouldn't be long before he was back in England; Glossop, in particular. United beat their rivals Blackburn in the Charity Shield at Wembley on August 14th 2-0, but it was nothing to write home about; another scrappy match. I remember thinking that we should do something special for these Charity Shield games. I had a great idea for the next time we got there.

The 1995/96 Season is the one where the great Scotland player Alan Hanson made a statement on Match of the Day after we had lost 3-1 at Villa Park in the opening game of the season. Alex Ferguson had decided to try out some of the youngsters from United's successful youth side. Alan Hanson said that you did not win leagues with kids. I will never forget how much stick he took for that statement! That same season Paul Ince was sold to an Italian club. I had a lot of respect for Ince, but I felt there was something about his attitude. I will always remember Mick Hucknall from Simply Red, who then lived in Milan, saying the same thing and that Ince had said to him "One day I will be with you in Italy." I will never forget those words. The West Ham fans I knew could not forgive him for having his photograph taken in a United shirt whilst still playing for West Ham. The fans accepted the loss of Ince, as I think they already knew that Roy Keane was ready to accept his new role. Bryan Robson had also decided to call it a day, to take up the role as Middlesborough's manager. Kanchelskis, Hughes and Sharpe were all to leave for various reasons. These three players had given me a lot of enjoyment and I was sad to see them all go. I knew that Alex believed in these kids and who were we to argue? Eric Cantona was banned because of his encounter with a fan in

93

the 1-1 draw at Palace in January. Some say that this cost us the league to Blackburn. Eric was special to the way United played their football. His vision and passing were superb. The electricity he generated, could be felt as soon as he took to the pitch. No one wanted Eric to leave, but credit must be given to Alex Ferguson for making Eric stay in England. No United fan would have blamed Eric if he had decided to play in another country. It would have been a sad and irreplaceable loss to English football.

After the Villa defeat, United won the next five games, then drew at Sheffield Wednesday before playing Liverpool on 1st October at Old Trafford. The buzz around the stadium and in the pubs was great. Eric Cantona was back. His exile was over. He had paid his debt to society. Now all the United supporters wanted, was for people to leave him alone, especially the refs and other players. All I can say is that it takes a lot of courage to come back to face the press and critics, who build you up then pull you down again headfirst. It's the English way of treating their superstars. Little did David Beckham know what he was going to go through in later years. The match ended a 2-2 draw, with Eric scoring the equaliser to the Scoreboard End from the penalty spot. K Stand's barmy army were going mad. I will never forget their fans singing 'Have you ever won the treble? Have you fuck'. This is another song they don't sing any more along with the Munich '58 song 'Always look on the runway for ice'.

After the Liverpool draw at Old Trafford, we won our next three games, which included a great 4-1 win at Chelsea on 21st October. I got a lift down with Steve Hepburn a financial advisor, Terry O'Neil and Peter Fallon (Strett). None of us were after any trouble. We decided to park up near the ground, find a quiet little pub around the corner and have something to eat and drink. Strett, against my advice, had his red United shirt on. Not the done thing at Chelsea; yes this is the same Strett I had seen at Leeds with spit all over his blazer. He never seems to listen. Anyway we walked into the pub. You could have cut the atmosphere with a knife. There were about one hundred of the craziest Chelsea lunatics you could ever imagine. Everything went quiet and if anyone knows Chelsea, they will know that they have a strong National Front element amongst their fans. I along with Strett was getting a lot of verbal. I was very relieved when the police arrived and advised us to move on. They had seen us enter the pub. Thank God they came in, as I think one of us would have been seriously injured. They told us where to find a pub that was a lot safer which we did. No harm came to any of us and United won the game easily 4-1.

We then lost 1-0 at Arsenal on 4th November, which was our first defeat since the opening game of the season. Late November and December was a bad time for United, and the pitches were very heavy. United drew the next three games 1-1 at Forest, 1-1 at home to Chelsea, 2-2 at home to Sheffield Wednesday then in December we had two hard away games at Liverpool and Leeds, losing them both — 2-0 at Anfield and 3-1 at Leeds. I was beginning to think we were playing too many kids in these matches and maybe Alex should buy some experience to help out with the defence and midfield. How dare I question Alex? Two home wins followed a 2-0 win against Newcastle and a 2-1 win against QPR but on 1st January at Tottenham, United got a hammering, which for me was well over due. It might teach us a lesson and keep the young lad's feet firmly on the ground. Fergie read the riot act. The display was totally unacceptable to any one wearing a United shirt and he was right! United then strung together a sequence of results that were truly magnificent. On 13th January we drew 0-0 at home to Villa, then won our next six games starting off with a 1-0 win at West Ham which is always a good result as we never get any favours from West Ham. Our rivals for the title were Newcastle. I could feel the pressure on their manager Kevin Keegan the ex-England manager. Alex was used to playing mind games with managers and Kevin Keegan wore his heart on his sleeve. Newcastle were odds-on favourites with everyone to win the league; all the other teams' supporters were sick of United winning all the time and all you could hear them saying was at least Newcastle play good football. I could go along with that, but United's tradition in the Theatre of Dreams has been to play good football. Could it be jealousy? You know as well as I do that it was. Wins followed at Wimbledon 4-2, Blackburn at home 1-0, Everton at home 2-0. Then things really started to happen. We were due to play a local derby at Bolton

Wanderers on 25th February. For some unknown reason to me Bolton fans absolutely hate United fans. The dislike is terrible. Once at an after-dinner speech, I listened to the great Nat Lofthouse, the Lion of Vienna, talk about his time at Bolton. He spoke of that famous shoulder charge at Wembley that lost United the FA Cup Final. So if any fans should have a grievance it should be us. It was a close game at Bolton. Ha! Ha! United won 6-0 in one of the best footballing displays I have ever seen. Bolton fans were leaving the ground with fifteen minutes remaining. I think it was to get at the United fans, as after the game there were running battles between both sets of fans. I have to admit that the Bolton fans were very annoyed; they were only interested in taking out their anger on any one in a red shirt. After over thirty years of watching football, you never see me wearing my colours. I sometimes wear a baseball cap with a United badge on it, or even just a badge. I know it shouldn't be this way but after what I have seen over the last thirty years has made me come to the conclusion that it is just not worth it. Looking at the Bolton fans as I walked back to the coach, made me realise I had made the right decision. A lot of my friends at MUFC share my feelings, so I hope we are not costing the club's commercial side any money. They already get enough out of us anyway.

After the 6-0 game at Bolton, I knew we could win the league, even with Newcastle's lead. I knew that if we beat them in our next away match at Newcastle, we had a chance, because psychologically Newcastle had bottled it! We went for a night out in Newcastle on 4th March, which was my son Robert's birthday. He knew I would make it up to him, so I went on the coach with the Stalybridge branch. What a game it turned out to be. Newcastle's new stadium was fantastic. The atmosphere was electric. United did not have many fans there and we were all penned in by the corner flag. For me Peter Schmeichel was 'man of the match'. He made some outstanding saves to keep Newcastle out, who in fairness, deserved something out of the game. Newcastle played well, but that's football. If you don't take your chances you get punished and there was Eric to the old Leezers End scoring with a shot into the side netting. United held on to a 1-0 lead and the title race was back on. Could Kevin Keegan handle it? United then drew 1-1 at QPR with Eric again scoring an important equaliser for us followed by four straight wins. Arsenal 1-0 thanks to another Eric cracker, Tottenham 1-0; both at Old Trafford and both winners from Eric. 'Is this man God' I thought! A 3-2 win at Manchester City followed by a 1-0 win at home to Coventry, where we had booked an executive box. I went with my head doorman Bernard Morgan, who now runs a club himself called Blues in Glossop. Can you believe it? It is not named after City but blues music. I am glad Bernard is doing well. He is a smashing lad and I wish him all the best in his new venture. There was about six of us in the box. We had a lovely meal along with drinks before the game. I have had my name down for a box for four years now. Who knows, one day my prayers might be answered. I will always remember it was the Easter holidays; a glorious day, but best of all United won 1-0. The game was spoilt by an accident to one of the Coventry players, Buust. He had an horrific break in the six yard box which upset Peter Schmeichel so much that I didn't think he would be able to carry on. My sympathies go out to this man, as anyone who has played football knows, it is the worst thing that can ever happen to you. I speak on behalf of every United fan when I say that I hope you are successful in everything you do after football because no one deserves to be out of the game once you have made it. We all know how hard it is to get there.

The title now looked like it was going to the last game of the season. United lost their next game 3-1 at Southampton leaving Leeds and Forest to be played at home and Middlesborough away on the 5th May. Leeds came to Old Trafford and played like every team does against United. They played like lions. Only a late Roy Keane cracker to the Stretford End broke the deadlock. Fergie started the mind games again by suggesting that the Leeds players had got their manager, Howard Wilkinson, sacked through lacking effort but somehow being able to turn it on again when it mattered. This upset a lot of people. Kevin Keegan took the bait again and sounded like a mad man cracking up when he was on television. He knew his team had to travel to Leeds and was accusing Fergie of playing dirty tricks, but Kevin should know that sticks and stones may break your bones but names will never hurt you. United only had to win their last two games at home to Forest and away to Middlesborough and the Championship was ours again. We hammered Forest 5-0 and so the mad scramble was on for Middlesborough tickets. The tickets were going for £150 each. We had a 52-seater coach going from the Stalybridge branch. I had managed to get tickets from Middlesborough through some friends I knew up there. It was a glorious day, so we stopped at a country pub on the outskirts of Middlesborough. I could sense that even the Middlesborough fans wanted United to win, as they hate Newcastle in the same way we hate Man City and I don't think that they wanted to take the stick all the way through the next season. The pub we stopped at had a massive beer garden with a huge chess set that was about twenty yards square; the pieces were made of concrete, which the owners thought were impossible to move. Tommy Price challenged me to a game of chess for £20. We started to play. I was winning the game when Tommy kicked my king over. It broke into pieces so we offered to pay for the damage but the landlord was ok about it. Each move on the chessboard took five people to move the pieces! After a lot to drink, we made our way to the Middlesborough ground. The support United had, was fantastic. The Riverside Stadium was packed, and the United fans sang through the entire match. As I said before, there were four of us sitting behind the Middlesborough goal. Tommy Price said to us "Let's try to get to where all the United fans are." Off he went, walked straight onto the pitch just before kickoff, so we all followed him. We walked to the United end and jumped in with the rest of the Reds. We could not believe that no one had stopped us doing this and joined in with the celebrations. United won the game easily with goals from May, Cole and Giggs. We had won the trophy we loved the most, the Premiership Championship, back from Blackburn Rovers who had it on loan from us the year before! Our travels were now back on for the European Cup which for Alex Ferguson and myself, is still our Holy Grail.

The FA Cup that year took us up to Sunderland in the third round after a 2-2 draw at Old Trafford. We found ourselves having to go up there for a night game which United won thanks to a great goal from Andy Cole, who was by now fast becoming not only a great goal scorer, but for me a far better footballer as well. His work rate is second to none. Although he and Eric don't always hit it off on the pitch, you never see him let it show. I feel Andy Cole is going to get better and better, but so are Manchester United. In the next round we drew Reading away winning 3-0. Then we drew Manchester City in a cracking game at Old Trafford. We beat the Blues 2-1, with Eric again getting the winner. In the sixth round we beat Southampton 2-0 at Old Trafford leaving us to play Chelsea in a tense semifinal at Villa Park. There were rumours going around that there was going to be a lot of trouble at the game, especially after all the trouble there had been at Wembley two seasons before. Our coach had arranged to meet in a pub in Birmingham town centre that we always used whenever we played Villa. We arrived at the pub at about 10 a.m. There were already about 200 United fans there. They were already drunk, singing and dancing, but they were only having a laugh. We knew it wouldn't be long before the police came along. The kickoff had been arranged for midday so as to avoid trouble after police advice, so really we were all breaking the law by being in the pub. When the police did arrive, it could easily have turned nasty. Tommy Price told the police it was a private party and that there wouldn't be any trouble. The police, not wanting to make a scene, decided to leave us to it, so after about an hour we all walked down to Villa Park together and to be perfectly honest never saw any Chelsea supporters. It would have taken a tough crew to have had a go at this mob! The match was a real thriller with another one of our idols, Mark Hughes who United fans felt had left too early, scoring the opener for Chelsea but two great David Beckham goals sealed victory for United, ensuring us a third Wembley appearance on the trot against our old rivals

Liverpool at Wembley on Saturday, 11th May.

United were now arranging VIP trips to the Wembley Hilton, which included a one night's stay after the game, plus a champagne reception and a free bar. So ten of us paid £120 a head to take advantage of this offer. United said we could make our own way, so we decided to travel down in style. The ten of us travelled down in a limousine with a chauffeur. We had the time of our lives. Every time we stopped at service stations, people were treating us like royalty! Someone would come to have a look who was in the limmo but all the windows were blacked out so we would wind them down a little and hand people bottles of Bud! We kept the champagne to ourselves though! We parked the limmo at the Wembley Hilton car park and went to book in. There was a bit of an atmosphere in the hotel bar as United fans and Liverpool fans do not often drink together. We took advantage of the free bar then made our way to the table in the big hall where the guest speakers, who were the ex-Liverpool player Phil Neil and the ex-United player Paddy Crerand, were ready to make their speeches. As soon as Paddy saw us all, he knew he was in for a hard time. He came straight over, sat down and had his meal with us saying you lads know how to enjoy yourselves, I'm going nowhere. All I can say is that Manchester United never made any money out of us; about five of us were licensees. Tommy Price had now decided to buy a couple of pubs in Denton, Manchester, starting with the Stamford Arms in Audenshaw then the Kings Head at Crown Point, Denton, which is named after my hero the Great Denis Law. There used to be a sign outside with Denis in his famous Scottish blue shirt scoring a goal and celebrating it with his famous one-armed salute. Tommy also bought the Top House in Denton where he now resides — three for starters, isn't bad is it! Tommy intends to build his empire, and no doubt he will. He is a very determined man. Phil Neil took some stick from us during his speech but it was all in good faith, there was no harm intended. The afternoon up to the kickoff passed without incident until last orders when everyone ordered everything you can imagine from bottles of champagne, doubles of every spirit to bottles of lager, Bud and

Stella. There was no more room on our table, it was just full of drinks. We were then asked to take our drinks into the bar as they wanted to get everything cleared up to get ready for the evening entertainment, so we ordered three trays to carry all the drinks into the main bar. They were so heavy that you needed to be a muscle man to carry one. Needless to say, Tommy carried one and Charlie Orr another. I volunteered for the third tray. When we managed to get through the main doors, I could not hold on any longer and the whole lot, with about £500 worth of drinks on it, went flying! We all know that the Hilton prices are not cheap. The lads were going mad at me but thank God we had two substitute trays left, so we could carry on drinking.

The funniest thing for me, was at about twelve o'clock, Tommy realised he had left his ticket at home in Denton. Can you believe that. We were all drunk in the Hilton, travelled down in a limmo, then Tommy decides he'd left his ticket behind. We all burst out laughing but Tommy was not amused. He quickly got onto his mobile to try to get one of the lads to bring it down in his jeep. The tickets from the touts were going at £500 each and Tommy would have paid that but they had all sold out. Luckily one of the lads from the pub said he would drive down with it to the Hilton for £50. Tommy said "No problem. Get down here with it as soon as possible." He took lots of stick from the lads, and at a quarter to three, the rest of the lads were off to Wembley to get ready for that famous song 'Abide with me'. I had heard and sung it so many times that I said I would wait with Tommy until his friend arrived with his ticket. I can't believe it but he arrived at three-fifteen after doing 110 mph on the motorway and getting a clear run. We rushed to Wembley. All the fans were there already, so we dived into our seats, only missing about twenty minutes of the game. According to most of the lads, we hadn't missed much, as it was a scrappy game. I could tell that only one goal was going to decide this game. With only minutes remaining, the god, Eric Cantona, scored a goal to the packed masses behind the United goal. It turned out to be the winning goal, making United the double winners again. In fact they were double

double winners which made Peter Fallon (Strett) come up with the idea of how we were going to celebrate. He said "Tonight lads, it's double doubles all round!" When we got back to the Hilton, most of the Liverpool supporters were, as their former captain Phil Thompson once said, 'as sick as parrots'. I felt sorry for them, so we did not take the piss; just drank and sang until the free bar closed at 8 p.m. We then ordered our chauffeur to take us around the sights of London. We went round Punch and Judy's in Covent Garden, then tried to get into Stringfellows, where we were politely refused entry. So we all ended up in a Chinese restaurant where we had a banquet for ten.

When we arrived back at the Hilton at about 1 a.m., the atmosphere had changed. I somehow knew it would be in the residents' bar, as there were United and Liverpool fans singing in there. For me the Liverpool fans were looking for trouble. I say this, because when Charlie Orr went to the bar to be served, some dickhead Scouser took his United baseball cap off his head and threw it behind to his mates. They didn't know that Charlie was with us. We joined up with some lads from Salford, who I knew, and we all started singing the famous 'Oh we hate Bill Shankly and we hate St John but most of all we hate Big Ron and we'll fight the Koppites one by one and throw them in the River Mersey. So to hell with Liverpool and Everton too, we will show no mercy and we'll fight fight fight with all our might for the boys in the red and white jersey' song. The whole room was now singing 'Manchester, la, la, la'. The Scousers were scared to death. They knew they would get a hammering and disappeared into the night. We ordered another six bottles of champagne, celebrating until about 4 a.m., before hitting the sack. Most of us missed breakfast the next morning which is nothing new for us. We got back into the limmo and headed home for Manchester. Another fine season behind us, again we were saying, "How can you beat that?" But nothing surprises you when following Man United.

United entered a weakened team in the Coco-Cola Cup. We were knocked out in the first round by York City losing 3-0 at Old Trafford, although we won 3-1 at York in the second leg. United were out, the only thing worth mentioning about this game was that we nearly had a mass brawl with about ten Cockney Reds who did nothing but slag United off the whole game. David Ashworth said to them "Why don't you fucking watch a London club you moaning bastards?" To which the mouthpiece of the group shut up, then the whole group started to get behind the team for the rest of the match. In the UEFA Cup Rotor Volergrad knocked us out on the away goals, as we had drawn 0-0 away and 2-2 at Old Trafford. We ended up with 82 points that season with 38 league games played. Not bad considering Blackburn had won the title the previous year with 89 points and 42 games played.

The 1996/97 Season started with a pre-season tournament at Glasgow Rangers featuring Manchester United, Newcastle, Sampdoria and Glasgow Rangers. I had never had any reason to go to Glasgow Rangers before, so decided to ring Lee Martin at Celtic and ask him to get us some tickets. I drove up for the weekend and went to meet Lee at Celtic Park on the Friday night. I took the godfather to my children David Clay, Tyson for short, with me. The reason we call him Tyson, is that he has a bigger neck than the boxer Mike Tyson. I think David's neck is about twenty-one inches! Anyway we met up with Lee, who took us round Celtic Park. We met most of the players including Charlie Nicholas, and had a good laugh. Lee told us to be very careful in Glasgow, as there was a curfew on at night after a certain time. The hatred between Celtic and Rangers fans was unbelievable. Lee even said that when he was out shopping with his wife and kids, if someone spotted him, if it was Celtic fans he would be mobbed and have to spend hours signing autographs, but if it was Rangers fans they would have to get out as soon as possible to avoid all the verbal abuse.

We booked into a hotel near to the Rangers ground. Lee stayed to have a quick drink with us but had to go as Celtic had a pre-season friendly on the Saturday. David and myself thanked Lee for the tickets, which were for two games on the Saturday and two on the Sunday. We decided to take his advice to stay out of Glasgow city centre and stay at the hotel, as there was a disco there as well. As usual, we both had a good drink and ended up meeting some genuine Glasgow Rangers fans who took it upon themselves to look after us. Let me tell you, the English think that they can drink, but these Jocks were hardened drinkers and drank the pair of us under the table. Anyone who knows David, will tell you that he can drink as much as the next man. We had a smashing night, so arranged to meet the lads the next morning. They said they would take us to some real pubs. As usual we missed breakfast, then we were picked up and taken to two great pubs full of Rangers fans. The first one was Alex Ferguson's old pub; the other was the great Scottish player, Jim Baxter's pub. We left the Rangers fans singing their songs without a word, as they hate United fans as much as Celtic supporters. To be fair, the Rangers fans we went to the match with, looked after us, taking us to the part of the ground where Lee had got us the tickets — called the Govan Stand. When we got to our seats, I thought this wasn't a bad ground. We had a great view on the halfway line and halfway up. David bought about six programmes for the lads back home and just put them on an empty seat next to him, when all of a sudden a big, really big Rangers fan said in a loud Scottish accent "I'm just having a look at one of these programmes" and started to flick through one. After about five minutes, David politely asked him if he had finished and could he have his programme back. "Not with a fucking accent like that" came the reply. "What the fuck are you doing in this stand? You'd better fuck off because when this ground is full, you are going to get your heads kicked in." I could now feel the hatred, so we both decided to head for the pitch. United were just warming up for their game against Sampdoria from Italy, who had Lombardo playing for them, who I gave 'man of the match' to. The second game of the afternoon was Glasgow Rangers against Newcastle. I think United were beaten, but I'm not sure as my mind was on other things. David and I walked down to the front of the pitch to ask a policeman for some assistance to get to where all the other United fans were behind the goal, even though there were only about two hundred of them, we felt it would be safer to sit in with them. Newcastle had the stand above us. I will always remember just before kickoff, the whole ground started singing the famous 'Stand up if you hate Man United' song. Both the Newcastle and Rangers fans sang it with a passion. Then the Rangers fans sang their anthem which echoed around the ground. I must say that they sang it with a lot of passion for their team just like Celtic do; they are both fanatical about their football. Anyway, my claim to fame at this match, is that the first shot Sampdoria had at goal, came flying straight for my face. I was sitting a yard away from the front post. I caught the ball and headed it back onto the pitch. It brought a cheer all around the ground but I just had to do it. If you buy a video of that match, the lads tell me it shows me heading the ball back! We did not stay for the Rangers against Newcastle game, as I thought why bother when the hatred is so bad. So David and I went back to the hotel by taxi and again waited for the Rangers fans to come back. I spoke to Barry Moorhouse afterwards and explained to him our situation sitting with all the Rangers fans was no fun at all. "The seats which were allocated to you were not supposed to be exchanged." But Barry said he would arrange for us both to have different seats the day after, especially as United were playing Rangers. Again I cannot remember much about the Rangers game, except that one of the Rangers players got Eric Cantona sent off and also in the Newcastle game in which I think we were beaten on penalties, their fans sang the Munich song, which is not like them at all. I think Sampdoria won the tournament, but to be honest, I wasn't really interested. We had a great weekend with the Rangers fans and still keep in touch by phone. You never know one day we might meet them in the European Cup, anything can happen in football!

Another good pre-season friendly we attended at about this time, was in Dublin, to play against the Republic of Ireland at Lansdowne Road. Nipper Royale said he would arrange a trip, so about twenty of us went for the weekend, going on the Friday and returning on the Sunday night. We went by ferry from Holyhead to Dublin. Going out there was a group of lads from Cardiff on a stag do to Dublin. Everything was ok going over, until one of the lads started to sing the Munich song very loudly. In fairness to the other lads he was with, he was quickly told to shut his mouth. One of our lads, John Redfern (Johnnie Red), a very tough United fan from Stalybridge who is a bricklayer, said to the lad concerned "You could have started a mass brawl on this ferry mate and I'm telling you now that when we get off this ferry I'm going to kick your fucking head in." I wouldn't advise anyone to fight Johnnie Red; he's awesome and very fast. He's also strong and fights better than anyone I know when he's drunk. All I wanted to do, was get some sleep! When we got off the ferry, John went straight over to those lads asking where the one who sang the Munich song was. The lads did not fancy a mass brawl on the platform but John spotted the lad and laid into him. After twenty seconds or so it was all over. No one else joined in. The lads from Cardiff helped their mate onto the train and went on their way. I don't think that lad will be daft enough to sing that song again, but you never know, some people never learn.

We reached our hotel in Dublin, then went straight out on the piss. Dublin is not a cheap city, but the atmosphere around the place is fabulous. The people are very friendly and what helps even more is that they worship Manchester United. We drank with them all weekend. The game was on a Sunday afternoon. We had arranged to meet the Belfast Kerry Duff branch at the ground, but their coach had taken longer than expected to get there. With most of these lads being Protestants, they were stopped every so often and to be honest were very lucky to get through at all. I met some cracking Irish people that weekend. I just wish that they could play pool. I won about £70, which isn't bad for me as I'm only an average player but the Irish are crap! Again the score was not important. We played all the kids and I think we drew. Considering we were playing the Republic of Ireland away, there were more United fans there than Irish. The support United have in Ireland is second to none. We all enjoyed ourselves that much, that we nearly missed the last ferry home, arriving with seconds to spare. Dale Ellis was on this trip with me and will be mentioned a lot later on, but he had us in stitches on this trip. He has a great voice and sings better out of a Pils bottle than some singers do with a backing group. I would encourage anybody to go to Dublin, but it is cheaper to go by air now. So anybody who likes real Guinness, Manchester United and the Irish people, try Dublin; it's something else!

The 1996/97 Season started with a 4-0 hammering of Newcastle in the Charity Shield at Wembley. My wife Carol, for all her patience of my football, no not football, but Manchester United madness, had always wanted to go on a cruise, and her brother Alan Hazlehurst, who also travelled with me to United, worked at Earls Court, Olympia, as a fireman which is owned by P&O Liners. He somehow managed to get us on this cruise. Alex was too young to go and stayed with my in-laws Joan and Graham, but we took the other two Robert and Natalie. Yes, to no surprise, it was a football cruise. Among the guests on board were the former England players Norman Hunter and Alan Mullery. Robert really enjoyed himself. We did not see him for the whole time, which was about seventeen days. We took in Portugal, Gibraltar, Madeira, Tunisia, Lanzerote and Tenerife aboard the fabulous *Canberra* that had also helped out our troops in the Falklands' crisis. I attended all the coaching sessions with Robert, who enjoyed Norman and Alan's coaching skills. I found that their knowledge of football was superb. Some of the stories they told me, were quite unbelievable. When we arrived in Lanzerote, Carol said she did not want to get off the ship. I knew United were playing against Newcastle, so I went on the ship's launch and straight to the first bar on the beach with a lad from Wales I had met on the cruise. Can you believe his name was David, he was a lifelong Leeds fan! As I said before, United were playing Newcastle in the Charity Shield. We managed to get into the bar fifteen minutes before kickoff, I could not believe my luck or eyes, the girls had given us six hours on shore; enough time to watch the game and have a few beers. In the bar it was full of Newcastle fans and all the other Manchester United haters but even the biggest anti-United fan in the world had to admire their football that afternoon. They absolutely slaughtered Newcastle, with Beckham, Butt, Keane and Cantona scoring. The Geordies were absolutely gutted. I ended up singing the famous anti-United song 'Who the fuck are Man United" and all the Geordies started laughing. We stayed and drank with them all afternoon, only arriving back to the ship with minutes to spare. The one thing I remember most, is a small Newcastle fan about ten years old crying at the defeat, with his dad trying to stop him, but he was inconsolable. That sight will stay with me forever. It shows what Bill Shankly the great ex-Liverpool manager once said is correct "Football is the difference between life and death". We all enjoyed that cruise, but it was now back to the league.

We kicked off with a game away at Wimbledon and if anybody had thought that United were not up for it, they had another thing coming. We beat Wimbledon 3-0 with David Beckham scoring from the halfway line; a truly great goal, not often tried by many players. The only two I can remember trying it for United were Bobby Charlton and the great Eric Cantona, who tried it at Chelsea the season before, but his effort hit the bar. David Beckham was now an established regular at United; his crossing, work rate, attitude and free kicks, had proved to me that no other team can compare to United's youth team set up. After that good win at Wimbledon on 17th August, United had a series of draws; 2-2 against Everton, 2-2 against Blackburn both at Old Trafford then a 1-1 draw at Derby where we were 1-0 down until David Beckham scored with a tremendous shot to the end where all the United masses were. After he had scored, he ran to the United supporters. I don't think he had realised what he was doing but the first person he ran to who was sitting on the front row was Tommy Price and myself. We nearly dragged him into the crowd with us! 1-1 was a fair result. When we got back to Stalybridge on the coach, Tommy realised that he had left his car keys at the pub where we had stopped at on the way back. We rang them up. So the next day Tommy had to drive back to pick up his keys.

Tommy had now decided to buy a bar in Stalybridge and

dedicate it to the Stalybridge Branch Supporters Club; the branch was by now one of the biggest branches in the country, boasting over 500 members, which isn't bad for a branch that started off with about twenty. Both Tommy and myself were original members. The Club Secretary is Walter Perjenko who dedicates all his spare time to the branch. They have a committee meeting every Tuesday to organise every game. Tommy had got a social club. He always wanted a bar purely for United fans, so he called it the Reds' Bar. In there was everything a fan could want. All around the walls were United paintings done by a local artist called Ian Gardiner. Behind the bar, were pictures of all the games the branch had been to. Pictures of different members at different matches. The club was massive. He installed a snooker table along with a table football machine. He also offered beer and lager at discounted prices for members. People from all over the country would come to see the Reds' Bar. When you go on the Manchester United Museum tour, the first thing you come across is Tommy Price being interviewed on the big screen showing some United officials around his bar. It was his pride and joy. The opening night was a great success. Alex Ferguson himself turned up to give a talk to the branch members; the tickets Tommy had distributed went very quickly, you could not move in the place. Tommy had even arranged for Alex to be piped in by Scottish pipers for a grand welcome. I think this took Alex by surprise. As soon as he started to speak, the whole place was in silence. His presence alone makes you feel proud to be a Red. He thanked us for our loyal support and spoke for about two hours recalling how hard it is for United to sign the right players; how agents and players are demanding ridiculous' fees and also how he had tried to sign Overmars the Arsenal winger before the Gunners did, but even a big club like United would not break the wage structure. What Overmars wanted, was just downright greedy. I'd like to add now that I am glad United broke the wage structure for Roy Keane; he is the only player who could have changed the Board's mind, and his displays for the club have earned him that right. I know that most United fans would agree with me when I say good luck Roy Keane.

The rest of the evening went well, with United even bringing the League and FA Cup trophies to the opening. You could have photographs taken with the cups. I have photos of me lifting both cups over my head. What a great feeling that is, I can tell you.

The next game for United was Leeds away, which only the die-hard fans go to. United won 4-0. That spelt the end of Howard Wilkinson's reign at Leeds. On 7th September, we won at Old Trafford against Nottingham Forest 4-1, then drew at Villa 0-0; then won our next two home games 2-0 against Tottenham and 1-0 against Liverpool with David Beckham scoring another great goal to the Stretford End. We then travelled up to Newcastle, who were after revenge for the 4-0 hammering in the Charity Shield. Again we took a 52-seater coach to the game. Newcastle played well. Everything went right for them and they ended up hammering United 5-0. We were out-classed. You could not argue with the result. As we were walking back to the coach together, about fifty Newcastle fans attacked us. Our coach was the last one parked outside this big pub which was where these Newcastle fans were when they saw us approaching. They all decided to attack. I think they thought United would run but they were in for a shock. That is something the Stalybridge and Ashton lads would never do, especially after a 5-0 defeat. We met the Geordies head-on with Eric Mitchell, David Ashworth, Tony Braithwaite and Ray Price in the front line. The Newcastle fans made a hasty retreat and all of a sudden there was a heavy police presence. The next thing I knew was a police dog was set on me and it was biting my new leather jacket. I tried to swing it off, but it would not let go. The lads said I looked like something out of a Batman film! The police then arrested me for fighting. I had done nothing. My mind went back to the time in Coventry when I was arrested. The police took me to the cells at Newcastle's ground, which are under the main stand and placed me in a cell with about twenty Geordies. I think skinheads had just come into fashion in Newcastle, because everyone had one; they also had Newcastle shirts on, which gave me away, as I didn't have any colours on. My new leather jacket was ripped to bits, so I sat down in a corner on my own. This Newcastle fan asked me where I was from and when I replied Manchester, he said it was good to find a MUFC fan actually from Manchester! After about twenty minutes, Big Nigel who runs the trips from Stalybridge, called in to try and explain that I had not done anything and that there was over fifty witnesses who would be prepared to verify the fact. The police, who wanted the United fans away as quickly as possible then said get him charged or let him go. Again I was charged with threatening behaviour and was bailed to go back to Newcastle two weeks later. When I returned to Manchester, I went to my solicitors to explain the situation, along with written statements from all the lads and from Newcastle fans I knew. The letters all said that I was innocent of the charge and that it was the Newcastle fans' fault for attacking our coach in the first place. Before I was to appear in court, my solicitor received a letter saying no further action would be taken and that they were sorry for any inconvenience caused. I was happy with that and put it all behind me. I still think the Newcastle fans are a bit behind the door with their dress sense; and in their belief that Newcastle are a good football team; the truth is that they cannot defend and are always vulnerable to concede goals at the back.

The next few games were a blip for United. We lost 6-3 to Southampton away; blaming our strip for a football defeat is a bit out of order but we never wore that grey away strip again. We then lost at home to Chelsea 2-1 on 16th November but were soon back to our winning ways beating Arsenal 1-0 at Old Trafford. We then drew 2-2 at Middlesborough where we were all on our best behaviour after receiving letters from Middlesborough Football Club regarding our behaviour from previous seasons. We ended November with a 3-1 win at Old Trafford against Leicester. December started with a 2-2 draw at West Ham. Again we all stayed at Cockney Mick's pub and we all had a great time winding all the West Ham fans up. Their favourite song is 'I'm forever blowing bubbles', our version is better 'I'm forever throwing bottles, pretty bottles in the air. They fly so high, they reach the sky, like West Ham they fade and die. Tottenham's always running, Chelsea's running too, and we're the Stretford enders, running after you!' I will always remember I saw the Wythenshaw gang led by O'Neil's mob, about 100 of them, all wearing black balaclavas. The West Ham fans stayed well away. These were United boys, who would have a go at anybody who wants trouble. They are well respected at every ground.

Just before Christmas, we drew at Sheffield Wednesday 1-1, followed by a 5-0 win over Sunderland at Old Trafford, and on Boxing Day we had a 4-0 win at Nottingham Forest. We had a bit of trouble with the Forest fans at their pub called the Avery, which is at the side of the River Trent. They did not like us singing in their pub which I suppose is fair enough, considering we had just beaten them 4-0 at their own ground. On 28th December we beat Leeds United 1-0 at Old Trafford. And so to the New Year. On 1st January, there was a boring 0-0 draw with Aston Villa at Old Trafford, then a great 2-1 win at Tottenham. United were now beginning to play good football. I could still tell that all the other clubs resented United. They always raised their games when they played against us but we were used to it by now. We then had a 2-0 win at Coventry, followed by three 2-1 wins at home against Wimbledon, Southampton and Arsenal. United were now getting ready for the run in. At the end of February, we then drew 1-1 at Chelsea where David Beckham equalised for the Reds. I could tell that Chelsea were going to be a force to be reckoned with in seasons to come. Although the atmosphere at Stamford Bridge is still very hostile, Chelsea still try to entertain. Newcastle were our closest rivals again this season but I always felt we would retain our title. On 1st March we beat Coventry 3-1 at home then lost 2-1 at Sunderland. This was our first defeat in about sixteen games. It just goes to show the strength of character these players have. I am proud of everyone of them.

We bounced back straight away, which is another good sign of any great side in how they handle a defeat and United know exactly how to respond. We beat Sheffield Wednesday 2-0 at home, then won 2-0 at Everton. On 5th April, we had a shock defeat to Derby, losing 3-2 at home. Had United lost the desire to win matches? I knew the answer. We went on to the end of the season unbeaten. On 12th April, we beat another one of our rivals Blackburn Rovers 3-2 at Ewood Park, but for me the result of the season was a great 3-1 win at Anfield. We were all packed behind the goal in the Anfield Road end, when Gary Pallister scored two great headers which totally silenced the Kop; they were two identical goals scored from the great crossing of David Beckham. Andy Cole sealed the game in the second half. This made up for all the stick we took off the Scousers the season we ended runners-up, when they sang 'You lost the league on Merseyside'. But we now reversed the song and going round the ground was 'We won the league on Merseyside!' My heart was beating like a drum to the sound. We totally outclassed Liverpool that day and I must say it took me by surprise to see United applauded off the pitch by Liverpool fans. Earlier in the day, the team coach had a window smashed with someone trying to spray Ryan Giggs with CS gas. It just shows that most of them are genuine fans.

We then drew 2-2 at Leicester, which left us with three home games to play. This was followed by a 3-3 draw with Middlesborough, which was a cracking game. The Middlesborough lads I knew wanted me to sit with them in the visitors' seats at Old Trafford. They got me four tickets, so I sat with David Clay, David Ashworth and the mad Middlesborough fan David Dyson. David Dyson has supported Middlesborough for thirty years. He goes everywhere with them. He knows all the boys, so we knew we were safe with him. The 'man of the match' for me was the little genius called Juninino. He tore United to shreds. I thought Ferguson might swoop for him but it never came to anything. I still think he would do a good job at Old Trafford but I am only a supporter and would never go against Alex Ferguson's judgement. On 8th May we drew 0-0 with Newcastle. Following that we beat West Ham at home and once again the Championship was at Old Trafford. I must be honest and say that I thought United would win the European Cup that season. The trophy was now an obsession with me. People were saying it was an obsession with Fergie, but nobody wanted that trophy more than me.

The test was on 11th September at Juventus, who everyone sets their standards by. The players like Del Piero are world class. It was only against this kind of opposition that you could judge your own team's ability. United's group consisted of Juventus, Rapid Vienna and Fenerbache. We travelled to Juventus on 11th September. About twenty of us had booked on the United day trip, which cost about £200. We were all dropped off just outside Turin. I couldn't believe it; the first bar we went in I bumped into some Reds I knew from Denton, Manchester. These lads were over there on holiday and I had not seen them for a few years. I used to play football with them on Sundays for Haughton Villa, a top Sunday team at the time. Their names were Billy Ollerenshaw and Clifford Crehan. We all got drunk together reminiscing about past games. We ended up missing the coaches back to the ground, so had to get taxis. It wasn't a classic match with United losing 1-0. The atmosphere was electric and these kind of nights are for me what football is all about. It was a glorious day. I even wore a bright yellow Sonetti tee shirt, but it did not help the result. We then beat Rapid Vienna 2-0 at Old Trafford. This was then followed by a trip to Turkey against Fenerbache on 16th October. The horror of my trip to Galatasaray still had painful memories for me. I felt it was not worth the hassle and bailed out of going. Tommy Price, along with Sammy Gilbey and Big Nigel, made the trip with the club. United won 2-0. Tommy said to me that it was nothing like Galatasaray. They seem to have sorted it out now but I was not prepared to take the chance. After this great win, United lost the next two games at Old Trafford. Firstly Fenerbache got their revenge for their defeat in Turkey by beating us 1-0, which was followed by a Juventus defeat on 20th November. This meant United had to win at Rapid Vienna in Austria to have any chance of qualifying. It was on 4th December and there was no way I wanted to miss this game. I rang United to try and get Ray Price and myself on the one-day trip, but it was full. Luckily, two days before, Barry Moorhouse rang me to say that Neville Neville, Gary Neville's dad and his sister could not travel, so without hesitation Ray and I took their places. It was the weather; we could not believe how cold

114

it was; minus seven degrees.

We arrived in Vienna at about midday, to be told that two United supporters had been shot in a disturbance in a bar, so we decided to keep our wits about us at all times. Vienna is a beautiful place but as always we only saw the bars. There was only one big bar there. When Ray and myself walked in, it was completely full of Reds. The first Reds we saw were the Macclesfield lads. They go everywhere. So we had a good singsong with them and were interviewed yet again by the TV crews. Outside, the riot police were keeping guard, but everything was going well. When we arrived at the stadium, we were freezing. I think it's the coldest I've ever been at a football match. United played well. They knew what they had to do and got a great 2-0 result, with goals from Eric Cantona and Ryan Giggs. The thing I remember most is the great save by Peter Schmeichel just before half-time with the score at 0-0. It was truly world class and kept us in the game. We arrived back in Manchester in the early hours with the team; Martin Edwards even had a smile on his face!

Our next European Cup opponents were the Portuguese champions FC Porto. The first leg was at Old Trafford on 5th March, the day after my eldest boy's birthday, so I took Rob to the game for his birthday treat. United were again outstanding. Without the suspended Roy Keane, Ryan Giggs ran the show. United won 4-0 and we all knew the second leg would be a formality. Everyone was booking a week's leave to celebrate the away leg, which was to played on 19th March. This trip was to be one of the best trips I have ever been on. The Stalybridge branch had booked a 52-seater coach. They had no problem filling it. We had one night's stop in the South of France at Biarritz where we introduced the locals to our anthem 'Oh ah Cantona!' It was drink, drink, drink all the way. I roomed with Steve Vance a good Red from Ashton, who has been going as long as myself. No one got any sleep that trip. Everyone was stealing everyone else's beer as soon as their eyes were shut. We eventually got to our hotel in Portugal, where we were to stay for two nights. I had arranged to meet some friends from Dukinfield, who had decided to make a holiday of it and stay for two weeks. I met these friends at our hotel. The food and drink was very cheap.

The night before the game, the lads I had met, Harry Gill and Sammy Gilbey, suggested we go into the town centre in Porto which was about fifteen miles away to celebrate Harry's birthday. We phoned a taxi from our hotel, getting to the centre at about 9 p.m., The attitude of the riot police was again disgraceful. United supporters were being attacked for no reason but we were used to this by now. Most of the bars were empty. The locals were out for blood too, so we decided to have one drink then get back to the hotel. It was Harry's round. The shock that was to follow even took me by surprise. "Bruce, I've been dipped" Harry said. "Someone's had my wallet." Considering we'd only been in one taxi and one bar, I said to Harry that he must be mistaken. I asked how much was in it, to which Harry replied about £600, credit cards and match tickets; even his passport. Harry was there for two weeks and considering what had just happened, was taking it very well. I would have been distraught. I said to Harry that he might have dropped it in the taxi. "Maybe" he replied, "but who is going to hand in a wallet with that much money in it?" We felt sorry for Harry. "What a birthday he was having. We decided to get back to the hotel and organise a whip round amongst the lads, saying to Harry, "Keep your head up, there's nothing you can do about it now." We got back to the hotel about midnight and headed straight to the reception desk to report the incident to the police, when to our surprise the hotel manager explained that the taxi driver had returned the wallet with all the contents intact to the hotel. We could not believe it. "What are the odds of that happening in Manchester?" Harry said with a big smile on his face. To his credit, Harry rang the taxi firm to thank the driver and to let him know there was a £30 tip waiting for him at the hotel. With the smile back on Harry's face, we continued drinking the cheap local wine until the early hours. We avoided the local lager called Super Block, as it was very strong!

The next day we caught the coach to the town centre where it didn't take us long to find the rest of the Reds. There were thousands of United supporters all massed around the Riberia

Square singing and chanting United songs. It was a glorious day. Riberia Square had about ten bars around it and it did not take long for the local bar owners to up their prices. The local lager had gone from 100 escudos to 500 a bottle but no one cared as we all knew that only a miracle could stop United going through to the European Cup semifinal for the first time since 1968. One of the first people I saw, was my old friend from Clayton Aniline, Doss (Twang Eyes) Maher, who was with another friend from Droylsden, Gordon Durward. We had a good laugh about old times then started to chant a City song we had made-up called 'City are a massive club' and before you knew it everyone was singing the song with us. Over 10,000 United supporters made the trip to Porto. Most of them well behaved, considering the beer that had been drunk. We all caught the local tube to the ground and went into a bar nearby, which was again full of Reds, I bumped into Tony McNelly in there. He is a very good semi-professional footballer living in Gorton, Manchester. Tony is one of the best goal scorers in the amateur league, who has won nearly everything you can in the non league game. I still don't know why he never made it at the top level, but again we spoke about the old days and had a good drink. Most of the United supporters got into the ground early, as we had heard that the riot police were working on a zero tolerance attitude. We were right, they were using their batons on everybody with a white face, hitting out indiscriminately. United defended well and came out with a creditable 0-0 draw. Everyone was now jumping up and down celebrating the forthcoming semifinal, which was to be played in Germany against Borussia Dortmund in April. The riot police were after trouble, suggesting that too many United supporters were trying to get out of the ground in an unsafe manner, so promptly fired rubber bullets into the Reds fans exiting near the corner flag. This caused a mass panic. The fans all turned around to try and get back into the stadium. We heard that at least four people had been shot. The stadium to me was totally unsafe to stage this kind of event and the police had been the main trouble causers. I waited until most of the people had left. I saw a young lad of about fourteen years of age who was very upset as he had been split up from his dad. I thought about my son Robert and what it would have been like if that was us, so I stayed with him. At least it was safe in the stadium. I told the lads that I'd get a taxi back to the hotel and to tell the coach to meet us there and not to hang about. My judgement was right. The dad came back when the ground was nearly empty, so everything ended up alright. I must stress that it looks to me that these kind of big games are not adequately handled like they are at Old Trafford. It seems like they are waiting for a disaster to happen; even the loss of life would not bother these people. I have now witnessed the two worst police forces describable, in both Istanbul and Porto. Their motto must be take no prisoners. Anyway we were not going to let this spoil our enjoyment and caught a taxi back to the hotel where the celebrations were in full swing. All the old sixties songs were sung with the hotel bar once again being drunk dry!

The next day saw a lot of bad heads, myself included, for the trip back, but when there are fifty of you, it does not take long to get your head right again. The return trip was planned to perfection. We'd booked the coach as a fishing trip to enable us to board the ferry in Bilbao in Spain. It takes you back to Portsmouth which is about a 24-hour crossing aboard the *Pride of Bilbao*. They don't like football coach parties but fishing trips are accepted. The *Bilbao* has everything you could dream of for a luxury holiday. It is the largest ferry sailing out of the UK. It boasts a line up of live entertainment, along with a nightclub, disco, casino, cinema, Jacuzzi, saunas and many bars. To us this was like being in paradise. So the trip back was great. We even had our own cabins if we wanted to catch up on some sleep, not that any of us took advantage of this! Everyone was in good spirits. The trip had been so well planned by Big Nigel of the Stalybridge branch, that on our return, we could go straight to the away game at Everton which we did — United winning 2-0 — but most of the lads were very tired; a week away on the booze was taking its toll. I must say I was glad to get home and see the children.

I knew my next excursion would be very soon and it was — the next month, on 19th April. We were drawn against Borussia

Dortmund, with the away leg being played first. This meant another week away. The plan was for me to drive my car down to my brother-in-law's in London, where one of his mates, a Watford fan, would drive us over in his car. I arranged to travel down to Alan's on the Sunday with two other lads from Ashton; Big Dennis a taxi driver and Wiggy a lad that went to school with Tommy Price. We all met up at a pub Alan knows in Watford for a drink. The cost of the trip was very reasonable, £40 per person for petrol but we did not have any match tickets. I knew we would get in. My record at United still stands at thirty years of going and only being locked out in the seventies at West Ham. Whilst we were waiting at the pub, a gang of Irish lads appeared from nowhere asking us if we were interested in buying any TVs or videos. I said no, but when they drew up in the car park with a Transit van full of gear saying, go on lads give us an offer, I ended up buying two TVs with remotes and two videos for £200. I was happy with that but the only problem I had now was how to get the gear back to Manchester. Then I remembered a friend of mine was relieving for a pub manager nearby so I rang him, and he met me at the pub. His name is David Turner (Harpo), who lives in Denton. He took the electrical items to his place in London, then when he was coming back to Manchester dropped them off at my home. I'd just like to say that all the equipment is still working, so I am happy with the deal.

I left my car at Alan's and on the Monday made our way to Dortmund via a one-night stopover in Ostend, Belgium. We managed to get bed and breakfast in a pub for £15 each, which again we thought was reasonable. We had a good laugh in Ostend with Dennis paying £20 for two dirty videos and we all did plenty of window shopping! I don't know if anyone did anything wrong but I heard Alan talking about having a double later on. I'm not sure what he meant, as he doesn't touch shorts! From Ostend we drove right through to Dortmund, near to East Germany, and it was one hell of a drive. We were also aware of Neo Nazis, who were after trouble with English supporters, again rumours were flying around of intended trouble with their fans. We arrived in the afternoon of the game.

I had arranged to meet Tommy Price and all the Stalybridge lads at the square in the town centre. The police had insisted that large screens were put up. They wanted a carnival atmosphere in the town. The first thing we needed was a hotel, which we found very quickly; paid for a twin room with five of us using it — the usual scam! Next was tickets for the game. No one fancied going into the German end, but they were the only tickets we could get for double the face value, which I didn't think was bad, so we purchased them from a German ticket tout which meant at least now we could relax and hit the beer!

By abut 2 p.m. we were all in the square along with 1,000s of others all enjoying themselves. The pubs were packed. We were all trying to find Tommy and the lads, when behind us we heard the sound of breaking glass. I looked behind and saw about fifty Dortmund skinheads attacking a pub full of United fans. Apparently they had arranged a mass brawl with the United fans who only wanted to get drunk. I could not believe what I was seeing. It was like something out of the 70s. The skinheads knew exactly which bar they were going to attack. I will not defend United fans if they are out of order. I will be the first to tell you, but that afternoon I knew there would be trouble. My motto in life is 'Never trouble trouble until trouble troubles you' but this was different. It was funny none of the skinheads entered the bar. They were bombarding it with bottles and bricks; the front windows were completely gone. All of a sudden I heard a voice saying "Have some of this you German bastards." Yes, it was Tommy Price. The United supporters started throwing bottles and glasses back at the Germans. They knew those skinheads had no intentions of attacking the lads inside. The only two people I saw throwing bottles from the inside were Tommy Price and a lad from Salford called Mike Grogan. I saw Mike get hit by a flying bottle, with Tommy carrying him away from the situation. After about ten minutes, which is a long time for a ruck, the German police arrived on the scene and to my surprise attacked their own fans with batons. In all my years of following United it was the first time I had seen riot police attack their own fans. The skinheads all disappeared, no one was arrested but the damage they had caused to their own bar was beyond belief. We didn't get involved with Tommy's situation as we knew he could handle it. My other motto is 'Always take care of number one', in this case we would have got hammered.

The five of us decided to get a taxi to the ground. I thought if they were like this before the game, what is it going to be like getting into the German end when none of us speak German. The taxi dropped us off near to the ground; it was bedlam. The German fans were up for it. One lad I saw was Del Boy, who follows United from the East End of London. He worked in Cockney Mick's pub the Prince Alfred. Del Boy had been stabbed in the stomach; he was bleeding from the wound. I knew it was bad. Del Boy is a tough person and I could tell he was in pain by the look on his face. I asked him if he was ok. He replied "Bruce the bastards have stabbed me." He was on his own outside the German end we were about to enter. I spoke in English to a policeman who radioed through for an ambulance. I think he knew Del Boy's condition was life threatening. Del Boy was taken in the ambulance before the game, treated in hospital then sent back to England on the first available flight. I have known Del Boy for over twenty years and he is as game for a fight as anyone, but to be stabbed is unbelievable. We all decided it was not worth taking a chance by going into the German end, so tried to get into the United end with our tickets. Again the German police were very helpful and they let us stand behind the net. The atmosphere was great. The first person I saw that I knew was Sammy Gilbey, who got security to let us into the top tier with the rest of the lads. All the United fans were doing the conga round the ground. Everyone was having fun. I spotted a girl wearing a Spice Girl Union Jack dress, which was not worth wearing as all the Reds were trying to get a grip of her! The match kicked off with a shock to all of us — the great Dane was injured, so Rai Van Der Gouw was to play in goal. United played well but missed some great chances to score an away goal. Nicky Butt hit the post but it wasn't our night. Dortmund scored a goal from long range that Schmeichel would have saved; we ended up losing the first leg 1-0. A draw would have been fair, but we all still felt very confident with the return at Old Trafford and thought United would go through.

We had arranged for a taxi to pick us up after the game, to take us back to the hotel as none of us wanted to hang around, especially after what had happened to Del Boy. The taxi was there waiting for us. We didn't see any trouble after the game but still took no chances. Back at the hotel we decided to stay in and drink the German lager which was first class. We also had a steak each which was massive. I must say the Germans take pride in their beer and food. We were made to feel very welcome, the manager even apologised for their fans' behaviour, explaining that they have a social problem with their youths just like we have. We enjoyed our meal, talked about what should have happened in the game, then went to bed at about 2 a.m., ready for the long drive home in the morning. We headed off back to Manchester after breakfast, which again was ace. No wonder most Germans are overweight! The journey back seemed to last forever. I swore that I wouldn't go that far by car again, but yes you are right, little did I know that I'd be going the same distance a year later, but this time to Munich.

The return leg was played on 21st April at Old Trafford. It was a great day — everyone had taken the afternoon off work and it was very sunny in Manchester for a change. About thirty of us caught the train into Manchester city centre to have a few drinks around town. Manchester was on red alert for any trouble from the Germans, but everything went ok. We had a great drink in Witherspoons, with everything £1.00 a pint. All the old songs were being sung by Tommy Price. The mood was that United were going to get to their first European Cup final since 1968. What a disappointment it turned out to be. A lad called Robert MacLean got me a ticket for the main stand. I have known Rob since we were both kids playing for the local and best Sunday morning side in Ashton-under-Lyne, Ashton Albion, which produced professional players for the likes of Arsenal, Nottingham Forest, Crystal Palace, Manchester City and many more. Rob himself wasn't a bad goal scorer. He was employed by Tommy to run the Reds bar in Stalybridge, but unfortunately got into marriage and financial difficulties. The last I heard he was in Spain with Tommy's takings. As you can imagine Tommy was not a happy chap, but says one day he will have to return. I sat with Rob in the main stand, cheering United onto the pitch. Everything was ok, until after the first ten minutes when Dortmund scored. Everyone around us was jumping up celebrating; we were right amongst about twenty Dortmund fans. 'How could they be in here?' I thought. I was not happy at all. Fighting broke out behind me and I went to help two United fans. United's security were quickly on the scene, but what I found hard to understand, was that the two United fans and myself were asked to vacate our seats. The Dortmund fans, who were now all laughing at us, were even happier as their team were winning 2-0 on aggregate. It looked like United were going out. I managed to get to a pub on Warwick Road called the Trafford to watch the entire second half on TV. United lost 2-0, but the chances they missed were untrue. It wasn't to be our day, as Fergie said, he was dead right, it wasn't to be my day either — my dream of European glory was again in ruins.

The Coco-Cola Cup that year, United were drawn away to Leicester City after beating Swindon Town 2-1 at Old Trafford. Again I went to the match with David Ashworth. Fergie kept with tradition playing all the kids and United lost 2-0 on aggregate. I was very impressed with their forward Emile Heskey, who now plays for Liverpool and England. I gave him 'man of the match'; he also scored a great goal. We were thinking is it worth spending all that money to go to a match, and watch most of the youth team. I made a decision that night to boycott the Coco-Cola Cup, as I felt United were not treating the competition seriously and my money would be better spent on future European adventures. Fergie has always taken the FA Cup seriously, as it is the platform that set United onto great things. After the Lee Martin winner against Crystal Palace in the Cup Final, we then won the Cup Winners Cup and there was no looking back from then on. On the 5th January we beat Tottenham 2-0 at Old Trafford. I have a lot of time for Tottenham, going back to the days when my wife was mad on Steve

Perryman. She had always liked him. I took her to Old Trafford one opening game of the season when United were 2-0 up at half-time, but yet lost 3-2, I think it was the 1976/77 Season, since then I have always had a soft spot for them. I also have a friend in Tenerife, where I am currently writing this book, who is a fanatical Spurs fan. His name is Paul, I have known him for over fifteen years and always take money off him when United play Spurs. There is always plenty of goals in the games, which goes to show you the entertainment value. Paul's brother sadly died from liver failure due to excessive drinking; he was also a Spurs fanatic. Paul now manages a bar on the island called Kormacks; as I write this book I am having a week with Paul and United's last home game is against Spurs, it is on live at 11.30 a.m., so we are going to have a drink on it and talk about the old times. After beating Tottenham, we were knocked out after a replay with Wimbledon; losing 1-0. United were once again crowned Premier League Champions that season, 1996/97, with 75 points. Things were just getting better and better.

After the usual summer break, the 1997/98 Season kicked off with a great Charity Shield match against Chelsea at Wembley, on 3rd August. United won on penalties, with the game ending 2-2; Ronnie Johnsen scoring a rare goal for the Reds. Our opening game was, yes you've guessed it, at Tottenham away. 'An easy start,' I thought; United coming out easy winners with goals from Butt and Beckham. I was beginning to think that this United side were beginning to jell together better than any of the other United sides. The movement off the ball was terrific, and David Beckham's crossing ability and free kicks were out of this world. He was certainly England class without a shadow of a doubt. The next two games were a scrappy 1-0 home win against Southampton, who I always wanted to get relegated because of the distance you have to travel; somehow they always manage to scrape through; then a hard-earned draw at Leicester City, who always work hard as a unit against United. I have a lot of respect for their manager Martin O'Neill. I rate him a top-class motivator and manager; I remember him from his early days at

Nottingham Forest. Now that Emile Heskey has gone to Liverpool, it will be interesting to see how he copes with Stan Collymore as a replacement. Collymore was once linked to United but I'm glad to say nothing came of it. Martin O'Neill has taken a big gamble on Collymore, I only hope he can repay the manager for taking a brave decision on giving him another chance in the premiership. Collymore has a lot of talent and it is always good to see class in our Premier League, which by now is easily the most difficult and best league in the world. My only worry is that we can still produce home-grown talent like the current kids from United's youth team. It is not nice to see all those foreign players on mega bucks like the current Chelsea team, but again that is another story.

United went through to the end of September unbeaten, before losing to Leeds 1-0, who like United had a lot of youngsters in their side. I knew then that Leeds would be a team to watch in the future. I also had a gut feeling that Arsenal would be up there too. United came back from the Leeds defeat like lions with their pride hurt. We beat Palace 2-0, drew 2-2 at Derby, where I thought we were very unlucky not to win, and then trounced Barnsley 7-0 at Old Trafford. It was good to hear the Barnsley fans singing their famous song 'It's just like watching Brazil', only this time intending it to mean United were like Brazil. Cole netted a hat trick with Ole getting a brace; Scholes and Poborsky getting the others. Following the hammering of Barnsley it was Sheffield Wednesday's turn to cop for another top class performance; United hitting six, winning 6-1 at Old Trafford with Cole scoring two, Sheringham and Solskjaer each scoring two. United's forwards were now buzzing, and everyone was saying the league title was already over — who can stop United after displays like this. The lads always used to bet on the scores at Old Trafford. David Ashworth and myself always had a £5.00 bet each on the correct score at every home game. Following the 7-0 thrashing of Barnsley, David said United would win 6-0, a score unheard of before, but now anything was possible. I had a 4-0 bet, so Sheffield Wednesday scoring cost us £400 at odds of 80/1. It was a big disappointment not being able to smile after a 6-1 win! The thing that cheered us up was a friend, a Barnsley fanatic who ran a bar in Piccadilly called the Waldorf. His name is Wayne Nuttall, and he made a stupid bet with us, saying "I will buy you a pint for every goal United score, as long as both of you buy me a pint for every goal Barnsley score." We took the bet without hesitation and now it was pay back time. We gave Nutty a lot of stick but he kept his word, buying us our drinks. The Waldorf was full of Barnsley supporters and can they drink. They were a good set of lads, I hoped Barnsley would stay up.

The test for me was the trip down to Highbury for the Arsenal game on 9th November. Everyone who knows football knows there is no love lost between these two clubs, following incidents dating back years, but now I was beginning to feel that Arsenal were moving away from their boring, boring, Arsenal days and had started to attack teams. They had signed good players like Overmars, Bergkamp, Petit, and Vierra, although I still maintain that their defence was aging. United knew they were in for a tough match. The game kicked off and before you knew it we were 2-0 down. Arsenal were unstoppable but United dug in. Teddy Sheringham took a lot of stick from the Arsenal fans, mainly from the North Bank, then proceeded to score two goals to their end to bring us back into the game. United went on to lose the game thanks to a goal from David Platt, the former United schoolboy and ex-England player. It was United's second defeat of the season, and I knew after that game that Arsenal would be up there challenging us for our title.

As always United came back from the defeat, thumping Blackburn 4-0 at Old Trafford, then it was time for another big game at Anfield on 6th December against Liverpool, who were now also trying to rebuild their team. United played excellently, coming out easily on top with a 3-1 win; Andy Cole scoring two and David Beckham one, keeping United up there. Another great win at Newcastle followed, which kept the momentum going. Since the Arsenal defeat United had won five games on the trot, but this run was ended at Coventry on 28th December. United were in complete control of the game. I never ever thought we were going to lose this one, but unlike United, they took their foot off the pedal and never killed Coventry off. They came back into the game to win 3-2. Their forward Darren Huckerby, who we had an interest in, was for me 'man of the match', scored the winner, he now plays for Leeds our biggest rivals. I always maintained he would do better at a bigger club. I had to hold my hands up to Coventry for their come back. You couldn't take anything away from them. They had battled well and got the three points.

This was the turning point of the season for me. Again we bounced back, winning 2-0 at Old Trafford against Tottenham, with both goals coming from Ryan Giggs. Another story I have about Tottenham is we once played them at Old Trafford in the early nineties. A funny thing happened to me; Lee Martin had got tickets for my brother Wallace, his son James, myself and my son Robert. We also had tickets for the players' lounge. When we entered the ground we heard a big commotion. A lady was very upset at being refused entry without her special pass. It was Nicky Barmby the Tottenham forward's, wife; apparently she is ten years' older than him and she was not happy at all. She was demanding that United's security should go and get Nicky from his changing room at 2.30 p.m., half an hour before kickoff! Wallace and I were in stitches but she was not joking. Her minder was insisting who she was, but the United security lads were dead right to be following their instructions. Anyway her minder made a phone call and one of the Tottenham officials came down to give her another pass. She was not amused and stormed off into the ground. My son Robert was playing football with Peter Schmeichel's children at the time, and still remembers it — it is his claim to fame! We met all the Tottenham players after the game. I was very impressed with Gary Mabbutt, he talked to us for ages and had lots of time for people with children; what a good professional he is. The plan after the game was to take the children home, then go on to a casino. Lee knows I don't gamble heavily, so just after half-time Lee, who was one of United's substitutes, asked me to look after £5,000 he had won on the horses; a treble had come up for him. It was a hell of a wad but I said I would give it to him later. He asked me if I was going to the casino, to which I replied "No, I have to get Robert back to Glossop, but do you want me to take any of the winnings home for you." Lee said no, he would be alright. Some of the United players used to have a few drinks in the players' lounge, then go to Sid's Casino where they could have a free meal with drinks and enjoy themselves. When I saw Lee on the Sunday, I asked him how he had got on. The look on his face said it all. He said "Bruce, I gave the whole £5,000 back. I wish you had taken some home with you, but anyway the meal was great. Easy come, easy go!" Lee is a great lad but he could not settle in Scotland after his transfer from United to Glasgow Celtic. Also his wife Kath, a local Glossop girl and the two children couldn't settle, so he was given a free transfer to Bristol Rovers. I felt that this situation did not help his football; his back injury was still bothering him even after several operations. How sad that the man who had changed everything for Manchester United, by scoring the winning goal against Crystal Palace that Thursday night at Wembley, was now struggling to keep his football career alive. Lee had been at United since he was eleven years old. He had signed on a YTS scheme; it is all that he knows. His wife is arranging a testimonial, Bristol Rovers against United, the date is yet to be confirmed. Tommy Price and myself have said we would also arrange a benefit night at our nightclub in Glossop, which is called Club 2000, formerly Dollars.

Back to the 1997/98 Season. After beating Spurs 2-0, United had a bad patch in January, losing 1-0 to our bogey team Southampton away, then a shock defeat by Leicester at Old Trafford. I must add that United were not playing the type of football that we had become used to, and I was also against Alex's system of freshening the team by dropping players, even if they had played well. I know the Premier League is the toughest in the world, but I was always a firm believer in picking your best eleven players at all times, but again I have changed my mind, the pace of the game is now so fast that you have to rest your players to get the best from them. After all it can't be easy, most of the United team are now playing at least two games a week. On 7th February we played our derby game

128

David Ashworth (Glossops World Champion dart thrower) with Tyson in the background, on our way to the airport for the Cup Winners Cup Final.

J

Istanbul — Galatasaray away: lunch in a Turkish bazaar before the infamous

Celebrations on Porto Square before the game.

Myself with T. Price and D. Clay (Tyson), before our meeting with Alex Ferguson

Our visit to see the Great Train Robber, Ronnie Biggs, with his dog 'Blitz'. Note Tommy holding a Royal Mail train replica with the working-class hero. This picture was taken during our trip to Rio de Janeiro for the World Club Championship.

Myself and my son Robert meeting the great Jaap Stam at the United hotel (The Inter Continental) in Rio de Janeiro. Big Nigel from the Stalybridge branch in the background.

*Eric Cantana meets **Tommy** for the first time at Adrian Dearnley's fortieth celebrations at Old Trafford. Keith Gillespie and Wilf McGuiness in attendance.*

against Bolton Wanderers at Old Trafford. Their fans sang the Munich song throughout the entire match, which we drew 1-1, with Andy Cole scoring for the Reds. United were still not playing good football but at least we had ended our run of two successive defeats, which is not often seen at Old Trafford. February was a good month for us with three straight wins; at Aston Villa 2-0, at home to Derby County winning 2-0 and a good win at Chelsea 1-0, where Phil Neville scored a rare goal which turned out to be the winner; Tore Andre Flo missed a lot of chances for Chelsea. United were back on track ready for the run in, or so I thought. March was a disaster, we went down 2-0 at Sheffield Wednesday, drew 1-1 at West Ham, with the turning point losing 1-0 to our rivals Arsenal at Old Trafford. They needed a win to keep their challenge alive and got their result. Arsenal played well, any team that attacks United at home deserves credit. It is not very often United don't score at home. So March was nearly over, with United getting only one point from three games. I was now starting to feel very nervous with Arsenal breathing down our necks. March ended with a 2-0 win against Wimbledon at home and a 3-1 win at Blackburn Rovers. Our next two home games against Liverpool and Newcastle were drawn 1-1. United were drawing too many games and Arsenal were closing the gap. They were in great form, no one seemed able to stop them. The final three games were all won by United, 3-0 at Crystal Palace, 3-0 at home to Leeds and the season finished with a 2-0 win at Barnsley, but United had paid the price of drawing too many games. Arsenal's great run continued and they overtook United, winning the Championship by one point. I remember being very disappointed but have to admit that you can't take anything away from Arsenal, they finished with a great run and I hold my hands up to them. I'm afraid I can't say the same about Tommy Price. When he met Paddy Chatburn, who is a fanatical Arsenal fan from Manchester, mouthing off about them being champions in a pub, Tommy went straight over to him and knocked him out; it took two people to pick Paddy up. I got him a taxi outside, where we went to another club. I told Paddy he should have expected that if he mouthed it off in one of

Tommy's pubs. Sometimes you can explain the consequences, only some people never listen and Paddy appears to be one of them.

Anyway Arsenal were in the European Cup, with United somehow being entered as runners-up in the Premier League. I think that the old European Cup where you had to be champions to enter, was a better way of describing the champions of Europe, but the European Cup was now about money as well — more matches with Sky TV rights, etc. In years to come I feel we will see a Super League, with all the top European teams competing against each other. You will see teams like Celtic and Rangers from Scotland, playing against teams from England, Spain, Italy, France and Portugal. The cost of travelling to these countries is now very cheap, with the airlines all competing with each other, so at least the supporters can travel relatively cheaply to watch their teams. The European Cup Champions Draw was made with United in a group with Kosice, Juventus and Feyenoord. I missed the Kosice away game which United won 3-0, as I was in Tenerife trying to open a bar called Besties. There is already a Beckham's and a Busby's there. I had no idea where Kosice was, but after talking to Walter Perjenko, the man who organises all the European trips for the Stalybridge branch, he advised me against going as it was too far to travel. After my experiences of travelling long distances with United, for example Honved, Dortmund and Porto, I decided to take Walter's advice and go to the next round instead. Walter is one of the founder members of the Stalybridge branch, following United for over thirty years. All his spare time goes into organising events for the branch, a lot of us do not realise how time consuming this must be for him; myself included, we take Walter for granted. I would like to thank Walter for all his efforts, without people like him a lot of United fans would not be able to attend so many games.

United won the away leg at Kosice 3-0, but the next match at Old Trafford against Juventus would be the test. Last year Juventus had the edge over United, winning both games 1-0. This time I knew the experience would do us good. The game turned out to be a classic, with United going behind early on to a Del Peiro goal, only for Teddy Sheringham to equalise. The crowd really got behind the team, with Paul Scholes coming on for Nicky Butt and then scoring to put us 2-1 in front. It was end to end stuff, but what really killed the Italians off was the goal scored by Ryan Giggs. He went on one of his runs on the left, skipped past the Italian defenders and blasted a rocket of a shot into the top corner; the crowd went bananas. I was jumping on the seats with Ray Price, we both knew then that United had learnt from past experiences. A few weeks later we played Feyenoord at Old Trafford, winning 2-1. What a great start to the Champions League, three straight wins. The next game was away to Feyenoord on 5th November. There was no way I wanted to miss this. The Feyenoord fans are supposed to be one of the worst crowds in Europe; I remember the Tottenham fans having a lot of trouble over there in the seventies. I had also been to their stadium when we won the Cup Winners Cup in 1991, but had not actually seen them play at home against United. I made a lot of phone calls as soon as I knew the dates, managing to book four seats with Easy Jet costing us £58 return. The only problem was that we had to fly from Luton. We caught the early plane on Monday morning and had booked to return early the following Thursday. The four in our group were Alan Hazlehurst, David Clay, David Ashworth and myself. On the day we were due to drive down to Luton, David Ashworth said that due to work commitments he couldn't go, so I rang Walter who managed to get three days' off work to take David's place. I drove us down to Luton, where we were met by Nick the Watford fan who had driven us to Dortmund the year before. He asked if he could come with us. As luck would have it there was room on the flight, so Nick became the fifth member of our group. As we were checking in, I was approached by two TV crewmen who were working for Sky News, asking us why we were using Easy Jet — Walter and myself replied because of the cost. What was actually happening was that the other air lines were lowering their prices to compete with Easy Jet, causing a price war. The only winners in a situation like this was the customer. My interview was shown around the world. I had phone calls from Tenerife and

America from friends saying that they had seen me on TV!

Alan had booked a twin room at the Marriott Hotel in Amsterdam for three nights. As usual the five of us would divide the cost between us. The Stalybridge branch had a 52-seater coach booked for a three-day excursion. I had arranged to meet Tommy Price who was driving with his two brothers, Ray and Paul, along with two of Ray's workmates. We caught a taxi from the airport to our hotel. All had quick showers and a change of clothes, then we were ready to see the sights. I was amazed to see how many Reds had made the trip, my estimates were about 5,000. The police were brilliant in their approach, keeping watch on the fans in this high-risk game. I didn't see any Feyenoord fans at all in the three days we stayed in Amsterdam. We met up with the Stalybridge crew who were all drunk from the coach trip, then toured the red light district of Amsterdam. This is one of the fastest cities in the world, where time just moves on without you realising it. We were all drinking in a bar near the canals, when we bumped into Kevin Booth, who runs the trips for the Middleton lads. We had a drink together, talking about old times and before you knew it the whole place was singing all the old songs; the atmosphere was fantastic. Everyone had their fair share of women, drugs and beer, what more could a man want? With United playing here it was like a dream come true! The day and night passed without incident. We got back to our room in the early hours, falling asleep very quickly.

The next morning we awoke to find we had missed breakfast as usual, so decided to have a walk around the red light district again. We had only been walking around for about ten minutes when I saw Tommy's jeep driving around the city like a mad man. We flagged him down and it turned out that they had driven through the night; they were not a pretty sight! Ray said to me "Never again Bruce. All we have done is argue all the way here." Apparently Tommy had thought one of Ray's workmates had stolen his money, which was about £2,000 — the lads had even stripped naked to prove their innocence. A few hours later, Tommy had found his money in his jacket pocket. You could have cut the atmosphere with a knife. As well as all this, Paul was not happy with Tommy for his driving, insisting that he should not drink and drive, which I have to say I support him on this. Anyway, I said "You are now in Amsterdam, so you might as well enjoy it." So they booked into a hotel for the night and off we all went for a good drink. I bumped into Wilf McGuiness walking around the streets with another master of ceremonies who works at Old Trafford, Alan Platt. We all had a good laugh until they both moved on. I then saw my older brother Wallace who had made the trip by car. The Stalybridge branch on tour is never short of excitement. In the early hours of the morning I spotted Addy Dearnley who was the club's president, driving a street cleaner back to the hotel. "Better than a taxi Bruce," he said. I replied "Addy you are mad. See you later!"

We all hit the sack, missed breakfast again, waking up at about dinner time on the day of the game. We decided to catch one of the trains that had been laid on for the United fans from Amsterdam Central train station. To my surprise no one was charging anybody for the journey, which took about an hour. I only realised the reason for this when we got to Rotterdam. The police had got it planned to perfection. They kept us all waiting for hours on the trains. We had all thought we could get drunk in the town centre, but the police had other plans for us. They said it was for our own protection and we found out later how right they had been. There were stories circulating that a group of about 200 United fans had attacked a crew of Feyenoord supporters in a bar in the town centre, causing thousands of pounds worth of damage. This came as a big surprise for me as most of the Reds I saw were drunk but well behaved. Whilst we were waiting on the train, a few Dutch lads, wearing United colours and speaking perfect English explained the hatred Ajax of Amsterdam have of Feyenoord; it is like a United City derby match. They said that hundreds of Ajax trouble makers had tickets for the match and were supporting the Reds. This explained why the police were keeping us all together at the station. When there was about 500 of us, they marched us off to the ground army style. The time was now two hours before kickoff. We knew we had no chance of getting a drink. The walk to the ground was about 300 yards, it was very intimidating. The Feyenoord fans were throwing stones and bottles at us. To their credit, the riot police were attacking their own fans with batons and tear gas to keep us together, protecting us from any harm. It is the first time I have seen the police attack their own fans with such force. I saw hundreds of their fans being attacked but had no pity for them, it reminded me of the seventies when United fans were regularly involved in this kind of behaviour, but not to this extent. These fans were behaving as if they had something to prove to the English, showing us that they could be just as daft as us. We were all glad to get to the ground in one piece but this was only the beginning.

All the United coaches had protection screens around them, to stop the windows being smashed; these had been fitted a few miles down the road by the police. One of the first people I saw get off the coach was my older brother Wallace, who said that the Dutch fans had attacked a coach full of United fans just as they were disembarking at the ground, so now the police were bringing the coaches directly into the ground through the entrance reserved for ambulances. By now it was forty-five minutes to kickoff. As there was no drink on sale in the ground, we decided to get into our seats. All the United fans were stuck together behind the goal. At either side of us were forty-foot plastic fences to stop the Dutch fans throwing missiles at us. This didn't deter the Dutch, they were attacking the police from both sides of the ground. They knew they had no chance of getting through to us, but even if they had of done I think the United fans would have won. There were thousands of us against hundreds of dick heads who were showing what I call Dutch courage. The police handled this with batons, which went on throughout the whole game. This put me off a bit as I had one eye on the game and one eye on the fans. The game kicked off with United giving a fine performance, winning 3-1 with Andy Cole scoring a hat trick. He was first class and deserved all the credit. The only disappointment for me was a horrendous tackle on Dennis Irwin late in the game. The Feyenoord player was substituted straight away but it was a deliberate attempt to break his leg, that could have ruined his career.

On 26th November we made it five straight wins by easily beating Kosice 3-0 at Old Trafford, this meant that United had a chance of eliminating Juventus from the competition on 10th November away. I went with the Manchester United Supporters Club tour, a day trip straight in and out. It is not often I travel with the club, as I like to make my own arrangements. We had a great day in Turin but the result went against us, we lost 1-0. Nevertheless we had got through to the quarterfinals for the second year running, this time drawing Monaco away on 4th March. Before the draw was made I had always wanted to go to Monaco. I had heard so many good reports from people who had been on holiday there, saying how good it was in the South of France, and here was my opportunity to be there. Monaco is only a small ground, I knew United would not get many tickets. I managed to persuade my partner Tommy Price that if I travelled over the month before the game, I would be in a position to buy many tickets for the lads, ensuring that we could arrange another great away excursion. Our local brewery Whitbread's were giving away air miles with every order, so after about six months we had managed to accumulate quite a lot. My wife Carol and I needed a few days' break from the nightclub, so I suggested to Tommy that we used the air miles for a trip to Monaco, and in the process get the tickets for the forthcoming match. Tommy was fine about this, so Carol had two days off work and we went off for a long weekend in France. We booked our flights through British Airways and flew from Manchester, Club Class, to Heathrow; from there we took a connecting flight to Nice. On the outward flight to Heathrow, I met an old friend of mine from my early days at Clayton Aniline, his name is Peter Wragg, who had become a very successful football manager at non-league level. He was now doing exhibitions for the Conference League and was on his way to London to do exactly that. In his day, Peter was a very good footballer who I thought should have made it to the top, but like thousands of other players, for reasons unknown, they don't make it. It was great to see him but even though the journey was only forty minutes we had a good chat about the old times. He could not believe I was going to Monaco for match tickets. I had arranged hotel accommodation for Carol and myself. I knew Monaco was going to be expensive, so I had asked for a list of five-star hotels that British Airways use and faxed them all, before we went to enquire if they did conference rates for any guests who were travelling out to see if the hotel could accommodate 300 to 400 for major private functions in the future. I received a few replies but the best one was from the Meridian Beach Plaza in Monte Carlo. They faxed back details, saying they would love to accommodate us, giving Carol and myself a double room with sea views for a special rate of £50 a night; they also said we could expect special privileges.

Once we arrived in Nice the look on Carol's face said everything, she was very excited. I think the break did her a lot of good, as it can't be easy working full time as well as looking after three kids. We then caught a taxi from Nice to our hotel in Monte Carlo where the manager, Mr Gilles Foureroux, was waiting to welcome us to the Meridian Beach Plaza. The hotel was out of this world; they even had their own private beach. Gilles had booked a table for two in the hotel restaurant at no cost to us. Up in the room was a bottle of champagne waiting for us. They really knew how to look after you, little did they know we were only there to get tickets for the United game. Gilles showed me around the conference rooms whilst Carol sunbathed on the private beach. The hotel didn't charge us for one meal over the three days we were there. Monte Carlo is only a few hundred yards long. The money there is unbelievable, people leave their Ferrari's open, but they never get stolen. I was beginning to wonder how they would cope with the Red invasion. The next day we decided to spend sightseeing. We walked into one hotel called the Lowes, which had its own casino with fruit machines that you could win thousands of pounds on. We decided to have £20 each on the machines. I lost mine very quickly but Carol won £100. I never saw any of it as she said we had not agreed 50/50 before we started playing. She won the money on her third attempt, then immediately cashed the tokens in, took the money and ran. "There's no way I'm giving it all back" she said. I would have kept playing, trying to win the jackpot but we had a good laugh anyway.

We then decided to visit Prince Rainier's Castle on the hill where the views are breathtaking. It is one of the most beautiful places in the world. I felt very lucky that I am fortunate enough to be able to see these places through watching United. We then walked down to the football ground, where we were disappointed to find out that the tickets were not going to be on sale for another two weeks; you also had to have a Monaco address to be able to buy them. Everything is done on credit cards here, they do not place their tickets on open sale. It was made an all-ticket game on the advice of the police, as they don't very often fill the ground which is built above a shopping precinct and sports centre. There is also a car park there with the ground on top of it all. It is a very unusual design, all the charges from the car park pays for the upkeep of the ground which was a gift to the Monaco team from Prince Rainier. I phoned Tommy to tell him the bad news. He was ok about it but said not to worry, we will get the tickets somehow we always do. When we returned to the hotel we enjoyed yet another meal, this time with Gilles as our guest. He asked if there was anything he could do to make our stay more enjoyable, so I cheekily enquired about tickets for the forthcoming game! I lied to him, saying that the rest of the committee members would need to view the hotel at around the time United were playing in the European Cup. Gilles took me by surprise saying that the Monaco team always stay at the hotel before every match and that it would be no problem whatsoever to get tickets for the game, as he knew most of the players. He asked me how many tickets I would like, to which I replied "Six please." I gave him my phone number and asked him to ring me when he had the tickets, then I would book another three twin rooms at the discounted conference rates. We had a great time in Monte Carlo, but I couldn't wait to get back with the lads a month later. Carol enjoyed herself too. She was a bit scared of it all blowing up in our faces but I assured her that I am now a professional at this type of thing. Gilles has been very helpful to me, as Meridian have hotels all over the world. He said it would be no problem to get me discounted rates at any of their hotels around the world. I kept this in mind for future matches, and on our return the first thing I did was to send him a thank you letter, accompanied by a bottle of Moet and Chandon. When we checked out of the hotel the only thing we had to pay for was the accommodation. What a successful trip this had been, not only did we have a great time but had also managed to secure six tickets for the Monaco game.

After about ten days, I received a phone call from Gilles to say he had successfully acquired six complimentary tickets from the Monaco team. The seats were situated in the main stand, where all the refreshments plus food would be taken care of by the club. I thanked him and immediately booked three twin rooms for three days to fit in with the match. The group of six included Tommy Price, Ray Price, Sammy Gilbey, Andre Shaha, Damion Dixon and myself. The next thing we had to do was book our flights with Easy Jet, as they flew to Nice from Liverpool. We were lucky again and managed to get the flights for £69 return. We arrived in Nice the day before the game. Tommy and Ray took the helicopter from the airport to the hotel at a cost of £50, but the rest of us caught a taxi. I had already briefed the lads to be on their best behaviour. If they were asked, they were to say that they were insurance workers coming to stay at the hotel to view the facilities for the forthcoming conference in September that year. When we arrived at the hotel Tommy and Ray were waiting for us outside. The lads could not believe how nice the hotel was! Once again Gilles wished us a happy holiday, thanked me for his gift then handed me the tickets for the game, which I then gave to the lads. He also pointed out that all the rooms had sea views, but his bosses had stated that only two out of the six could receive the corporate hospitality with regards to drinks and meals. I thanked him, saying that it would be no problem. The two would be Andy Shaha and myself as we both worked for the same insurance company, the others could view the facilities at their own pleasure, which would be better as they could form their own opinions. I had told Gilles that the decision rests with these people and that it was narrowed

138

down to two hotels, the Meridian and the Lowes Hotel. Gilles believed this story, so over the next three days made us very welcome. He even introduced us to the Monaco team who stayed over the night before the game. I remember having a chat with John Collins, the ex-Celtic and Monaco midfielder who now plays for Fulham. He told me how good the money was over there and as football is only a short career, he has to make the most of it for his family. We also spoke to Barry Venison who was covering the match for television. Barry is another ex-England player who also played for Liverpool and Newcastle. He enquired how we thought United would go on, so we told him in no uncertain terms that the game would be easy, 4-0 to United. Barry just smiled, I bet he thought typical biased Reds!

The day before the game we walked up to the ground. There were no tickets on sale. The club had been very careful of their distribution, a lot of United fans I spoke to had paid £100 for match tickets. We saw Strett who had snatched four tickets from a ticket tout. "Serves them bastards right. They are always ripping the fans off" he said. I told him to stay out of the way as these touts worked in groups, so Strett said goodbye and went back to his hotel. All the lads were down in the harbour in Monaco. I could not believe some of the boats moored up there; there must have been millions of pounds worth of yachts. One we saw belonged to the racing driver David Coulthard. Tommy decided to climb aboard to have some photos taken! There was a nice bar in the harbour called the Ship, where we had a few drinks outside. Tommy advised the owner how many Reds would be over the next day. He seemed shocked as to exactly how many would be travelling and at £4.00 a pint told the owner he would make a fortune. Tommy even offered him £3,000 cash to own the bar for the day of the match, but he politely declined the offer but asked Tommy if he would keep an eye on things in return for a few free drinks. As we knew most of the Reds it was an offer we could not refuse, so again we had saved some money on the day of the match. We left the marina telling the owner of the Ship that we would see him at midday tomorrow. The lads all agreed to try our hands at the Lowe's Casino, pooling together £20 each for the fruit machines, but Tommy had other ideas. He decided to try his hand at roulette. He didn't know what he was doing but placed his chips on a few numbers that came up at 14-1. At one stage he was about two thousand pounds up, but ended up giving it all back like all gamblers do. We stayed at the Lowe's Hotel until about midnight, then made our way back to our hotel where we had a few drinks before retiring to bed in readiness for a heavy session on match day.

We all awoke early for a grand buffet breakfast; the best thing for us in readiness for the day ahead! Most of the Stalybridge lads were flying over on the one-day trip with United, so we arranged to meet them at the Ship. We were at the bar for opening time 11 a.m. It was a glorious afternoon with all the United fans sitting drinking outside the bar. There were hundreds of Reds singing songs from the sixties and there was no trouble whatsoever. I met three lads from Dukinfield, which is not far from me. They are known for doing stupid things at United matches but only for a laugh. Their names are Dale Ellis, Sammy Craggs and Barry Graham. Dale has been watching United as long as I have. Recently I have heard he has to wear a tag along with Paul Hands whom I mentioned earlier. Sammy Craggs is an HGV driver who travels everywhere with Dale. The third lad, Barry, is a die hard City fan, but always wants United to do well in the European Cup. Barry has followed City since the sixties, once having a dart thrown in his head at Anfield when City were there. They had to take him to hospital with the dart still stuck in his head to avoid any brain damage. Barry took some stick about this, we told him it must have been the *News of the World* darts champion to have been able to pick him out of the crowd. We had a great laugh with these three, they also had another lad with them but I didn't know his name; they said it was Barry Graham's cousin. Anyway these four had driven over; they had bottles of white wine with them, so not wanting to pay the Ship's prices we were secretly opening the wine and filling our glasses. After about four hours of drinking the four lads decided to strip off. Sitting at their table completely naked drinking their wine, it was so funny everyone was laughing even the police and the bar owner. They then all decided to jump into the sea where all the yachts were moored. By now everyone was following suit, the sea was a mass of United supporters skinny dipping. I remember thinking 'No way'; the water looked beautiful but it was freezing. Then everyone started throwing everyone else in fully clothed, so I said to Tommy and the lads that it was now time to make a move to get into the ground. The owner of the Ship said it was ok for us to go back after the game, the police had told him to close to avoid trouble, so he asked us to use the side door and keep our voices down, which we said we would do. I thanked him again, then we set off to the ground which was only half a mile away.

United had a great following as usual. It seems that people are following United from all around the world, which is great, they are now extending Old Trafford, but the atmosphere seems to have gone. People have told me recently that United are trying to have an end just for people to sing in, to recreate the atmosphere I revelled in in the seventies. In those days we all sang to get behind the team, which is why I like European and away league games. At United matches you hardly see any trouble at all. Children are encouraged to attend, with families also attending, which they hardly ever did in the sixties and seventies. Footballers are now like film stars, under pressure to perform at the highest level. Sometimes I think how do David Beckham and Ryan Giggs cope, but then in the same breath I wish it was me. I'd be able to handle it for the money they are paid nowadays. Gilles did us proud, we were situated in the best seats in the ground with the best view, but unfortunately it was a scrappy game. Monaco seemed happy with the 0-0 draw. I remember thinking that we would win the return at Old Trafford. After the match we headed straight back to the Ship. The owner had also been to the match. He did not feel very confident for the second leg, but to give him his due he said that he would be going over to Old Trafford, so I swapped phone numbers with him and said we would meet him in a pub near to Old Trafford. Later in the night we caught two taxis back to our hotel for a drink, then we all fell straight into our beds.

In the morning I thanked Gilles for all his hospitality and said I would fax him the following week with the committee's decision. I also stressed to him that it was not just down to me, but everyone on the committee. I made him aware that he had my vote. We said our goodbyes and caught taxis back to Nice Airport.

The return leg was played at Old Trafford on 18th May. In the opening ten minutes disaster struck as Monaco scored a great goal to the Scoreboard End, which meant that United had to score two goals. We had met the owner of the Ship in the Trafford pub, he was staying overnight at the Copthorne Hotel. We all had a drink with him and I told him to expect a thrashing of at least 4-0 and said goodbye. I could not believe what was happening, could my dream be over yet again? United missed chances; they should have won easily. Ole Gunnar Solskjaer equalised for the Reds, but to no avail. Monaco held on, so went through on the away goals ruling. The score ended up 1-1. I now had the feeling that United would never realise my dream of winning the European Cup, but as luck would have it, even though Arsenal had won the league and I had taken a lot of stick from Ralph (Paddy) Chapburn, the only Arsenal fan I know who lives in Manchester, United gained entry into the European Cup through the back door, as the new ruling was that the runners-up in the Premier League also qualified, so I was happy with that. This took away some of the pain of losing our title.

In the Coca-Cola Cup that year, United were beaten 2-0 at Ipswich and I kept my word about not attending. In the FA Cup, United were drawn away to Chelsea on the 4th January in the third round. Over the years I have witnessed some classic encounters between these two teams, but this game was something else. I travelled down with the Stalybridge branch. By now we knew what to expect at Chelsea — a hostile atmosphere. We also knew that David Beckham would get slagged off for his relationship with Posh Spice. In one of the great games of previous years we beat Chelsea 4-0 in the 1993/94 FA Cup Final, with Eric Cantona scoring two dubious penalties; then beating a Mark Hughes' inspired Chelsea at Villa Park in the 1995/96 FA Cup semifinal. We had also beaten them at Wembley on penalties in the 1997/98 Charity Shield, so this third round draw had me thinking that they were due a win against us, and having been drawn away, I must admit that I did not feel as confident as I usually do. As it happens United proved me wrong, the display was one of the best I have ever seen from any United team over the last thirty years. They totally out classed Chelsea in every department. David Beckham who took tremendous stick from the Shed End at Chelsea was marvellous. United's passing and movement was a sight to be seen; before Chelsea knew what had hit them, United were up 4-0 which silenced the Chelsea hordes. With Beckham scoring two and Cole two, Chelsea snatched a goal back, but two more goals from Teddy Sheringham had the score at 6-1. The United fans were all celebrating loudly along the touch line — I would have said there was about 7,000 there. Ten minutes before the end the Chelsea fans emptied their own ground to the chants of the United supporters singing part time supporters. Chelsea pulled back two late goals to make the score 6-3. Some United fans were confused as we did not know if Teddy Sheringham's goals had counted. We had lost count with how many goals we had scored and did not know if the score ended up 6-3 or 5-3. I'd like to think it was 6-3 so that is how I am writing it! The police did a great job at Chelsea, they kept us in the ground for over an hour, then when we were given the all clear, they marched us through the streets, even a grave yard, to avoid the Chelsea fans who wanted revenge for the hammering. It was a great day, with the coach stopping off at Beconsfield on the way back, where we had a good drink before heading back to Manchester.

The fourth round, we had an easy 5-1 win at Old Trafford against Walsall, then we played Barnsley in the fifth round at Old Trafford, drawing 1-1, which was a massive improvement for Barnsley who had taken a 7-0 mauling earlier in the season at Old Trafford. I had to admire their character; for me they were worthy of the draw but I was still convinced that United would easily win the replay, especially after that great performance at Chelsea. I have to take my hat off to Barnsley, as they beat United 3-2 in the replay, so that was the end of United's cup run, which tells you that you can take nothing for granted in football — always expect the unexpected.

The 1997/98 Season ended up with United runners-up, and what could have been another great season finished with United winning nothing, which is unheard of after their successes over recent years. I still knew United were a great side but I felt we needed one or two good signings to help the side overcome the loss of the great Eric Cantona, who had decided to call it a day to take up acting. Knowing Alex Ferguson's judgement on players, I also knew he wouldn't rush into the transfer market, so I would have to wait and see if in the close season anything developed.

In the pre season I decided to take Carol and the kids to Disneyland in Florida. After all they never stopped me going to any United matches, no matter where the Reds were playing, so I planned the holiday for late July and we all had a great time. You hear a lot of stories about America and how big headed the Yanks are, but once you get over there you have to admire their organising skills, as everything is planned to perfection. What surprised me was as we were walking around Universal Studios, all around us were people wearing United shirts. Again I was surprised at how many people from around the world follow United. Universal Studios is absolutely massive, there are thousands of people in there. All of a sudden I heard some one shout my name. I looked around to see a United supporter and his family from Denton in Manchester, who must have had the same idea as me to take his family away in the pre-season. I had a quick chat with him then said goodbye.

On our return to England the fixture lists were out, and United were to play Leicester at home in their first game. The Charity Shield was to be played at Wembley against our rivals Arsenal on the 23rd July, which was my fortieth birthday and Carol enquired if I wanted a party. I said no, but I wouldn't mind going to the Charity Shield against Arsenal as my birthday present. So I booked two limousines; they were massive — one was black, the other white. I invited eighteen of my friends down for the trip. I also rang United to see if I could have eighteen tickets together, which they provided at a cost of £30.00 each. On the day of the match I was very excited like a school kid going to his first game. I had even arranged for a full English breakfast at a pub in Glossop, Derbyshire, called the Nags Head at 7.30 a.m. John the landlord laid on a superb champagne breakfast. This was the perfect start to a great day. The weather was red hot and we loaded the limos up with cases of champagne, along with boxes of Buds, bought from the cash and carry. The next stop was at the Wembley Hilton, where I had arranged for us to have a meal, also the limos were to be left there, picking us up at 7 p.m. after the game when all the traffic had died down. I found that my arranging skills were becoming nearly as good as the Yanks! The two limos set off with all eighteen of us. I was in the front car along with Tommy and Ray Price, David Ashworth, David Clay, Rob Clorley, Keith Gratix, Bernard Morgan, Mark Coxan and his brother Carl. We had a great laugh all the way down the motorway; people were staring to see who it was in the limos. When we stopped at the service stations to use the toilets everyone was taking photos. We were telling people that we were Simply Red's backing group, going down to the Wembley Hilton to meet Mick Hucknall! We were even giving old ladies glasses of champagne; it was one long laugh from start to finish. We arrived at the hotel at 12 p.m., in time for our lunch. To my disappointment, Ned Kelly, who is United's head of security was not there, so we could not use his room number as on previous Wembley excursions, but we did not care as most of us were drunk by this stage! The lunch provided was very nice, all in all it had been a great day so far, but the best present I could have had would be to beat Arsenal at Wembley, then wind up that Arsenal fan from Manchester Ralph Paddy Chapburn!

We made our way to our seats. The day had a pleasant atmosphere about it and I was looking forward to seeing our latest record signing, £10 million for Jaap Stam, a centre half from Holland. I had watched him in the World Cup, but said I would make my judgement like I always do when they wear a red shirt and no other. He had not had a great tournament, a lot of people were already questioning Fergie's judgement; as usual the critics were out to get him. David Beckham had been sent off for England against Argentina for retaliation on Simeone. I thought it was a harsh decision but the rules say he had to go and off he went. England lost the game on penalties. I must say that I was very impressed with Liverpool's Michael Owen who scored a great goal, but the stick Beckham took for his sending off was disgusting; it compared with the stick Eric Cantona took and in some cases it was worse. I was praying that Becks would not turn his back on United, as there was talk that he might say "To hell with it all" and go to Italy or somewhere. That for me would have been a disaster for the Reds, as David Beckham is still one of the best crossers of the ball I have ever seen in my life. He is also one of the best free kick specialists I have seen. I can only compare him to Zico the Brazilian who I was lucky enough to meet on my travels a few years later. This treatment of Beckham promoted United fans to sing 'You can stick your fucking England up your arse'.

The Charity Shield kicked off. Arsenal yet again surprised me by attacking United from the start. They outclassed United, which is rarely seen and they deserved their 3-0 win. The result for me did not matter, it was the way United had played that gave me concern. I felt that we still needed a great player to fill the hole in between the forwards and midfield, but who was available at this late stage? We all headed back to the Wembley Hilton. It didn't take us very long to get back to our smiling ways again. The old United songs were now being sung. The Hilton staff were fantastic as they are used to this kind of behaviour by now. We left there when all the traffic had gone, stopping for a curry on the way back, then dropping all the lads off in Glossop town centre. It had been a great fortieth birthday for myself; one that I would never forget, only the result spoilt it.

The next big game for United was the week after, when we were to play LKS Lodz in the UEFA Champions League second qualifying first leg at Old Trafford. LKS Lodz were the Polish champions and although United had gained entry through the back door, having finished runners-up, it was no easy game. The attendance at Old Trafford was nearly 51,000. United had to win the game, played over two legs, to progress to the Champions League proper. In all honesty LKS Lodz came for a draw, packing their defence, which enabled United to attack at will. United poured forward from the off. Only bad finishing and a great display from the Lodz keeper, Wyparlo, kept the score line at 2-0 with goals from Giggs and a late header from Andy Cole. I thought this would be an acceptable cushion for the second leg

Jaap Stam, by now the world's most expensive defender had a good game and it was great to see Roy Keane back in action after his lengthy injury lay off. I knew United would have tougher tests ahead but thought 2-0 should be enough to get us through.

After our Wednesday night's win at Old Trafford, it was the opening match of the season against Leicester City on Saturday 15th August. I knew that Martin O'Neill's Foxes would not come and lie down. I was very disappointed with the Leicester City supporters as they booed and called David Beckham throughout the entire ninety minutes. I felt sorry for Becks; would he have to put up with this for the whole season? Only Becks knew the answer, the best way to silence your critics is to play well and David Beckham had a fine game. Leicester caught United with an early goal after ten minutes from Heskey, it was a below par United team performance. The newly formed defensive partnership of Johnsen and Stam clearly needed more time to gel and the old man Tony Cottee silenced the Old Trafford crowd by making it 2-0 on seventy-six minutes. With only fifteen minutes remaining Teddy Sheringham nudged a Beckham shot wide of the Leicester goalkeeper, and it was left to David Beckham to strike a great goal with almost the last kick of the game to save United from an embarrassing opening home defeat. United must have been poor for Alex Ferguson to admit that it was debatable whether United deserved a point. The only thing that came out of this game for me was David Beckham is going to come in for a rough ride where ever he goes, I only pray that he handles the situation, but only time will tell.

The following Saturday United were at West Ham for our first away trip of the season. It was on 22nd August with Fergie making another secret move on the transfer market, breaking the record again for the United signing of Dwight Yorke. I did not think he was worthy of the money we had paid for him, but again said I would reserve my judgement until he had worn the red shirt. United supporters know after a few appearances whether a player is going to fit into the system or not. We knew West Ham would make it hard on Beckham. I remember when they threw bananas at Paul Ince when he left them to join us. I travelled down in my car and sat in the Bobby Moore Stand hoping United could secure their first win of the season. In normal circumstances the debut of a £12.6 million player would have come in for close scrutiny from the West Ham fans and the media, but it was David Beckham who is now going to be in the spotlight wherever he goes. He was persecuted by a hysterical section of the Hammer's supporters as a result of his World Cup sending off. Becks showed great character and passed his test with flying colours; refusing to be provoked by the same fans that were cheering him on a few months earlier. 'How fickle football fans are' I thought; they booed his every touch of the match. It was a scrappy affair with West Ham pushing forward in the first half, but with little threat to the United defence which had Roy Keane in there to replace the injured Stam. United should have had a penalty when Ruddock handled Giggs' cross, but in fairness to the referee he was unsighted. The game ended goalless; a boring 0-0 you might say, but I knew West Ham always make it very hard for United. Like every other team in the Premiership they try to raise their game against us, but we are used to that by now. I was happy with the result for the white shirted heroes.

The following Wednesday, on the 26th August, was the away leg of our UEFA Champions League qualifier against LKS Lodz. I did not fancy going to Poland to watch this game, which United drew 0-0, but a few of the lads from Stalybridge went to the game. They said the beer was very cheap but the game was crap. I was glad I saved my money but at least United were through from what could have been a tricky game. August ended with United in fifteenth position; Liverpool were top. You also have to remember that the Reds had only played two league games. I was very glad for Becks who was concentrating on his football, that was the best way to answer his critics. The next game was on the 9th September on a Wednesday night, when the new boys Charlton Athletic were visitors to Old Trafford. I remembered watching them in the play-off final, beating Sunderland on penalties; it was a thrilling end to end game. I felt sorry for the Sunderland full back, I think it was Gray, that missed his penalty, but I had no tears for the ex-City players Peter Reid, Niall Quinn and Nicky Summerbee. I was particularly impressed with the Charlton forward Clive Mendonca, as I thought he could be a handful to the newly formed partnership of Johnsen and Stam. The talk in all the papers now was the intended takeover bid from B Sky B, as well as what the press were calling a bad start to the season. What United needed now was a good win to keep the hounds at bay and we got it with two goals each from Dwight Yorke, on his home league debut, and the ever popular Ole Gunner Solskjaer. Although I must say that United let Charlton take the lead through Kinsella, this was getting a bit scary as not many teams attacked at Old Trafford, but now both Leicester and Charlton had visited and scored first. The Reds finished the game easy 4-1 winners. Another player made his league debut that day, it was Blomqvist who settled well on the left flank. I remembered him from a few seasons earlier, where he gave a 'man of the match' performance for Gothenburg against the Reds. He gave David May of United the run around and obviously Fergie had not forgotten that game in Sweden either.

On Saturday 12th September Coventry were the visitors to Old Trafford. I have a lot of fond memories of Gordon Strachan and hope he does well at Coventry, but not at the expense of United! It was a one sided affair. United scored after twenty minutes, with Ronny Johnsen making it 2-0 just after half-time. It was good to see Johnsen scoring at Old Trafford and you could also tell that he was communicating well with Stam. Stam in particular was beginning to impress me. It was another full house at Old Trafford over 55,000, but the man who stood out the most was Dwight Yorke. He has a tremendous touch just like Eric had. The ball appears to be glued to his feet and he also has great vision and pace. I knew then that Fergie had done his homework; how many times does he have to prove me wrong? I laughed when I read the Sunday papers the next day as Gordon Strachan had compared Coventry's approach to that of a dentist's patient who knew that pain was coming soon!

The lads were looking forward to our EUFA Champions League group D clash, on Wednesday 6th September, against Barcelona. To progress in the Champions League you have to play against the best and you don't get many bigger names than Barcelona. This was football the way it used to be played; it was a night of pure entertainment; end-to-end football that delighted the 54,000 crowd, with the crowd really getting behind United. Giggs opened the scoring, after seventeen minutes, with a rare header after Solskjaer had rattled the crossbar. Paul Scholes made it 2-0, slotting one home after a great overhead kick from Yorke, which bounced back off the Barcelona keeper and fell in front of him. I had memories of that great United fight back many years before in the Bryan Robson era, when we came back from 2-0 to win 3-2 at Old Trafford against Barcelona. They would not do the same again, as Barcelona changed their game plan and began attacking the Reds. Rivaldo had a goal disallowed for offside; I thought this was a bit dubious but who cared. The Reds held on until half-time. I remember saying to Ray Price that we needed a third goal to kill them off. To which Ray replied "You are right, but we must keep it tight at the back." When Ray and I watch the Reds together, it is like we are actually playing for United and kicking every ball. The second half started with confusion in United's defence and Barcelona pulled back a quick goal, two minutes after the break. The game was again wide open. Now I know why they say 2-0 is the worst lead you can have. Barcelona were now on top and were awarded a penalty, after sixty minutes, when Rivaldo took a dive after a challenge from Stam; it made amends for the goal he had had disallowed. Giovanni scored from the spot, it was now 2-2. United were at sixes and sevens, but after about seventy minutes United were awarded a free kick twenty-five yards out. David Beckham produced another one of his specials from the top draw and the Reds were back in front 3-2. The game was far from over. In the last twenty minutes Barcelona piled on the pressure. Nicky Butt handled the ball during a goalmouth scramble; an offence for which he was sent off. Luis Enrique made it 3-3 and that's how it stayed. I was a bit disappointed at throwing a 2-0 lead away, especially at Old Trafford but all credit has to go to Barcelona. In the end it was a fair result. No team had deserved to lose. Here's one to remember, can you tell me the last team to get two penalties at Old Trafford? If you can you are better than me. I think it must have been before my time!

The following Sunday, United were at the holder's Highbury ground to play Arsenal. The Barcelona game must have tired out the Reds; we could have done with an easier game. I thought now knew why Alex Ferguson likes to freshen things up, as the pace of the game is a lot quicker and players are picking up more injuries than before. United played the Gunners on 20th September. The Gunners had beaten us in the last three previous encounters and I was wondering if they were becoming our bogie side. This was the home of the newly crowned Premier League Champions. I decided to drive down to the game taking with me my son Robert, along with the Arsenal fan, Ralph Paddy Chapburn, who also brought his two sons Danny and Ross. Paddy got us the tickets but told us to keep quiet or we would be thrown out. United kicked off in their black strip. Right from the start Arsenal came at us in a determined frame of mind. They knew they had the psychological edge over us. United showed no movement up front with all three forwards, Giggs, Yorke and Blomqvist having quiet games. Arsenal's defence were outstanding, particularly Adams and Keown. Adams out jumped Stam to score a header after fourteen minutes. Arsenal made it 2-0 just before half-time. In the second half United attacked but then Nicky Butt was sent off for the second time in four days, for fouling Vierra. Ljungberg made it a miserable afternoon for the Reds, coming on as sub for Anelka. He chipped Peter Schmeichel for the third goal and that's the way it stayed. Robert and I took terrible stick all the way home. 'How could United do this to me' I thought, especially when Paddy was there.

'You are only as good as your next game', is another famous football saying and United's next visitors to Old Trafford were Liverpool, our old rivals. It was played on Thursday 24th September, with a 55,000 full house, that created a terrific atmosphere. The games between United and Liverpool have something special about them; the rivalry between the two sets of fans borders on hatred. The Liverpool fans were singing their famous song 'Have you ever won the treble, have you fuck'. There was also fighting outside Old Trafford, which is something you rarely see nowadays. A lad from Salford who I knew from the sixties, had been slashed down his face with a Stanley knife, which is, from my experience, an old Liverpool trick, his name was Teamo, word was going round the ground that the Scousers were up for it. The game kicked off with Liverpool playing the better football for the first twenty minutes. Then after that United were awarded a dubious penalty for handball. McAteer was harshly judged and Dennis Irwin netted from the spot. We don't get many penalties at Old Trafford over the season, so I was not complaining. Again I was very impressed with Liverpool's new kid on the block Michael Owen, but Stam and Gary Neville handled him well. In the second half United were let off the hook again when Riedle had a strike disallowed for offside. Paul Scholes killed Liverpool off with a great shot from just inside the box, to make it 2-0, after eighty minutes. Everyone thought there would be trouble with the Scousers after the game, but everything was ok. I didn't see any trouble although I felt for Teamo. A few weeks later I was told by Wilf McGuiness that when the Liverpool supporter appeared in Court in Salford for the attack on Teamo, before he could enter the Courts he was attacked by a gang of lads and badly beaten up. I did not feel sorry for him. I hope he gets locked up and they throw away the key.

United had bounced back from the 3-0 defeat at Highbury and it was now time for my first EUFA Champions League adventure in group D. We were due to play Bayern Munich on Wednesday 30th September, at the Olympic Stadium, Munich. It coincided with the October beer festival. I had always wanted to go to the beer festival and with United there as well it was like a dream come true. So I asked Carol if I could go for the week, and as usual she didn't stand in my way. United didn't have a game on the Saturday following the 2-0 win over Liverpool, so five of us decided to drive over in my car from Manchester. The five of us were Tommy and Ray Price, a lad from Ashton called Hassey and a young lad called Duncan Cox; it was his first European trip and his Dad who also follows United asked me to keep an eye on him. The plan was to drive to Dover, catch the train through the tunnel, drive to Belgium and then straight through to Munich. After the Dortmund trip I vowed I would never go on another massive jaunt overland, but time is a good healer and it didn't take me long to change my mind. The travelling was a bit of a bind but the laughs we had were well worth the pain. I drove down to Dover. I don't like driving abroad, we were very lucky to have Tommy Price with us, he speaks good German and is used to driving abroad after his days as a bricklayer in Germany. He drove us the entire way. It was over 1,000 miles, but with a few stop offs along the way, we arrived in Munich on the Sunday.

When we were about ten miles from Munich, which is where the 1958 team perished (incidentally the word Munich means to United supporters Manchester United Never Intended Coming Home), Tommy saw a sign for Dachau, where the Germans had their concentration camp. Tommy suggested that we stop to have a look around. We were all tired but realised that it was a piece of history, so decided to stop and take a look. The place is something else, it will haunt me to the end of my days. We spent hours walking round the camp, seeing the gas chambers where all the Jews were killed. The whole area was grey and still had a fear about it. We saw thousands of pictures of Jews being tortured; children being gassed; the sight of it was all too much for me and I found myself crying, thinking how lucky we are today and how fortunate I am to have three children in a different situation than these innocent children found themselves in. I saw maps of all the concentration camps across Germany, there were thousands of them, Auschwitz 1,2,3, Belsen 1,2,3, and many more. The one thing I could not understand, is that if they were killing this many people, the German people must have known what was happening. Surely the smell in the air would have told them. I just wanted to get out of the place, so I said a prayer for the people and felt that the hatred for the Germans is understandable. I also prayed that United would slaughter Bayern Munich. When we got back to the car all the lads had a go at Tommy for taking us there. Ray said it was the most depressing place he had ever seen and I had to agree with him.

We were all in desperate need of cheering up, so we booked into the first available hotel, had a quick shower then made our way to the beer festival, which was in the town centre. Tommy had been to the festival years before, but what I saw opened my eyes. There were thousands of people walking between three huge marques, each one had over three thousand people in it. They were all drinking lager from steins and enjoying themselves. The lager tasted better than anything I had tasted before, there

153

were no chemicals in it and it was very strong, but went down like milk! There was a band in the middle playing all the German tunes, so we quickly found a table and joined in the festivities. Sadly Dachau was now out of my mind, but I vowed to ensure that I would not forget the sights I had seen, and always be very grateful to the soldiers of the Second World War who gave us our freedom. After five or six steins each we were all joining in the fun. I was surprised how many people from different countries were there, with everyone behaving themselves, even though they were all very drunk. Can you imagine something like this in England? They would be fighting each other within the hour! Outside the tents was a massive funfair with rides for all ages, so we all ended up having a go on everything.

After our first night the aftereffects of the long drive was taking its toll. We did not wake up on Monday until 4 p.m., and the plan was to go straight back on the beer. We had asked one of the waiters to reserve us a table near to the bandstand, as that is where the atmosphere is best. Tommy had remembered an old song that they used to play at the beer festivals in the seventies, so asked the band leader to play it. Everyone in the marquee knew the song. The Germans were suddenly jumping on the tables, steins in hand, singing along with the band. It was a very catchy tune and the atmosphere was truly amazing. The food available in these marques was superb, you could buy huge legs of lamb, full roasted chickens and large frankfurter sausages. This trip was turning out to be well worth the drive half way across Europe. Whilst you are in these tents enjoying yourselves, you tend to lose all track of time. We had entered there at 5 p.m., and before you knew it it was closing time — the hours had just flown by, so we all returned to the hotel.

On the Tuesday, the day before the game, we walked to the Olympic Stadium, which is fantastic. It is now a few years' old. I think it was built for the 1972 Olympics. We toured the stadium hoping to catch a glimpse of either United or Bayern Munich training, but unfortunately saw neither team. In the afternoon we went on a boat trip around the River Rhine. We saw some lovely sights. Germany has some beautiful valleys, hills and castles; I must say I was very impressed. By 6 p.m., we were back at our favourite place and table in the beer tent. We sat at our table with a gang of girls from England. As the tables sat twenty on either side, and there were only five of us, we were heavily out numbered! It didn't take Tommy long to get the girls going. Within two hours one of the girls had her tits out for the lads. Again we all enjoyed ourselves; had plenty to eat and drink, then headed back to the hotel. The plan on the day of the game was to meet at the beer tent to see if any of the United supporters were allowed in. The local German police, who knew our faces after a few days, were very wary of the potential trouble you could encounter in these big marquees. They also told us that large groups of German supporters always visited the festival, so they had to carefully monitor the situation. I have to admit that the German police again handled the situation to perfection. They had selected one marquee out of the three, segregating it into two sections, one for the United supporters and the other one for tourists. Just after midday the United fans started to drift in. Within a few hours there were hundreds, all singing and dancing, enjoying the carnival atmosphere. I bumped into Barry Moorhouse's brother who was in fancy dress; he was dressed as Bart Simpson! He was with all the Langley and Middleton lads. Everyone was well behaved; the Munich fans were coming over to shake hands with all the Reds, this was a far cry from the Dortmund trip where there was lots of trouble. We had heard from some other United fans that trouble had kicked off the night before in one of the other beer tents between United fans and Germans. They said that it had got a bit nasty, but I can only give my version of the trip and we never saw any trouble whatsoever. We all had a good drink, then walked to the stadium with some Munich fans we had met in the beer tent. They spoke perfect English and we were lucky as we had Tommy who could speak German. They took us on a short cut through a park, then even walked us to our entrance.

The Germans really got behind their team; there was a 55,000 full house at the Olympic Stadium. This for me shows the drawing power of Manchester United. Bayern Munich still had that old warhorse Luthar Matthaus playing number ten for them, along with great players like Babbel and Effenburg. We knew we were in for a tough game. United played in their white strip, starting brightly but it was the Germans who scored first, after ten minutes, from a long throw which Stam failed to reach and Elber the brilliant Brazilian scored from close range. United then started to play some decent football and after thirty minutes Dwight Yorke equalised with a diving header from an exquisite David Beckham cross. The Reds were now beginning to control the game, with the first half ending 1-1. United started the second half in the same vein, taking the lead after a few minutes with Paul Scholes beating the German keeper Kahn courageously in a fifty-fifty challenge, before walking the ball into the net. The weather had changed, it was pouring down with rain. The Germans were now pressing for an equaliser, but United's defence held firm until the ninetieth minute, where an uncharacteristic late blunder by Peter Schmeichel let in, yet again, the Brazilian Elber to equalise with his second goal. It again came from a long throw, Schmeichel attempted to punch the ball completely missing it, leaving the Brazilian with an open goal that even I would have scored. The referee blew for time and we were all terribly disappointed. I would have settled for a draw beforehand, but you can't help feeling the pain when Munich had scored so late in the game. I was convinced United had the three points in the bag. Another worrying aspect of the game was a needless booking of David Beckham which would keep him out of the next UEFA Champions League encounter.

We soon forgot about the game once we had got back to the beer tents. It was our last night and I must be honest when I say I was dreading the return journey home. We set off back to Manchester on Thursday morning after a continental breakfast; a few of us myself included had sore heads from the night before! Tommy again drove us all the way back to England. It took us about sixteen hours including stops. It was a miracle that he got us through Brussels without crashing as I have never seen so many mad drivers before in my life. Tommy just behaved as if he was one of them, so we survived. I was wondering if Tommy would drive the same way in his own car, but Ray said he would have driven worse. " Bruce, you can be sure of that. I was in his car going to Feyenoord remember!" We arrived back in

Manchester late Friday afternoon.

United were due to play our bogey team Southampton at the Dell on the Saturday. Being the fanatical Red that I am, I drove down to Southampton with Ray and Paul Price and Nigel Roberts, a Red from Stalybridge. For once United enjoyed a good day at the Dell, where they had lost on their three previous visits. Arriving this time without the injured Peter Schmeichel, Giggs and Scholes; this demonstrated the strength of United's squad, as we won comfortably 3-0, leaving Southampton bottom of the table. It was United's first away victory. That lifted them to second place in the Premiership. This would not please the press I thought. Southampton are one of the teams that always struggle to survive in the Premiership. I have nothing against the Saints, except the travelling; it would make my life a little easier if they went down! The return journey that day was unforgettable. I was still tired after the Munich trip, so Nigel Roberts drove my car back to Manchester, whilst I slept in the back all the way home. Ray Price tells me that he got us back in two and a half hours, which has to be some kind of record. Apparently he was doing 140 mph at some stages of the journey. Anyway I was just glad to get home in one piece and to see my children. On the Sunday we went out for a family meal, they knew that I had missed them very much.

The following Saturday, Wimbledon were the visitors to Old Trafford. This was Manchester United in all their power and glory, very close to their best. United scored five, hitting the woodwork twice and only the brilliance of Wimbledon's goalkeeper Sullivan, who was celebrating his Scotland call up, prevented the Reds from reaching double figures. I was very impressed with the goalkeeper's performance, saying to Ray Price that he could be a good signing for the Reds, as it would keep the injured Schmeichel on his toes. There were stories circulating Old Trafford that Schmeichel's back had gone and he could be nearing retirement. Cole scored two and Yorke got one. Their partnership was beginning to flourish; they were also good friends off the pitch. 'That can only help their game' I thought. Giggs and Beckham scored United's other goals, with Euell scoring Wimbledon's consolation goal. Keano's rehabilitation was complete, and another United youngster made his debut at right back, his name was Brown. Alex Ferguson had unearthed another gem, Joe Kinnear, the Don's boss, summed up after the game "There is no shame in being beaten by a great team" and I had to agree. Fergie's pre-season signings were beginning to blend into the team. I felt that this United side could do perhaps as well as past double winning sides United had fielded, I also remember thinking that this team might grant Fergie and myself our obsession of winning the Champions League, but only time will tell.

Wednesday 21st October, we entertained Brondby at their Parken Stadium in Copenhagen. This time I decided to go on the one-day 'in and out' trip with United. After two draws against top quality opposition United were desperate for their first victory of the European campaign. Brondby were perceived as group D's weakest side. The United fans were dropped off at Copenhagen's Square, where the Danes made us very welcome. The support for United over there again borders on fanatical; all the fans drank together and enjoyed each others' company. The Reds got off to a flying start after only two minutes, with Wes Brown tearing down the right and delivering a perfect cross for Giggs to score with ease. Giggs then scored his second goal twenty minutes later from a Blomqvist cross, with Cole making it 3-0 after half an hour; for me the game was now over. Brondby scored just before half-time and the Reds went into the interval leading 3-1. It was very encouraging to see the Dane Peter Schmeichel returning in goal for Raimond Van Der Gouw, who is a very good keeper. Schmeichel has to be the best there is; in my opinion he is world class and I have not seen a better keeper in thirty years. In the second half Roy Keane made it 4-1, then further goals from Yorke and Solskjaer, who scored with his first touch after coming on as substitute, made it 6-1. Brondby were dead and buried but scored an injury time goal. United finished the game winning 6-2. This for me showed the other teams in our group that United meant business; also thanks to Bayern's defeat of Barcelona, it left the Reds at the top of group D.

It was now back to the bread and butter. The Reds were playing Derby County on Saturday 24th October, at their new ground

Pride Park, and after the stroll against Brondby I thought we would win this game easy, but again I was proved wrong. Jim Smith's Rams played as if their lives depended on it. They worked relentlessly. United were sluggish, indeed for most of the afternoon their normal zest and aggression was absent. Derby deservedly took the lead after seventy-five minutes. Fergie was furious and made what I thought was a strange decision, a treble substitution, he took off Giggs, Butt and Gary Neville, replacing them with Blomqvist, Scholes and Cruyff to try and salvage something from the game. With five minutes remaining the Dutchman saved the day, scoring the equaliser. I have my reservations about Jordi Cruyff, as it must be very difficult having such a great footballing father to live up to, but in saying that I have watched him in the red shirt in his every match for United and it is my opinion that we should let him go. The game ended up all square at 1-1 and in fairness I was happy with the result. United had got out of jail. United were now playing twice a week and it was time for the Worthington Cup third round.

Again it gave Alex Ferguson a chance to give the squad members a full game, and also try out some of the kids in the youth team. We had drawn Bury at Old Trafford, I know I had said I would miss this competition, but my sons Robert and Alex wanted to go, so I took them in the family stand. I ordered my tickets through Walter Perjenko at the Stalybridge branch. There was a crowd of over 52,000 at Old Trafford, which I found amazing, with Bury bringing over 10,000 fans. It is good to see small clubs like Bury get some much needed revenue. United won the game 2-0 after extra time, with goals from Solskjaer and Nevland. Only the torrential rain, which we are used to in Manchester, spoilt the occasion for Robert and Alex as we all got drenched! The Shakers had done themselves proud and I must say that I was impressed with some of their youngsters.

The last day of October, United were at Everton where they produced a stunning performance, hammering an Everton team that had gone ten games without defeat. Ferguson's decision to rest players, then bring them back fresh, certainly brings results. United ran out easy 4-1 winners, with Duncan Ferguson netting Everton's consolation goal. The United scorers were Yorke, a

Short own goal, then two in six minutes from Cole and Blomqvist, his first for United. This ensured United stayed second in the Premier behind the leaders Aston Villa, who had made a great start to the season. I was happy with United's form and especially happy for Roy Keane, who had taken some six weeks to regain full fitness following the lengthy lay-off from a challenge on a Leeds defender in the previous season. His dynamic thrusts from deep have laid the foundations for United's success; it was also good to secure our first away win of the season.

November approached with our UEFA Champions League group D game against Brondby, which was played at Old Trafford on Wednesday 4th November. I must admit that everyone I spoke to was expecting an avalanche of goals, especially after the 6-2 demolition over there in Copenhagen and I'm glad to say they were proved right. United turned on the style, scoring three times in the opening fifteen minutes. David Beckham scored first with a delightful thirty yard free kick, which raised the roof of the 53,000 packed Old Trafford ground. Andy Cole made it 2-0 after thirteen minutes and Phil Neville made it 3-0 with a rare goal. Yorke made it 4-0 after half an hour, then Paul Scholes ended the nightmare by making it 5-0 after the hour. To be fair to Brondby they never abandoned their own attacking formation and the score remained the same until the final whistle, sparing them any further embarrassment. Counting the pre-season hammering we gave them, United had now scored seventeen times in three meetings with the Danes. It is hard to believe that they had beaten Bayern Munich earlier in the competition. Years earlier I remember them beating Liverpool at Anfield, so for me this was a great result for the Reds, proving to our critics that we are now ready to take on the best in the Champions League.

On Saturday 8th November 1998, the Reds entertained Newcastle in front of a 55,000 full house at Old Trafford. Newcastle were to me very disappointing. Ruud Gullit's side were in the process of reconstruction after the departure of Kevin Keegan. The Magpies crowded the midfield. Newcastle teams of the past always placed the emphasis on attack, but this team had come with the only intention of getting a point and cancelling out a United attack, which had scored twenty-six goals in their last seven outings. The only shot Newcastle had on target was from Alan Shearer, who again came in for a lot of verbal abuse from the United fans, who had still not forgiven him for choosing Newcastle rather than the Reds. The crowd were singing 'There's only one greedy bastard'. Shearer handled the pressure well but the afternoon's entertainment was very disappointing and the Geordies scraped the point they had come for.

It was now time for the Worthington Cup fourth round. United had drawn Nottingham Forest at Old Trafford. The only game I had missed so far was the UEFA Champions League qualifying round second leg at LKS Lodz. I was beginning to feel guilty about missing that game, as I could sense United were onto something special. The team were playing well and the players were working together. It hurt me to miss any game, so I changed my mind about not watching the reserves in the Worthington Cup, taking Robert and Alex with me to the Forest game. We watched the game from the family stand; I had expected Alex to field a virtual reserve side, which he did, yet we still defeated our Premiership strugglers 2-1, with two second half goals from the 'assassin' Ole Gunner Solskjaer. Stone pulled one back for Forest after seventy minutes, but the Reds' reserves held on, which meant United were through to the last eight of the Worthington Cup. Robert and Alex enjoyed the game so much that I promised them that whoever United drew in the last eight I would take them.

The following Saturday, 14th November, Blackburn Rovers were the visitors to Old Trafford. United were again on fire. Scholes put United in front after half an hour and Yorke made it two just before half-time. Minutes into the second half Sherwood received his marching orders for a 'handbags at dawn' clash with Beckham and on the hour Scholes got his second. You would have thought this incident would have opened the floodgates, but Blackburn came at the Reds, scoring two goals in ten minutes. In the end the United fans were shouting for the final whistle. I must say I was very relieved when the whistle came. United had kept their run going, having only been beaten once at Highbury to Arsenal in the Premier League.

It was now time to visit Sheffield Wednesday; not a good

ground for the Reds, a record of one win in our last eight visits to Hillsborough tells its own story. I travelled to the game on the coach with the Stalybridge branch. Every year when we go to Wednesday we stop at a little pub in a village called Otters Bridge. The landlord makes us very welcome, even laying on pies and sandwiches for the lads. We always have a good drink then go to the game. United were rubbish, with Sheffield Wednesday deservingly beating us 3-1. The less said about this game the better; once again Hillsborough had proved to be an unhappy hunting ground. I must say that I was more concerned about our forthcoming visit to the Nou-Camp to play FC Barcelona the following Wednesday.

Again I had a week off and decided to travel by plane with Tommy Price. The plan was to fly by Easy Jet to Nice, because their normal flight to Barcelona was full. We were going to have a night in Nice, then get the night train through to Barcelona. We enjoyed ourselves in Nice and tried most of the pubs in the city centre. Tommy had travelled this way years before, which convinced me to travel with him. Let me tell you there's no way I will travel this route again. The train journey took eighteen hours and we hardly got any sleep. The train was packed with United supporters. It was that bad you had to sleep on your own bags to prevent them from being stolen. We arrived at Barcelona train station at about 11 o'clock on the day before the game. We both had a shower at the station; left our bags at the left luggage then headed straight to 'La Ramblers', where it was our intention to meet all the lads from the Stalybridge branch, who had travelled with United on the one-day 'in and out' trip. 'La Ramblers' is about two miles long; full of bars and restaurants. The place has a buzz about it; everyone who visits Barcelona always heads for 'La Ramblers'. It didn't take us long to meet the lads. They were in a pub called the Robin Hood. Tommy and I hired a horse and carriage to tour the square; everyone was enjoying themselves, there were United supporters all around. Barcelona had given us about 10,000 tickets. There were about forty of us walking down the Ramblers when we spotted a sex shop at the bottom. We all decided to pay a visit. There was a bar in there where you could pay 200 pesetas to watch a live sex show, or pay 100 pesetas to watch a blue movie on the big screen. The forty of us took over the bar area. There were groups of us sat talking about the game against Barcelona, none of us were singing any songs or behaving badly. Tommy Price was at the bar wearing the biggest sombrero I had ever seen. He had met two French International rugby players and they were having a laugh, when all of a sudden I noticed four Spanish police entering the narrow entrance to the sex shop. They were holding their three foot truncheons in their hands; one of them was tapping his truncheon against the wall. I knew something was going to happen, these riot police had not entered the premises to say 'Hello lads, how are you'! They walked to the middle of the bar, looked round, saw all of us sitting at the tables drinking our beer. You could cut the atmosphere with a knife; there was a deadly silence. They then indiscriminately, without checking the situation, started to lash out at anybody in their sights. This soon turned into a very ugly situation. Everyone left everything they had, even their belongings, and ran for the exit. I jumped up and ran to Tommy at the bar, who told me to go and sit down. I said "Thanks mate" then I noticed the bar owner, so I shouted to him "Spanioli. Spanioli" pretending to be Spanish. He grabbed me and took me behind the bar. The whole bar area was cleared in minutes; it was a very scary moment. Later we asked the owner why this had happened? He could not explain it, but he had lost a lot of custom. About an hour or so later, the lads started returning to gather their belongings. The bruises I saw on some of the lads was disgusting; this again shows to me how the Spanish riot police work, they don't help the situation but make it worse. I felt especially sorry for Gordon and Nick the Greek, as they had taken a bad beating. Out of the forty lads that were in that sex shop, only two people didn't get touched, that was Tommy and myself. Although I had a narrow escape, I still had a right go at Tommy who said "Everyone for himself in a situation like that Bruce" and burst out laughing!

We decided to retrieve our bags from the train station and book into a hotel on 'The Ramblers' where all the action was. I also knew that the European Cup Final was to be staged at Barcelona and wondered how the riot police would handle the supporters that would converge there in their thousands. I had already made my mind up that if United got to the final that year, we would stay outside Barcelona until the day of the match. Apart from that incident with the riot police, we saw no other disturbances and had a very enjoyable time.

On the day of the match we arrived at the Nou-Camp Stadium with plenty of time to spare. I had a good walk around this truly magnificent stadium; these were the games when you could tell if United had moved forward in terms of European experience. I was a bit disappointed at the attendance of about 55,000, the game was a classic even out stripping the contest between these two attack-minded sides at Old Trafford back in September. Barcelona scored in the first minute; I had visions of a humiliating repeat of the Reds' Nou-Camp nightmare in 1994, when we were hammered 4-0. Rivaldo was running the game. Barcelona had to win to remain in the competition and they had certainly set about it in the right way, however United stood firm with Peter Schmeichel outstanding. The Reds settled into their stride when Dwight Yorke equalised with a low drive from the edge of the box. Both teams missed chances and the score at half-time was 1-1. In the second half with the United hordes shouting them on, Andy Cole gave United the lead after a great one/two with Yorke. Cole finished with precision and the game had now changed yet again. Barcelona now had to come at us, which always suits United's style of counterattacking and then catching them on the break, however our lead was short lived. Barcelona were awarded a free kick, then the brilliant Brazilian Rivaldo equalised with a curling shot that left Peter Schmeichel rooted to the goal line. The scores were now level, yet still the action moved from end to end. The Reds then regained the upper hand; Beckham crossed and Dwight Yorke scored with a powerful header that gave the Barcelona keeper no chance of saving. The Reds were back in front 3-2, but Barcelona kept searching for the equaliser and it came from a stunning overhead kick from Rivaldo; his second goal of the game. He nearly scored his hat trick, hitting the bar from almost thirty yards, but United held on to celebrate one of our finest hours in European history.

We quickly headed back to the Robin Hood Bar on the

Ramblers, where we sang into the early hours. This was truly a great night, and I was now beginning to think this is THE year! The morning after the game I said to Tommy that I didn't fancy the long train journey back to Nice. He didn't either as we were drained from last night's entertainment, so we rang Easy Jet and as luck would have it we managed to change our return flight tickets, so caught the afternoon plane from Barcelona to Speke Airport in Liverpool where Tommy had left his car and returned to Manchester. What more could you ask for? The two games we had played against Barcelona were well worth the money. United only needed to draw against Bayern Munich at Old Trafford and we would both be in the quarterfinals.

It was now back to the Premiership and our visitors to Old Trafford were Leeds United for a 4 p.m. kickoff on a Sunday. The atmosphere around Old Trafford was brilliant, as it always is against Leeds. To my horror Leeds silenced the crowd by taking the lead after half an hour through Hasselbaink. United equalised dead on the stroke of half-time, and within a minute of the restart were in front through a Roy Keane goal. The United fans were delirious. David O'Leary's Leeds side was full of youngsters and they fought for every ball. They never gave up so it came as no surprise to me when Kewell, who had tormented the United defence all afternoon, equalised with a delightful chip. He certainly caught my eye and was easily 'man of the match'. I could tell that he was one for the future as he had pace, vision and could run at defenders. This only made United step up a gear and ten minutes from time Nicky Butt silenced the 3,500 travelling Leeds supporters by grabbing the winner. United won the game 3-2. Nicky Butt is a Gorton lad, born in the heart of Manchester, which is a predominately Blue area. His brother Simon plays amateur football on Sunday's for a pub side called the Royal Oak. Their manager is a man called Tony Etchells, a bricklayer, who had followed United through thick and thin in the sixties with Tommy Price. Tony has built up a formidable side through his hard work in the amateur league and I wish him all the best. I still think that my old Sunday team, Haughton Villa in the eighties would have beaten his side of the nineties, but that is just my biased opinion!

165

November ended with United having played the same number of games as our rivals Aston Villa; fourteen. We were one point behind them. I quite liked it that way, as we were tucked in behind them, as I knew they wouldn't be able to handle the pressure. For me Villa's squad was no way big enough to maintain their great start to the season, but again only time would tell. It was now time for the quarterfinal of the Worthington Cup on 2nd December. We had drawn Spurs away. Carol gave me permission to keep Robert and Alex off school, so I drove down with David Clay who did the same with his son James, and headed off to White Hart Lane. I know United's team is impressive, but Spurs were up for it, coming at us from the off. I was relieved to go in at half-time 0-0. Spurs piled on the pressure in the second half, deservingly taking the lead through Chris Armstrong. He then scored again ten minutes later to make it 2-0. Teddy Sheringham, who took plenty of stick from the Spurs fans, pulled one back for the Reds with a neat header. The Reds now went in search of the equaliser, leaving gaps at the back. David Ginola took advantage of this by going on one of his mazy runs in the last five minutes and unleashed a twenty-five yarder that flew into the back of the net, giving Raimond Van Der Gouw no chance. United were out and the long journey back was made in complete silence. The kids were all knackered; they slept all the way back, we didn't want to disturb them as they had school in the morning, but they had thoroughly enjoyed the occasion. It was another game Robert and Alex could say they had been to in later years. I knew that they both would not forget this game .

December approached and it was time for the top two to clash at Villa Park; only one point separated United from Villa. The Reds played in their white away strip, and the afternoon began with plenty of jeers for Dwight Yorke from his former fans. I had expected this as no fans like their former idols going to another team, even if that team is the biggest and best in the country. It was a scrappy affair. I was again disappointed, I had expected Villa to go for it but it became a midfield battle with neither side pressing forward. United took the lead through Paul Scholes just after half-time, then Villa equalised through Joachim ten minutes later, and that's the way it stayed until the final whistle.

I was happy with the result. Having watched Villa, my opinion of them had not altered, they wouldn't last the pace. United had one eye on their UEFA Champions League game with Bayern Munich on Wednesday.

We could not afford to lose this match at Old Trafford, as Bayern Munich had progressed to the quarterfinals thanks to a draw with the Germans and some favourable results elsewhere. The Reds went through as one of the two best group runners-up and top scorers to date. It was far from the classic encounter we had witnessed against Barcelona previously. Keane gave United the lead just before half-time, with the Germans equalising ten minutes into the second half. I must admit that the teams must have known the results elsewhere were going in their favour, as the last fifteen minutes of play was like a friendly. Both teams kept possession without trying to penetrate. The whistle finally came and both teams had qualified for the quarterfinals. I remember thinking that this could make a great final. At least the Reds had a break until March next year, that would also give me time to save some money! United were draining my resources; I had still only missed one game all season, away to Lodz, the lads were winding me up calling me a part-time supporter, but I knew different.

United could now concentrate on the league, and I was now making my second trip to White Hart Lane. I usually miss this fixture as for some reason every time we play Spurs I happen to be on holiday in Tenerife with the family. I have some friends over there who are fanatical Spurs fans, they are two brothers called Paul and Lee who have a pub on the island called The Boozer. Unfortunately the last time I spoke to Lee he informed me that his brother had died from sclerosis of the liver, due to excessive drinking. The news of Lee's death upset me as I have had some great times over the years with these two in Tenerife. I offered my condolences to Paul, Lee was only aged thirty-eight when he died; it is a great regret to lose a friend especially through excessive drinking. I travelled down to the game with the Stalybridge branch on the coach. Again the Spurs fans gave Teddy Sheringham a hard time, which was expected, but United started the game brightly going two goals up in the first twenty minutes. Both goals came from the assassin Ole Gunner Solskjaer. Rumours were circulating that United might be doing a deal with Spurs that might take Sol Campbell to Old Trafford. I rate Sol Campbell very highly but in all honesty would prefer Ole to stay. I have seen some great finishers in my time, including Denis Law and Jimmy Greaves and Ole is right in there amongst them. The United fans idolise him myself included. The game was going United's way when the referee evened things by sending off Gary Neville, just before half-time, for a second bookable offence on the Frenchman Ginola. It was a bad decision as Ginola was having a good game giving Gary the run around, I felt that he had been harshly treated. United went into half-time leading 2-0. The referee was Uriah Rennie who is a good ref, but at times tries to be bigger than the two teams actually involved. I once saw him signing autographs before a game at Old Trafford, that for me tells you a story. The second half kicked off with United withstanding tremendous pressure, they did well to hold out until the last twenty minutes considering they only had ten men. Tottenham reduced the arrears when Sol Campbell headed in powerfully from a Darren Anderton free kick. I still thought that United would hold onto their lead, but in the ninetieth minute Campbell popped up right at the death to equalise with his second of the match. United had thrown away a two goal lead which you rarely see and also had a man sent off, but the point we gained was still enough to send them to the top of the Premiership for the first time this season.

Our next game was again against London opposition; this time it was Chelsea who were visiting Old Trafford on a cold December night. Chelsea had assembled a side with undeniable class. I could see that they were emerging as genuine title contenders. United surprised me by leaving both Beckham and Giggs on the bench, but nevertheless they started brightly. Andy Cole missed a good chance in the opening ten minutes. Chelsea then began to take control and play some neat, controlled football that impressed me. They were knocking the ball around very well, but it was against the run of the play when Andy Cole gave us the lead on the stroke of half-time. In the second half Chelsea continued to press forward and it came as no surprise when

Zola neatly chipped over the advancing Schmeichel to level the scores with five minutes remaining. I couldn't argue with the result. Chelsea had kept the game open and were well worth the result; they had matched United in every department.

Just before Christmas, Bryan Robson's Middlesborough came to Old Trafford. My old friend David Dyson from Teeside, rang me to ask if he could stay over for the game. I took him to the Reds bar in Stalybridge and he was very impressed with all the hard work Tommy had done to make the pub like a Manchester United shrine. The match was an occasion to thank Gary Pallister and Clayton Blackmore, who was one of the subs, for their past efforts in helping to make United a formidable force. The fans gave both players a great reception. Middlesborough took the game seriously and before we knew it we were three goals down with less than an hour played. It's years since anything like this had happened at Old Trafford. The United defence was missing the injured Stam. United came back into the game with two goals from Butt and Scholes, then put the Middlesborough defence under virtual siege for the last twenty minutes but Middlesborough held out for a 3-2 win. It was United's first home defeat of the season, they had also drawn their last four games, I knew it would give Alex Ferguson cause for concern, he had to miss the match due to a family bereavement. It was obvious that Alex had a lot of hard work still to do.

After the Christmas festivities, Nottingham Forest visited Old Trafford on Boxing Day, when United returned to winning ways, hammering them 3-0. Ryan Giggs scored an absolute gem of a goal. On Tuesday 29th December we were at Chelsea, who had by now overtaken us in the league. Villa were still the leaders but Chelsea were second and Arsenal third with United fourth. We needed to get something out of this game. Also news was out that Peter Schmeichel had made his own decision to leave Old Trafford at the end of the season, this was disastrous news for United. 'How can you replace a keeper like Schmeichel?' I thought, and this game told me why you can't. Schmeichel was magnificent he stood between the Reds and a rout. Some of his saves were world class. I knew that when he was on this kind of form it would have to be a great goal to beat him. He made some great one on one saves from the Chelsea forwards Zola and Flo, with one save from Zola still staying in my mind today. Again United were lucky to earn a draw. The Reds had to be satisfied, they had not played particularly well but had battled. For me that is the sign of a great team, never buckling under pressure. I also thought that Frank Leboeuf, who had already been cautioned, was very lucky to stay on the pitch when he floored David Beckham who was heading for goal.

The year ended with United in the quarterfinals of the European Cup and well placed in the league. It was now time for, what I can only describe as the best knock-out tournament in the world, the FA Cup. It is every fan's dream to see their team at Wembley. I know as I have been very lucky to have watched United at every Cup Final since 1963, when they beat Leicester City 3-1 with goals from Denis Law and two from David Herd. Incidentally the great Gordon Banks was the Leicester goalkeeper. United had not drawn an easy third round game; Middlesborough were the visitors at Old Trafford and it was a chance to get revenge for our league defeat back in December. This game was played on Sunday 3rd January, with a 4 p.m. kickoff. The critics were asking whether United were still interested in the FA Cup with their other commitments. My answer would have definitely been yes, after all this cup was the one that started all Alex Ferguson's successes. People forget how it was my old friend Lee Martin who scored that memorable winner against Crystal Palace in the FA Cup Final replay in 1990. 'How times fly' I thought. Middlesborough came to Old Trafford and played some entertaining football. They even took the lead early in the second half through Andy Townsend. I was beginning to have fears of a repeat of their pre-Christmas league success, but with Alex Ferguson back at the helm, Andy Cole equalised and further goals from Dennis Irwin and Ryan Giggs knocked the wind out of the Teesiders; the Reds were in the fourth round draw.

Sunday 10th January and West Ham were the visitors to Old Trafford. The match might have been abandoned due to a power failure which had delayed the kickoff by one hour. It also gave me the chance to see West Ham's teenage prodigy Joe Cole who came on as substitute for Trevor Sinclair. The game itself was a one-sided affair with United winning the game easily 4-1. The Reds' forwards were on fire, with Andy Cole scoring two goals, one in each half, Yorke scoring one and the assassin Ole Gunner Solskjaer putting the final nail in the coffin. Lampard scored a consolation goal for the Hammers in the last minute. This performance had me thinking that another double could be on the way to Old Trafford, but there was a long way to go yet. United's next game was away to Leicester City. It was the first time Tommy Price and myself were unsuccessful in United's postal ballot, so this left us with no option but to ring a friend of mine called Martin Boucher who is a ticket tout. Martin provided us with two tickets at double face value which we thought was well worth the money. A lot of Manchester United supporters call ticket touts, but I look at it differently. I feel they are providing a service. It is like supply and demand, if the supply is low the demand is high. Leicester City don't give us a big allocation of tickets due to their small ground. Martin never lets us down whenever we call upon him, he follows the club everywhere. He knows Tommy and I are loyal Reds and he could earn a lot more from the tickets than what we gave him. I drove down to Leicester in the car and the Reds continued where they had left off against West Ham. The forwards were by now on fire, everything they hit went in. Dwight Yorke scored a hat trick, Andy Cole scored two and even Jaap Stam got his name on the score sheet, scoring United's sixth goal in the final minute. The Reds had massacred Leicester City 6-2 and they could so easily have scored ten. Suddenly United's form of November and December was now a distant memory.

Sunday 24th January is a day I will always remember. The Reds had drawn Liverpool for a 12 o'clock kickoff at Old Trafford in the fourth round of the FA Cup. It was the Reds' third Sunday game in January. I would still prefer to play on a Saturday at 3 p.m. along with all the other FA Cup ties, as I feel that the excitement of the FA Cup is all about listening to the results on the radio and then waiting for the next round draw, as you always knew who was in the hat and out at the same time. But with Sky TV now showing at least two games a week, it was only my opinion that the FA Cup with all its great traditions was becoming devalued. United had drawn another Premiership side in the cup, but at least we were at Old Trafford. I felt we should go for broke as I didn't fancy going to Anfield for a replay. The game had to be won at Old Trafford. Liverpool started off well and took the lead in the first few minutes through Owen. They then packed the midfield, playing three central defenders, inviting United to come at them. The Liverpool game plan nearly worked. United totally dominated the second half and two goals in the last two minutes from Yorke and Solskjaer silenced the Liverpool fans that were whistling for the game to end. Old Trafford was alive with fans going berserk. I now know why they call this stadium the Theatre of Dreams, as what I had just witnessed was a dream come true. This team never knows when to give up. Liverpool had battled bravely but it was the Reds from Manchester that were in the hat for the fifth round.

Our next game, can you believe, was on another Sunday at Charlton Athletic. United had now played four Sunday games in January and I was thinking was this some kind of record. Years ago you could not have imagined that Premier League football would have been played on a day of rest — how times have changed! I had also noticed that the standard of the non-league game had gone down. A lot of Sunday players were now only interested in watching the games instead of playing it. In football you are always told to play for the full ninety minutes, but I had noticed that over the last four United games a goal had been scored in the final minute — Ryan Giggs in the ninetieth minute at home to Middlesborough in the FA Cup third round, Lampard for West Ham in the league, Jaap Stam at Leicester City and Ole Gunner Solskjaer at the death against Liverpool — this for me is always the sign of a good team. We did exactly the same at Charlton Athletic, leaving it to Yorke who secured the points for the Reds scoring in the last minute. I felt that Charlton were unlucky and maybe a draw would have been fair, but another saying in football is that you make your own luck. The Reds were certainly beginning to enjoy theirs, as United had now won all of their five games during January. I was also pleased for Henning Berg who had fought his way back into the side with some outstanding performances. The Reds were now top of the table with Chelsea moving to second place, a point behind. Villa had dropped to third. I remember thinking had the bubble burst at Villa?

February approached with Derby County visiting Old Trafford. They played one man up front with six in midfield. This killed the game off as a spectacle, but United eventually broke them down and Yorke scored the winner in the second half. Saturday 6th February was the 41st anniversary of the Munich disaster and the Reds were playing Nottingham Forest away at the City Ground. I had still only missed the Lodz game; this was my 37th game of the season and it was only February. I was determined not to miss any United games and set my own standards. I know myself that when it comes to following Manchester United I am up there with the best of them. I will always remember a great Red called Gordon Signett, who is one of the old school, who was at the Waterford game saying to me "Bruce, the only good Red is the one that goes tomorrow." Those words have always stayed with me. The Forest game produced a display by United that was for me one of the best away performances I'd ever witnessed, even surpassing the 6-2 win a few weeks earlier at Leicester City; this side was reaching new heights. It was the Reds' most convincing away win I'd ever seen in my thirty years. They won 8-1, Yorke scored two, Cole scored two, but the 'man of the match' was United's substitute Ole Gunner Solskjaer, who replaced Dwight Yorke. Poor Forest, who were rooted to the foot of the table, had no answer to him. He scored four times in the last ten minutes, prompting a statement from Alex Ferguson that had me in stitches, "The boy's not a bad substitute" he was quoted to have told the press. Meanwhile the former United manager Ron Atkinson, now the Forest boss, took it in his stride and could still raise a smile. When he was quizzed after the game about Solskjaer's finishing, he too was quoted to have said "It's a good job they didn't put him on earlier, or we would have been in real trouble!"

On Sunday 14th February United had drawn Kevin Keegan's Fulham in the FA Cup fifth round at Old Trafford. Our third home draw. It was Valentine's Day, and what better way to treat my wife Carol and all the children than going to this match. At first Carol was not amused, but eventually came round to my way of thinking, as it was the first time that all five of us had visited Old Trafford together. Walter Perjenko got me five tickets for the family stand, so the plan was to go to the game, then take the children tenpin bowling at White City, which is very near to the ground. We all went to the game as a family, but I have to admit that it is not easy to watch a game and keep your eyes on three children at the same time. It is also a very costly experience, so I was grateful that Carol had had the sense to bring some sandwiches and drinks with her. Fulham brought a great support to the game, but they were beaten 1-0 with Andy Cole scoring the winner in the first half. The Reds were now in the quarterfinals of both the European Cup and FA Cup and also top of the league. People were now whispering about the possibility of a treble. We went bowling after the game, having a great family day. Carol won the bowling contest but I have to admit that I had my mind on the next game at Old Trafford, which was the following Wednesday night against Arsenal.

Arsenal had shot up the league into fourth place, two points behind the Reds. I took my son Robert along with the Arsenal fans Ralph Paddy Chapburn and his two sons Danny and Ross It was a top of the table clash as Arsenal were the reigning champions and I wanted revenge. Before the game I asked Rober who he thought would score the first goal, to which he replied Dwight Yorke, so I put a £10 bet on him at 9-1; Andy Cole wa: the 6-1 favourite to get the first goal. The Gunners were improving on their current form and I felt that if we could win this game i would create some breathing space for the important matche: ahead; notably the quarterfinals of both cup competitions. The game was a closely fought contest. Yorke missed an early chanc to win me some money, but after half an hour I was jumping o my seat as the Reds were awarded a penalty. Ray Parlour wa judged to have fouled Ronny Johnsen and Dwight Yorke steppe up to take the penalty in the absence of our regular penalty take Dennis Irwin; to my horror he missed it. Robert was devastate as I had promised him half the money if Yorke had scored. Padd was laughing his head off. Yorke had lost all confidence, whicl is his trademark. The Reds had not quite clicked and the score stayed 0-0 at half-time. In the second half Arsenal's new strike force of Kanu and Anelka combined to put Arsenal in front. It was hard to say but Arsenal looked the more balanced side at times and it was left to Andy Cole to equalise on the hour. In the end, despite an impressive late assault by the Reds, the score remained the same, leaving the title race wide open.

The Reds then, as Alex Ferguson described, 'ground out a result' at Coventry; Ryan Giggs scoring the winner after eighty minutes. This was followed by another win at home to relegation haunted Southampton. The Reds won 2-1 with all the goals coming in the last ten minutes. Yet again the changing point of the match for me was the introduction of Roy Keane in the second half. He put us in front after eighty minutes and Yorke made it two five minutes from time. Le Tissier grabbed one back for the Saints and when the final whistle came I breathed a sigh of relief. February ended with the Reds still top of the league on fifty-seven points; Chelsea were four points behind but had a game in hand.

The time had now come for our EUFA Champions League quarterfinal first leg. The Reds had drawn the star-studded Italian side Internazionale Milan, with the first leg played at Old Trafford. The match was to be played on 3rd March, the day before my son Robert's birthday, so as a treat I took him to the game. I was very interested to see how David Beckham would handle his clash with the Argentine Simeone and also how we would handle the Milan forwards Baggio and Zamorano. The Reds played with no thought for Inter Milan's reputation. David Beckham had to be congratulated for his sparkling display, he crossed perfectly for Dwight Yorke to score in the first five minutes with a glorious header. The crowd went ballistic then he did exactly the same right on half-time for Yorke with yet another header to make it 2-0. Simeone never went near Beckham who was without a doubt my 'man of the match', followed closely by United's Roy Keane. The Reds had won 2-0 and also denied the Italians the luxury of an away goal. I could not wait to go to the San Siro for the second leg, but before that we had to play our FA Cup quarterfinal on 7th March against our rivals Chelsea at Old Trafford.

It was played on a Sunday yet again, with a 2 p.m. kickoff. People were saying that United had the gods on their side, with all our FA Cup games being drawn at Old Trafford, but people forget that barring Fulham the three other teams were all from the Premiership. Chelsea came to Old Trafford with the backing of 8,000 die hard supporters who seemed intent on causing trouble. There were groups of rival supporters fighting all over the place. I thought we had seen the end of this sort of thing at Old Trafford but I'm afraid that it has only been swept under the carpet. You might not see much trouble in the ground as it is well policed, but I have to admit that it is still going on outside the grounds, maybe not to the extent of the 1970s but it is definitely still happening. I was hoping that United would take care of Chelsea at the first attempt. If I was honest I didn't fancy going to Stamford Bridge for another night game, as I had already done that in December for our league game where we drew 0-0. United had a good record against Chelsea in the FA Cup, having beaten them on a number of occasions throughout the nineties. I'm afraid I was very disappointed, Chelsea battled bravely with ten men; Di Matteo was sent off just before half-time. Their goalkeeper de Goey was also in magnificent form along with their centre half Desailly. He had United's prolific goal scoring duo Yorke and Cole in his pocket, I had to give him 'man of the match'. United still had the better chances, but it wasn't to be our afternoon. With five minutes remaining, Paul Scholes was dismissed for two bookable offences; the same thing had happened to Di Matteo earlier so we couldn't complain. The only positive thing to come out of the game was the display of United's young Wes Brown, he proved an able deputy for the suspended Jaap Stam.

The replay was played on the following Wednesday night, so I asked Carol if I could take Robert with me. She said it was ok as long as he didn't miss school the next day. My friend David Clay decided to come along with his son James, so the four of us set off at lunch time on the Wednesday. When I picked up the ticket from United I was disappointed to find out that they had no junior tickets, so all our tickets were priced at £25 each. Thank God United don't treat their fans this way, I felt we were paying towards the upkeep of Chelsea's expensive foreign contingent. The match kicked off with United making a splendid start. Dwight Yorke scoring in the opening five minutes, this completely silenced the Chelsea hordes. I was very surprised at how many United supporters had made the journey down south; there were about 8,000 of them situated down the touchline. United had taken control of the game, which was played in typical European fashion. Yorke made it 2-0 after an hour, when he delivered an instant chip with the outside of his foot, which went over de Goey to nestle in the top corner of the net. It was a moment of true brilliance, a truly classic goal which settled the game. Chelsea huffed and puffed but it was to no avail, United went through 2-0, this was in fact the fourth defeat we had given Chelsea in the last six seasons. The journey back home was a happy one; Robert and James were now our lucky charms.

We were now into the last third of the season and had to travel to St James Park to play Newcastle on Saturday 13th March. The once idol of the Geordies Andy Cole scored two great goals after Newcastle had gone in front through Soland. It was a precious victory for the Reds, which preserved our four-point lead at the top of the Premiership. Now it was time for the Champions League second leg against Inter Milan, and there was no way on God's earth I was going to miss this.

I had arranged a five-day trip for the lads, who were David Ashworth, Alan Hazlehurst, Tommy Price, Sammy Gilbey, Jeff Clayton and Denis Cocker. There were seven of us in total, but we only had four tickets between us. I had received them from United, so they were given to Tommy, David and Sammy. I gave my ticket to Alan who lives in London. I said to Jeff and Denis who came without tickets that we'd have no problem getting tickets once we had got to the ground. We again travelled with Easy Jet from Liverpool to Geneva, where the plan was to have two days in Geneva, then catch the train to Milan. Stay two nights before returning back to Manchester on the Friday morning. It was another fantastic trip from start to finish. These European trips just seem to get better and better. Our hotel in Geneva was basic, but when you look at the prices for hotel accommodation and the cost of the beer you will know why we only booked two twin rooms and all seven of us shared them.

Geneva is in Switzerland, it happens to be one of the nices
but most expensive places imaginable. I put it in comparison t
Monte Carlo. The first day there we spent walking around Lak
Geneva looking at all the millionaires' mansions that wer
overlooking the lake. I said to Tommy Price that this should b
the place to live. "Maybe, one day" was his reply! Geneva ha
plenty of nightlife so we all decided to sample some of it. W
tried out most of the bars and were then told by some locals t
try out the nightclubs on the other side of the town. By midnigh
Tommy, Denis, Sammy and David were very drunk, so caught
taxi back to the hotel. Big Jeff who is six foot six, Alan and mysel
decided to catch a taxi to the nightclub. We were escorted to ou
table. I knew that it must be a very expensive place, as there wer
no prices to be seen at any of the bars, also you could not pa
with cash but had to use your credit card. A lady approached m
wearing hardly any clothes asking if we required any drink:
The only drink you could order was champagne, so I ordered
bottle and she took my American Express Gold Card to pay for i
All three of us were very drunk and did not realise that we wer
in a brothel. Suddenly three girls came out of nowhere and joine
us at our table, they even helped themselves to our champagn
Jeff was enjoying all the attention they were giving him an
quickly ordered another bottle. Before you knew it mor
champagne was being ordered. The girls were now toples
pouring champagne over each other then licking it off. I sudden
became aware of how much all this was going to cost, so
enquired about the bill. We had been in the place about tw
hours and drank three bottles of champagne. I nearly died
shock when one of the waitresses approached me to say th
the bill was so far 7,680 Swiss Francs. I quickly sobered u
asking Alan how much that was in English pounds. "Fuckir
hell Bruce, that's over £3,000." The problem was that they ha
taken my card which has no limit on it, so I quickly borrowe
Alan's mobile phone to call American Express. I explained
them the situation and that we were being ripped off. The girl c
the phone asked me if they had debited the card to which
replied "No not as yet." She then explained to me that if I cou

get the card back off the manager without it having been debited, I could then question the amounts being charged. It was now time to do some quick thinking, so I said to the other two that I was going to try and get my card back. "How?" said Alan. I said "I'm going to tell him I've given him the wrong card. As luck would have it I also had my Master Card on me, so when or if he gives me that card, I'm going to do a runner. So you two had better sober up. Get ready" I told them. "We will meet back at the hotel and good luck. It's every man for himself." I confidently approached the manager at the bar and told him that I had mistakenly given the waitress the wrong card earlier in the night. I had my Master Card in one hand. He replied "No problem sir" and handed me my American Express card. Without a moment's hesitation I was off faster than Ryan Giggs and so were the other two. I didn't look round but just kept my head down and ran. I think I would have beaten the 200 metres' record that night! I remember what was only a few minutes running seemed like ages. I thought I must be unfit but you have to take into consideration that I am forty. Alan shouted at me saying "Bruce, you can stop now. No one is following." Jeff was a few yards behind Alan. All three of us walked into the nearest hotel, I then ordered a taxi to take us back to our hotel. We waited there until the taxi arrived about ten minutes later. On the drive back none of us spoke a word. I thought Jeff, who is thirty-eight, was going to have a heart attack. All three of us went to bed; the time must have been about 4 a.m.

The morning after we all got up for breakfast and had a good laugh about the previous nights events. I told the lads that there was no way I was going back to that end of town where all the nightclubs were! After breakfast we again walked along Lake Geneva, having a few drinks at the local bars. Tommy and David said they would have to make up a song about our antics from the previous night. The song they wrote was to the tune of 'Roy Keane's fucking magic'. It went like this ' Bruce is fucking tragic, he wears a tragic hat and when he saw the brothel he said I fancied that, they asked him for some champagne, he said Dom Perignon and when they brought the bill round the Bruce was fucking gone!'. In the afternoon we caught the train to Milan.

We had loaded up with booze and were on our way. The journey to Milan was breathtaking; the views were fantastic. The song was sung for most of the journey, but I can take the stick as there was no way I was going to pay that bill. On our return weeks later, I received a phone call from American Express. They enquired about the bill in the nightclub, so I again explained to them the circumstances. Apparently the Dom Perignon we were drinking was vintage and from a very rare year, costing over £1,000 a bottle. She then asked if I was prepared to replace the bottles I replied yes, but was very disappointed about being ripped off, but to my surprise she said "No problem sir. We have taken care of everything for you, at no cost to yourself." I never heard anything about the disagreement again, but must admit that famous American Express saying 'That will do nicely' really does work. I wondered if Master Card would have done the same thing.

We arrived in Milan on the afternoon of the game; went straight to the hotel, quickly showered and were then straight out on the town. Milan is a beautiful city, the only thing that spoils it is that it is full off Italians! Some Reds told us that you could get tickets at the ground, so we decided to stay drinking in Milan's square where hundreds of Reds were enjoying the occasion. The Italian police surprised me with their low-key attitude. They kept a low profile as I think they realised that we were only having a good time. We all headed towards the stadium about two hours before kickoff. Inter's stadium is fabulous. There were about 5,000 United supporters who had made the trip and hundreds outside without tickets including the three of us. The Italian ticket touts were all on scooters and motorbikes asking £100 for match tickets. We saw a gang from Salford steal a bunch of tickets from a tout and run off. I approached one of the Italian ticket touts asking how much for three tickets, he replied so many Lira. His English was not very good and neither was my Italian, so I asked him "How much in English money?" He said "£100." There were seven of us around him; Denis and Jeff both gave me £50 each, I then took £50 from my own wallet and handed the Italian £150 in English pounds, but only when I had the match tickets in my hand. We then quickly walked away, he was shouting something in Italian; words to the effect of English bastards but we just ignored him and made our way to the United fans at the other end of the ground. The three tickets we had were for the Milan end but when Tommy Price handed them in at the turnstiles along with the other four tickets the operator just let us in. I don't think he wanted any hassle by trying to explain to us in English that three should be in another section of the ground. The atmosphere in the ground was electric. United had a 2-0 lead from the first leg but was it going to be enough? I knew that they would have to come at us which could then in turn leave them wide open for a counter attack. If we could get an away goal the game would be over. Like we were expecting, the Italians put United under constant pressure. Peter Schmeichel and Jaap Stam were outstanding and also the referee was having a great game. The Italians were trying to gain an advantage at every opportunity by cheating. A lesser man may have swayed but United stood firm. The Chilean Zamorano dived in the box in the first fifteen minutes, but this referee was standing for no nonsense and clamped down on the Italian's play acting. Inter even gambled by playing an unfit Ronaldo, but saying that even an unfit Ronaldo is better than a lot of fit Premiership players. The Brazilian is a world class player but you could definitely tell in his performance that he was struggling. United survived the first half, going in at half-time 0-0, but the Italians had the better of the chances and it came as no surprise to me when they took the lead after about an hour's play. Schmeichel then pulled off a wonderful reflex save from Ronaldo. Inter were now being urged on by their fanatical home fans and were all over the Reds in search of the equaliser. To be perfectly honest they missed some easy chances. They pushed forward in suicidal numbers, United caught them on the break and with a few minutes' remaining Paul Scholes equalised. As if by magic the stadium started to empty, leaving the jubilant Reds to their ecstatic celebrations. All seven of us were jumping about like school children, embracing each other. United were now in the semifinals of the Champions League for the second time in three years. It was the first time that I felt my dream of European glory could come true.

We all celebrated United's achievement until the early hours, then the next day we made the journey back home, which is always a delight when your team has won.

The Reds' next game after the daunting Milan trip was at Old Trafford against Everton on Sunday 21st March, and I was honestly thinking that with all the circumstances surrounding the Milan game, that the Reds might feel a little jaded from their midweek excursions, but this team loves to prove me wrong. Everton held out until the second half and were then hit with three goals in ten minutes. The game was over apart from Hutchinson pulling one back ten minutes from time, but the Reds won easily 3-1. March finished with United still top of the Premiership, four points in front of Arsenal after thirty games played. There were eight games remaining and I was beginning to feel confident that we could win our title back off the holders Arsenal. In early April United travelled to Wimbledon who always work very hard against us. They snatched the lead after five minutes through Euell. The Reds worked relentlessly to score through Beckham on the stroke of half-time. Sullivan the Don's keeper had another outstanding match and the game ended in a 1-1 draw. United had to be content with stretching their unbeaten run to twenty games. Again the only thing I could concentrate on was next week's semifinal first leg at Old Trafford against Juventus; I couldn't sleep at night!

United had drawn another Italian giant. I was glad that their star player Del Piero was still injured, but they still had world class players like Zinedine Zidane who would easily get into United's side; I rate him that highly. They also had players like Didier Deschamps the Frenchman who Eric Cantona used to call the water carrier, not to mention Edgar Davids and Filippo Inzaghi, so I knew we were in for a tough game. The Theatre of Dreams was about to witness another great European night. The atmosphere was electric but United were finding it difficult to handle the Juventus midfield and I have to admit that for well over an hour the Italians outplayed the Reds. Their side oozed quality. They had eleven stars out there on the pitch and took the lead after half an hour with Conte scoring. This gave them the benefit of an important away goal that I thought could prove fatal. In the second half the Reds raised the tempo. The Italians are masters at defending, so you always know it is going to be difficult when they go in front. I had to admire them as they were playing very good football and were not out to con the referee as some teams do. United replaced Yorke with Teddy Sheringham for the last ten minutes, and the Reds were now gathered for a final assault to try and break down the Italian defence. It seemed to have worked when Teddy Sheringham equalised with a good header but the referee was well placed and judged him to be offside. The fans were willing the Reds on, and it was into injury time when Ryan Giggs half volleyed home from about four yards, to the Stretford End, which had me punching the air with delight. I never ever leave Old Trafford until the final whistle has gone, as you always feel that the Reds will score or that something will happen right at the death. Like I said earlier, the sign of a great side is when they can play for ninety minutes, this United side certainly does that.

I knew I had to go to the away leg, even though I didn't feel very confident. Juventus had certainly impressed me, but this game was quickly put on the back burner because it was now time for our FA Cup semifinal on Sunday 11th April, with a silly 12.30 p.m. kickoff. The Reds were again drawn against London opposition, this time we were playing the mighty Arsenal. Because of the strange time of the kickoff I drove to the game with Tommy Price. United had the best of this semifinal clash, creating more chances than the Gunners but failed to take them. What annoyed me most is when Ryan Giggs skinned the Arsenal full back Dixon before crossing for Dwight Yorke to flick on into the path of Roy Keane, who unleashed a terrific half volley that gave Arsenal's David Seaman no chance, the referee David Elleray disallowed Keane's effort for apparently being offside. I was furious at him; how could he disallow a goal like that in a semifinal I screamed but the decision had been made and nothing I could say would change it. You only had to look at the United players' reaction to his decision that told you something wasn't right. Every outfield player was arguing with him; eventually he booked Dennis Irwin and play continued. The game ended up a stalemate 0-0, so extra time was to be played. Then an off the ball incident between Nicky Butt and Arsenal's Vivas resulted in the Arsenal number seven receiving his marching orders for apparently elbowing. Arsenal then regrouped and their ten men defended bravely against a strong United attack, but the game ended a 0-0 draw resulting in a replay to be played again at Villa Park.

My son Robert would not let me forget that he had been to the Chelsea away game in the quarterfinals and was begging me to take him to the replay. His best friend, who is a very good footballer with a lot of professional teams watching him, wanted to go as well. His name is Daniel Cuddy, he follows United but had never been to a United game, so I asked Dave Clay if he wanted to take his son James. He said yes, so this time Dave would drive down in his Space Cruiser and the replay would be a lads' and dads' day out! We arrived at Villa Park and parked up near to the ground, then went to a pub called the Cap and Gown. It was already full of United fans singing the latest song about our brick of a centre half Jaap Stam. The man leading the singing was a lad called Peter Boyle, he makes up some great songs about United and it's not long before all the fans are singing them. The song went like this ' Yip Yap Stam is a big Dutch man, get past him if you think you can, try a little trick and he'll make you look a prick, yip yap Jaap Stam'.

Over the contents of this book you will have read me describing some fantastic matches that I have been lucky enough to have seen, but this game was something else. It was the best game of football I have had the pleasure to see. Both teams gave their all and it was with great sadness that one team had to lose. It was an epic roller coaster of a contest. David Beckham gave United the lead after about twenty minutes with a delightful twenty-five yarder that bent past Seaman, giving him no chance. Both teams were at each others' throats and the game was played at a tremendous pace. Arsenal scored their equaliser through Bergkamp which took a wicked deflection off the magnificent Stam. The children were thoroughly enjoying the game and were even joining in with all the songs, but in the seventieth minute David Elleray, the same referee who had disallowed Roy Keane's effort in the first game, was now red-carding our skipper for two bookable offences, and it was now United's turn to hang on.

The look in Robert's and the other children's eyes told the story. They were all nearly in tears, but this was nothing to what happened in the ninetieth minute; Philip Neville, the Reds' full back, brought down Arsenal's winger Ray Parlour and up stepped the Dutchman Dennis Bergkamp to take the spot kick. The United fans enmassed behind the goal were whistling to try and put him off. I could not bear to watch, so closed my eyes and prayed to Saint Jude, asking Robert to do the same. Bergkamp stepped forward and blasted the ball, all I can remember is Robert jumping on me saying Dad he's missed. Peter Schmeichel had apparently made a great save. The game went into extra time yet again, but I could sense tiredness in the Arsenal team. They looked as if they had run out of steam, never taking advantage of the extra man. I am not a believer in fairy tale endings but this game had one. Ryan Giggs seized possession in his own half from Vierra, he raced eighty yards, leaving five or six Arsenal players in his wake before hitting a cracking shot over Seaman's head from about ten yards. It was a truly great FA Cup goal, possibly the best. The fans were now on the pitch, this excitement was too much to bear; the happiness on the children's faces will stay with me forever. This match had had every kind of emotion imaginable. United held out to win 2-1 after extra time to reach our fifteenth FA Cup Final. Robert and his friends thanked David and myself for taking them to such an exciting game and I knew that in years to come Robert would be able to describe the game in detail as I have done here. He said to me "I will never forget that game Dad. I love you." Words like that to me make it all worthwhile.

In their next game I expected United to struggle after the two titanic battles against the Gunners. I had also tried to get in touch with that Arsenal fan Paddy Chapburn, but he was not taking any calls, but I knew he couldn't hide forever. Our next game was at home against Sheffield Wednesday. I had no need to worry as the Reds won 3-0 easily, hardly having to break sweat, it was now time for the second leg against Juventus. I booked with Tommy and Ray Price to go on the day 'in and out' trip with United. There was at least twenty from the Stalybridge branch who also made the trip. I had still only missed that one game at LKS Lodz, and had decided I would not miss any games until the end of the season. The Stadio Delle Alpi in Turin was packed with 60,000 fans; little did I know what was in store for us. The Wednesday before against Arsenal I witnessed what I described as one of the best games I have ever seen, I didn't think anything could ever equal it, but ask any United fan to choose between these two matches and I can tell you there wouldn't be much in it. For the second time in two weeks United had to rise to supreme heights. Juventus were 2-0 up before United had got out of first gear, I couldn't believe what I was seeing, it looked as if we were dead and buried. After all not many teams beat Juventus on their own soil, let alone come back from 2-0, but miracles can happen and it is of my opinion that one happened that night. The Reds rolled up their sleeves. Inzaghi had hit the net twice in the opening ten minutes and United did the same in the twenty-fourth and thirty-fourth minutes. Roy Keane brought United back into the game with a bullet header from a David Beckham corner, then Dwight Yorke equalised with another header, this time from an Andy Cole cross. 2-2 would have been enough to take United through to the final, but the Reds were not interested to go through on the away goals' ruling. They steamed right into the heart of the Juventus side, hitting the woodwork twice once by Yorke and then by Irwin. In the last five minutes I was on my seat screaming for a penalty after Yorke had been fouled; the referee played the advantage and the loose ball fell to Andy Cole who slid the ball home from a narrow angle. The Reds had gone in front for the first time, thousands of fans were celebrating hysterically. Sadly bookings for Paul Scholes and Roy Keane had ruled them out of the final, but I had no time to worry about that as this was a night for pride, joy and celebration. I embraced Ray Price saying that it has been well worth waiting thirty years for and it was now time to book a week's holiday in Lloret De Mar. The talk of the treble was definitely on, especially after our two great semifinal results over Arsenal and Juventus.

Our last game in April was played at Old Trafford against Leeds on Sunday 25th April. The young Leeds side took United on and attacked from the kickoff, they even deserved to take the ead through Hasselbaink. Kewell was having another utstanding match, this Leeds team is certainly one for the future, ney all work as a unit. United equalised through Andy Cole and ne game finished 1-1. April ended with Arsenal leading the remiership by one point, having played a game more than us. I vas wondering if maybe we had done them a favour by knocking nem out of the FA Cup. It was now May and the climax to the eason was Aston Villa entertaining United at Old Trafford on May Day. Villa had made a great start to the season but could ot maintain the pace; their squad is not big enough to sustain serious challenge for the Premiership, although saying that ney still have a few players worth watching in Southgate, Dublin nd Paul Merson. The game was far from a classic, but after the xcitement of recent games we couldn't grumble. The Reds took ne lead after twenty minutes with an own goal by Villa's Watson. pachim equalised just before half-time and it was left to David eckham to score with one of his specials from twenty-five yards ut. It surprises me why some teams don't place defenders on ne line, surely they should know by now how deadly accurate eckham is; in their case Villa didn't even think a defensive wall as necessary. The game ended with the Reds winning 2-1 and e now had to travel to Merseyside to face our archenemies iverpool at Anfield on a Wednesday night.

Tommy Price said he would drive, so took David Ashworth nd myself to the game. We needed to win at Liverpool as rsenal were breathing down our necks. The Reds of Manchester arted well and Yorke put us in front with a good header after venty minutes. Then Dennis Irwin scored a penalty in the second alf to make it 2-0; we were now in complete control. That is until ne eccentric referee, yes you guessed it, David Elleray made pme strange decisions. I still hadn't forgiven him for disallowing oy Keane's goal in the FA Cup semifinal, then sending him off the replay, and now here he was sending off Dennis Irwin for vo bookable offences. The second offence was for deliberately icking the ball away, when in fact he was genuinely making an tempt to keep it in play, but to make matters worse he gave iverpool a penalty for what he thought was a foul by Blomqvist. was a diabolical decision. Redknapp converted the penalty and United's ten men were under pressure from then on. I thought we would still hold out but the Guv, or Champagne Charlie as Alex Ferguson describes him, scrambled home the equaliser. I have nothing against Paul Ince, he did his bit for United, I just think he has become a bit bitter because Alex Ferguson never took up the option to resign him from Italy on his return. The way he celebrated his goal told every United fan in the ground that he has no love for United any more. I was very disappointed with the referee David Elleray, this man could have cost Manchester United the Championship. It is not very often you hear United's chairman blasting the referee, but in this case he did, making it very clear to everybody who he thought could cost United the league and I had to agree with him.

The tension was beginning to build up in the Championship race. The Reds had fallen three points behind Arsenal and the pressure was on. Our next match was away to Middlesborough on Sunday 9th May. United needed a victory and also to win well, as a few goals would do our goal difference no harm at all. Tommy drove Jeff Clayton and myself to the game. We had arranged to pick up David Dyson, a Middlesborough fan that have mentioned earlier, at his local pub near to the ground. We reached Middlesborough at midday, then Dave took us in a few pubs. We could not believe how cheap it was — £1 a pint! It took me back to the eighties but we were not complaining. We drank with the Middlesborough fans who made us feel very welcome. The game itself was a scrappy affair. United had what looked like a perfectly good goal by Teddy Sheringham disallowed for offside, then United took the lead on the stroke of half-time through Dwight Yorke with a well-placed header. The second half commenced with both sides squandering chances. The final whistle brought a huge sigh of relief from us all. United had secured the points, winning 1-0, but our goal difference was equal to Arsenal's; a nail biting week lay ahead.

Our last away game of the season was against Blackburn Rovers at Ewood Park on Wednesday 12th May. Both teams needed to win. The Reds' supporters were packed in their thousands behind the goal. The new Blackburn boss was our old assistant manager Brian Kidd. Anything less than a win for

Rovers would take them down. I still have fond memories of Kiddo. I remember him scoring one of the goals in the 1968 European Cup Final on his birthday and can also remember the Stretford End crowning him the King of Old Trafford. Brian Kidd is United through and through. I also know his brother Bernard, a bricklayer, who used to live in Moston way back in the seventies. No one at United wanted to lose Kiddo, as we all thought that he was being groomed to be Alex Ferguson's successor, but I knew he wanted to see how he could do at being number one and wish him continuing success. United took the game to Rovers and went for the jugular from the kickoff, but wayward finishing let us down badly. Blackburn played with a lot of spirit, but ended up being relegated. The game ended in a 0-0 draw.

United now required a victory in our last game at Old Trafford against Arsenal's North London rivals Tottenham Hotspur to make sure of the title. I was even getting phone calls from Spurs supporters hoping that they would get beaten. Paul rang me from Tenerife to say "Please don't let Arsenal win the league, as I will never live it down if they win the league two years in succession" but there was no need to worry, United secured their fifth Championship triumph under manager Alex Ferguson, although it was the first to be clinched at Old Trafford. Spurs took the lead in the first half against the run of play through Les Ferdinand, who brilliantly chipped the ball over the advancing Schmeichel. United continued to pressure the Spurs defence and only some fine saves from the Spurs goalkeeper, Ian Walker, prevented us from equalising, but there was nothing he could do about the build up leading to Beckham's equaliser. Giggs and Scholes combined well on the left, threading the ball to Becks who finished with a powerful angled drive, that Walker somehow got a hand to, but the sheer power of the shot took it into the net. The score stayed 1-1 at half-time and the crowd were becoming a little hesitant. The atmosphere was suddenly transformed just after the break, when Andy Cole flicked the ball from a Neville clearance over Walker's head to put the Reds in front. Old Trafford went crazy. News was going around the ground of an Arsenal goal at Highbury, I remember thinking that years

189

before Arsenal had snatched the title off Liverpool by winning at Anfield, one mistake by the Reds and the Gunners would be celebrating their second successive Championship. The game ended 2-1; Manchester United had secured their twelfth Championship success, keeping up their thirty-one match unbeaten run in the process. Roy Keane held up the trophy to the Old Trafford faithful who now had next week's FA Cup Final to look forward to against Newcastle.

I had another game on my mind. It was the testimonial game for the ex-Red Lee Martin, to be played at Bristol Rover's stadium on Thursday night 20th May, Alex Ferguson had promised to take a strong United team down for Lee and kept his word. He himself led the team out, signing autographs after the game along with all the United players for well over an hour. United's team consisted of both youth and established players. Out of the youth team was John Curtis and Jonathan Greening; the more senior players that turned out for Lee was David May who captained the side, Paul Scholes, Ole Gunner Solskjaer and the brilliant David Beckham. The Rover's ground was packed to capacity, all the tickets had been sold out two months before the game. I was pleased for Lee and had a drink with him after the game along with all the other players. Lee gave me a United shirt signed by the United team. I told him I would wear it for the Cup Final on Saturday against Newcastle which I did. The people who made the trip down to Bristol with me were David Ashworth, Lee Hamilton, Alan Hazlehurst and David Clay. We stayed the night at the Bath Hotel in the town centre. Bath is a beautiful city. I had also arranged a benefit night for Lee Martin at my nightclub in Glossop where Lee lives. He arranged for Ryan Giggs to appear. It was another great night and the place was packed. My partner and I had also arranged a special presentation to be made to Lee. We had a local artist called Ian Gardener paint a picture of Lee holding the FA Cup high in the air. Ian had excelled himself, the painting is one of Lee's treasured possessions. The game for Lee gave Alex Ferguson the time to select his Cup Final team, choosing four of the players that had played in the 2-2 draw at Bristol Rovers. They were David May, Paul Scholes, Ole Gunner Solskjaer and David Beckham.

FA Cup Final days are always special for me. The Reds were going for their third double which isn't bad by anyone's standards. Again we all travelled down to the game in style. We hired our regular stretch limmo. The lucky lads that made the trip were Tommy Price, Peter Hazlehurst, Simon Howarth, Jeff Clayton and myself. I wore my treasured United shirt signed by all the players. We drank champagne all the way to the Wembley Hilton, who by now were on first name terms with us all. The FA Cup Final was played in the glorious Wembley sunshine. United dominated the early proceedings and even over came the loss of our skipper Roy Keane to what I can only describe as a late Gary Speed challenge. Only ten minutes had been played when our super sub Teddy Sheringham put the Reds in front. Paul Scholes made it 2-0 early in the second half. Rarely have I seen such a totally one-sided final, and to be perfectly honest I was very disappointed with Alan Shearer and his Newcastle side; they just did not want to compete. They threw on Duncan Ferguson for the second half but it was to no avail, their best scoring opportunity fell to the number ten Ketsbaia, who hit the outside of the post when it seemed easier to score as Peter Schmeichel was stranded in no-man's-land. Teddy Sheringham was also very unlucky not to score his second goal, with the ball bouncing back off the Newcastle bar. Our third double had been achieved and it was now on to Barcelona for the treble.

This game was to be played on Wednesday 26th May, which ironically was Sir Matt Busby's 90th birthday. This was my sixty-first game of the season, which I feel will be hard to equal. I would like to know if anyone has beaten me and gone to all sixty-two games! I'd arranged for the lads to fly to Barcelona on the Monday before the game, then get the train to Lloret De Mar on the coast; have three days there, returning back to Manchester on the Friday. If anybody missed the European Cup Final there is nothing I can say which will be able to describe the events that occurred that night. The people who made the trip with myself were David Ashworth, Tommy Price and Alan Hazlehurst. Alan had again found it very difficult to obtain a match ticket and the Spanish touts were asking anything up to £600 for a Cup Final ticket. We fell lucky whilst we were drinking at a bar in Lloret, as Tommy and Dave, who speak very good German, became friendly with some Bayern Munich supporters who had a spare ticket and sold it to them for £100. Alan did not want to sit with the German supporters, so I swapped my ticket for his, and was now sitting in the Munich end. There must have been literally 20,000 United supporters in Lloret De Mar and over 80,000 in the Ramblers on the day of the game. The local bar where most of the United supporters were drinking in Lloret, was the Piccadilly bar in the town centre. There were a few clashes with the German supporters but nothing drastic occurred. We met most of the Ashton mob there, then we caught the early train to Barcelona where we headed straight for the Robin Hood pub in the Ramblers. Once there I bumped into Twang Eyes (Doss Maher), who I hadn't seen for a long while. We had a drink together talking about old times, the thirty years have flown by. "Doss" I said "let's hope we do it tonight" to which Doss agreed. The singing then started. Tommy Price got the atmosphere going with all the old songs. It was like one big carnival. It was also good to bump into John Shorrocks with his wife Carol, who had made the trip. John was Tommy's best man at his wedding; they both went to the games together in the sixties. I couldn't help thinking how Eric Mitchell, Tony Braithwaite and John Bent would have loved to be here savouring this tremendous feeling. Something told me that afternoon we would win the treble. I know this sounds incredible but it is true; the scale of the glory and the manner in which it was achieved was hard to take in.

We all arrived at the Nou-Camp Stadium with hours to spare. After the game we had all decided to meet back at the Robin Hood bar on the Ramblers. 91,000 fans were packed into the Nou-Camp and there were thousands more locked outside. People had bought forged tickets for the game at silly prices, so just before kickoff all hell was breaking loose at the turnstiles. One story I have to tell is of Mick Cox and Ess Cox who travelled to the final with their wives and Mick's son Duncan Edwards Cox; the young lad I took to the Bayern Munich away trip in the earlier rounds. He is named after the great man himself. They travel everywhere with the Reds, purchasing their tickets for his game from United. Somehow the Spanish police said their tickets were forgeries and wouldn't let them gain entrance to what should have been their finest hour. They all had their tickets confiscated and had to watch the game in a local bar near to the ground. I felt sorry for this family as their oldest brother Joe Cox was tragically killed outside a pub in Glossop over a fight about match tickets for a United game. It happened on what should have been his forty-ninth birthday. Why should this happen to a nice footballing family like the Coxes? I don't know, sometimes life can be so cruel.

The Germans had made the better start, taking the lead through an early Basler free kick after only six minutes; it somehow deceived the Reds' goalkeeper Schmeichel, who only moved when it was in the back of the net. The Germans all around me behind the goal were going ballistic. I remember thinking how the Reds had it all to do now. They had no Roy Keane or Paul Scholes, but the magnificent David Beckham was controlling things in his unaccustomed central role. The score remained 1-0 as half-time approached. In the second half the Reds began to press forward and were hit with a series of counterattacks. Peter Schmeichel had to make some great saves to keep us in the game. My heart nearly stopped when they hit the post after eighty minutes and then with barely five minutes' remaining the German Janckers' overhead kick crashed against the United crossbar. The game was now into added time. I was praying to Saint Jude for a miracle — thank God it occurred. Beck's drove in a corner which Ryan Giggs miskicked, the shot ran to Teddy Sheringham who steered it home from just inside the six-yard box. The crowd went wild. I looked around the German end and there were Reds celebrating everywhere. The Germans were devastated but more was to follow. Again Becks swept another teasing cross into the German's goalmouth, Teddy flicked it on and who else was arriving at the far post unmarked but the 'Assassin' Ole Gunner Solskjaer who volleyed home the winner. It must go down as one of the greatest escapes of all time. Alex Ferguson had finally achieved his Holy Grail and so had I. The Reds had also won a remarkable treble that I don't think will ever be witnessed again in my lifetime. Tears were streaming down

my face. I said a prayer for Sir Matt on his birthday; Eric, Ton
and John were also in my thoughts along with Joe Cox. Tw
other great United supporters came to mind as well, they wer
big Paul and Bernard Ringland, these two friends of mine died o
heart attacks watching their team at Old Trafford. Due to th
excitement this match nearly had me joining them.

The celebrations were now beginning, a football fairy tal
was complete. I walked back about six miles to the Rambler
The first people I met there were Ray Price, Sammy Gilbey an
Rob Radcliffe. We drank well into the early hours of the mornin
Unlucky Rob had had his wallet stolen, but this didn't deter hin
We all ended up in a disco by the harbour, at the bottom of th
Ramblers. To my surprise Bryan Robson and Viv Anderson th
Middlesborough duo and both ex-Reds celebrated ecstaticall
with us all. If nothing else in life is absolutely perfect, this late
United campaign came pretty close. By the time we arrived bac
at our hotel it was breakfast time. I had breakfast with Tomm
Price then slept for twelve hours. Looking back on the season
successes how could I ever forget the two thrilling 3-3 draw
with Barcelona, the great 3-2 come back at Juventus as well a
our clashes in the FA Cup with both Arsenal and Chelsea? Th
fight back at Old Trafford against our rivals Liverpool, and Gigg
goal against the Gunners will stay in my memory bank foreve
along with all the other memories described in this book. Ale
Ferguson has deserved his Knighthood, even the loss of Bria
Kidd didn't deter him.

All this that had happened did not prepare me for the shock
was about to hear when I arrived home. My intentions were
take the whole family to United's homecoming on the Sunda
following our great European victory. My wife Carol, after ov
twenty years of marriage, had decided that we should have
trial separation. I had known her twenty-seven years in total an
although in the first six months I found it very hard to come
terms with, I accepted her wishes. Manchester United were n
at fault, she said she just needed some space and time on h
own. No one else was involved, we had become more like be
friends. The treble season ended in disappointment for me, b

knew only one thing would make me feel better and that was to cheer my favourite team on in Europe yet again.

This might mean that I would have to miss a few league games I thought, but the two places I intended to go to were Tokyo for the World Club Champion's game against the South American champions. The Brazilian team Palmeris and also to travel to Rio to watch the FIFA World Club Championships in January 2000. We sold our home in Glossop, Derbyshire, and I moved back to my parents' in Ashton-under-Lyne, Lancashire. My friend, the Arsenal fan Ralph Paddy Chatburn, also separated from his wife Lorraine at about the same time. Carol and I decided to still go on the family holiday I had booked, again to take the three children to Florida in the pre-season. The children loved the holiday but my wife Carol had already made her mind up about the forthcoming divorce before we went. Nothing was going to change her mind. Life must go on, my main priority is to ensure that it will not affect my children. At this moment in time I am glad to say it hasn't. Carol lets me see the children whenever I like, so I can't complain, things could be a lot worse I thought. Our American holiday clashed with the Charity Shield game with Arsenal — bad planning on my behalf. Anyway the Gunners, which pleased Paddy, beat the Reds but I'm glad to say I was too far away for him to get in touch with me!

I arrived back in England in time for our opening game of the 1999/2000 Season at Everton on August 8th — ironically a Sunday game. We were used to playing on Sundays by now. The game ended a scrappy 1-1 draw with Dwight Yorke scoring the goal for the Reds. They then went on a great run through August, winning the next six games on the bounce. Ferguson had made for me a strange signing as he brought in another goalkeeper to keep the pressure on Bosnich and Van Der Gouw, it was the Italian keeper Taibi. What better game to give him his debut than Liverpool away at Anfield — talk about being thrown in at the deep end! The Italian survived a nightmare early error which resulted in a Liverpool goal, but then redeemed himself with a 'man of the match' display making some outstanding saves to keep the Liverpool forwards from scoring. The Reds kept up their good start to the season with a good 3-2 win. Sadly

I was finding it very difficult to maintain my standards from the season before. I was missing not seeing my children through the week and the weekends were the only time that I could see them. Something had to give, so I decided to concentrate on United's away games and also decided to miss the early round of the Champions League, as I knew that I had to save for Tokyo in November.

The Reds made a bit of a disastrous start to the Champions League, drawing 0-0 at home to Croatia Zagreb, then winning our next two matches 3-0 away to SK Sturm Graz and 2-1 at home to Olympique Marseille, finally losing the away leg 1-0 where was convinced that tactics played a big part in our defeat. In between this, the Reds took a savage beating at Chelsea, losing 5-0. November approached and we were playing the Italians AC Florentina away on Tuesday 23rd November, one week before our game with Palmeris in Tokyo. I booked to go on the one-day 'in and out' trip with United, along with Tommy and Ray Price. The Reds had told us we were to be penned in the ground for our own protection, and that the views would be obstructed but it was a lot worse than even I expected. We arrived in Florence about midday. It is a beautiful place with more restaurants than bars. Barry Moorhouse had warned us all to be aware of trouble. Apparently Florentina have a hooligan element attached to them similar to what United had in the seventies. This did not deter us. Tommy Price said he was starving "Let's have something to eat first." He suggested a pizza restaurant, so the three of us entered the restaurant. We had an excellent meal along with couple of bottles of Italian wine. After about an hour or so looked out of the window and spotted two lads walking past. was convinced I knew them but these people were wearing blue caps in Florentina colours. I approached the door and shouted out their names. They both turned round it was Pete Fallon (Strett) and Nick the Greek. They came walking back so Tommy ordered another couple of bottles of wine. "What's going on Strett? Why the Florentina colours?" I asked. They were on three-day trip, and had caught the train down from Rome. Both were a little scared of any problems that could arise on the way back to the train station after the match. These two had to go

ack to Rome to catch their plane, so they were taking no chances.
said to Strett "Nick the Greek will pass off as an Italian, no
roblem, but you have no chance you are English through and
hrough." We all had a good laugh; finished our wine then went
ff to tour the city.

The coaches picked us up in plenty of time to see the game.
The Italian police escorted us to our section of the ground,
which I can only describe as a Perspex container. You could
hardly see the pitch through the plastic. Every United supporter
who was at that game had to watch from this plastic box for their
own protection, even some of the United players' families were
in our enclosure. I had a brief chat with Ted Beckham, David's
father, who I found to be a decent chap whose knowledge of
football would leave some people for dead. The game kicked off
with the Italians on the attack, they played with only two up
front, one of them was the brilliant Argentine Batistuta who
Alex Ferguson had tried to sign a few years earlier. Both forwards
worked extremely hard and closed down United's back four,
preventing the Reds' full backs from attacking. I was still
convinced that the Reds would get something out of the game.
We were playing controlled football, finding space for each other,
but all this was ruined when the normally reliable Roy Keane
tried a back pass to the United keeper without concentrating on
who was around him. It was what he described as a Sunday
morning error. The Argentine Batistuta wasted no time in picking
up the loose ball, then crashing an unstoppable shot from about
twenty yards that nearly brought the net down. The Reds pushed
up in search of an equaliser, you would have thought we'd have
learnt from the Roy Keane mistake but we hadn't. Berg played a
loose ball across the goal and they made it 2-0; match over. The
Reds had lost by two dreadful mistakes, and had to take it on the
chin.

The next Champions League game was a fortnight later, but
before that they had what I considered to be their most important
game after winning the European Cup Final. It was the World
Club Champions Final to be held in Tokyo on 30th November
1999. Our opponents were the South American champions
Palmeris of Brazil. United had played in this tournament way

back in the sixties. In those days the games were played over two legs. The Reds were playing another South American team called Estudiantes, I think it was Willie Morgan's debut. He scored for the Reds in a 1-1 draw at Old Trafford, but we lost the away leg in South America. Both matches were ill-tempered games that the great Pat Crerand still talks about today. The Reds had both Nobby Stiles and George Best sent off. It ended our chances of becoming the first English team to be Club Champions of the World. No English side had managed to win this tournament but many had tried and failed, including the great Liverpool and Nottingham Forest sides of the eighties. Because of the amount of games teams were playing in recent years, the World Club Final was now decided over one game, and what better place in the world to play the final than in Tokyo.

Tommy Price, along with Simon and Derek Howarth, had paid £800 for a three-day trip; I said this was too expensive especially with the FIFA World Club Championships to be held in South America in January. So with that in mind I asked my brother-in-law Alan Hazlehurst to surf the internet to try and get us a cheap flight to Tokyo. Alan rang me back a few hours later saying the cheapest flight he could get us on was with Pakistan International Airlines, going from Manchester on Friday 26th November returning back one week later at a cost of £398 each. This was half the price of Tommy's trip. I knew I could stay in Tom's hotel in Tokyo, so I told Alan to book the holiday. Alan was due to come with David Ashworth and myself, but due to work commitments had to cancel. If anybody in the whole world can say that they have encountered a trip which I am about to describe, then I would like to hear from them.

A friend of mine called Adam offered to take us to the airport. Because Adam had undertaken a lot of building work at my house, in return I said he could look after my new BMW. All he had to do was drop us off then pick us up on our return to Manchester. We arrived at Manchester airport with plenty of time to spare. We were checking in at departures, when we were told that it was a dry flight due to the fact they are a Muslim country and also to be extra careful as a few weeks earlier there had been a military coup and the army were now running the country. You would not believe the route we had to take to watch a football match in Tokyo. What had we let ourselves in for? The girls at the airport, they said that we have a good drink before boarding. Pakistan International Airlines are a nightmare, they never leave on time due to the fact that every member of the families turn up at the airport to say farewell. The check in girls had given us some valuable tips. "Always board last" they said. We also had the best seats on the flight near the emergency exit where we had plenty of space, but to my horror the space was used to let the Muslim's pray at least five times a day. David and myself boarded the plane last, having had a good drink in the departure lounge. We departed after a two-hour delay. David had another problem as he only likes English food, so this trip was going to lose him a lot of weight. The flight was nine hours to Karachi, where we were due to have a two-day stopover at the airport hotel which was included in the price. Having travelled all over the world with various airlines, staying in five-star hotels what was in store for us was beyond belief. When we arrived at Karachi Airport we were told that we would have to hand our passports to the airport authorities, who would then return them to us on our departure. There was a bus service from the airport to the hotel that took about ten minutes, the problem was that there must have been 150 people crammed onto the bus. Dave said he wanted to get his head down for a few hours after all the disturbances and praying on the aeroplane. I had to agree with him so when we had checked into the hotel and entered our room we just burst out laughing. There were two single beds in the room; one sink with one toilet, but the problem was that there was no water; you had to use a bucket and a tap that was outside. We were both too tired from the journey to complain so we went to sleep; the time was about 7.30 a.m. on 27th November.

We both slept well waking up at about 2 p.m. The sunshine was blazing in through our window that didn't even have any curtains. We both quickly got washed and changed into shorts and tee shirts. Dave suggested we have a walk around the place to get acquainted with the locals. Within seconds we were surrounded by the locals offering their services as tour guides. I recognised the coach driver who had driven us to the hotel in the morning, he was also the night porter at the hotel. We started to talk to him and he told us that he had six children, which meant he had to work very hard to make ends meet. Some days he had to work twenty hours. His wages were about £8 per month. In all my travels I have witnessed many things, but nothing can compare to the sights we saw in Karachi. The chap's name was Larbi and he also asked if he could be our tour guide. David asked him how much it would cost, to which he replied "Just give me whatever you think." We both felt sorry for him and said ok. Larbi's car was an old banger, but when you see Karachi town centre you know why every car looks the same. The unusual thing about his car was that it had a Manchester United sticker in the back window. Larbi told us that one of his sons supported United. He didn't know that we were Reds going to Tokyo, our trust in this man grew from then on. There are ten million people living in Karachi, it is a very depressing place. Beggars stop you in the street and the cars and motorbikes are packed with friends and families. The record amount of people we saw on one motorbike was six. Everyone uses their horns, you just drive the best way you can. Surprisingly we never saw any accidents, so they must know what they are doing! We had two days to kill. David wanted something decent to eat and we had also asked Larbi to take us somewhere for a drink. "No beer in Pakistan" he explained, but with a wink in his eye told us to follow him. We both kept very close to Larbi, but David stood out like a sore thumb. We walked for about fifteen minutes through the crowds, where Larbi pointed to a Korean restaurant across the road that had a soldier in his uniform guarding the door. He had a machine gun and looked as if he would have no hesitation using it. Larbi said he would have no problem getting us in, but would wait for us outside as it is against his religion to drink. David walked in first, with me following closely behind. The place was jam-packed with foreigners; Americans, English, Chinese, Japs you name it they were in there. When David entered first everyone looked around for a glimpse of his white face then carried on with what they were doing. We were both escorted to a table in the corner of the room where David enquired if we could have a drink of beer. I said to him "There's no chance of a beer in here Dave." Looking round the other tables all you could see were cups and saucers, but to my surprise the man came back with two large cans of Heineken wrapped in towels. We were delighted, it tasted terrific, so we also ordered some food. David had to make do with fish but this didn't bother him, but two days without beer would have killed him. I had been wise enough to have my inoculations prior to the trip, but David hadn't, saying that he would be all right. We stayed in the Korean restaurant until well after midnight having consumed about eight cans each. By this time we were both pissed. The waiters had witnessed us getting slowly drunk and by the end of the night we were singing all the old United songs to the waiters — even the soldier outside came in to tell us to quieten down. The Korean owners were bribing him to allow drinks to be served. We both thanked them for their hospitality, paid the bill which was about 500 rupees (£6.00) for both of us, we then fell into Larbi's car which he had moved right outside the entrance to the restaurant. We both knew we would sleep tonight, so arranged for Larbi to wake us up at 10 a.m. in the morning. The plan was for him to take us to all the five-star hotels in the town centre, where we would use the facilities to freshen up.

Larbi arrived the next morning dead on time, we were both up and ready with our holdalls. The first hotel we arrived at was the Sheraton. Larbi again said he would wait for us outside. The commissioner on the door bid us a welcome, then we proceeded to the pool area. It was a beautiful hotel, the first thing you noticed was the air conditioning. You could also order alcoholic drinks at the bar, but the problem was you had to charge them to your room which was no good to David and myself. There were also three restaurants serving English and Chinese food. I could see that this pleased David, he said he would have something later. At the pool area we were given fresh towels, then escorted to our sun loungers. We were receiving five-star treatment. We felt like movie stars. We both had a dip in the pool, visited the spa pool and the sauna where we had a shave and got changed ready for the afternoon's entertainment. David bought himself a meal at the restaurant, it was an English Sunday lunch, roast beef with Yorkshire pudding; this I can tell you made his day.

Larbi had promised to take us to some beautiful beaches in the afternoon that were about an hour's drive away. The weather was again very hot, it must have been in the 80s. The Pakistan people certainly love their cricket, everywhere you turned you would see hundreds of children playing cricket matches all over the place. The beach Larbi took us to was very beautiful. To our amazement we saw a giant shark washed up on the beach. It was about ten feet long, all the children were gathered round it, the sea was deep blue. Larbi told me it was the Indian Ocean. David again was the only white face for miles around. I noticed a man about 100 yards away spot David, he then started to run forward in our direction. He was carrying a bag in one hand and appeared to be dragging what looked like a ferret on a lead in the other hand. Straightaway I asked Larbi what was going on? He then said "Mongoose fight snake. Would you like to watch?" I said "No way" but Dave asked how much it would cost. "100 rupees was the reply." "Give over Bruce, it's only £1.00. I can't miss this." I decided to watch the event from the safety of Larbi's car. Dave was very excited and paid the man his money. He then proceeded to take out a large silver snake from his bag, within seconds a crowd of small children appeared from nowhere to watch the fight and formed a circle. The snake tried to put up a good fight against the mongoose but the tactics used against it gave it no chance. The mongoose kept biting the snake's tail until it became worn out, then suddenly attacked it's head. The fight was over in about one minute. If I had been David I would have demanded my money back. As Dave was returning back to Larbi's car the old man asked if we would like to watch the mongoose fight a cobra? "Better fight" he said. To which Dave replied "No thanks."

We then made our way back to the Korean bar where again we drank Heineken, but this time we did not get too pissed; just enough to help us sleep. Our flight from Karachi to Tokyo was leaving at 6.45 a.m., on 29th November the day before the game. We were to make two stops on our way, one was at Islamaba where fortunately a lot of people left the aircraft, and the other was at Lahore. Larbi took us to the airport where our passport were returned to us. We both gave Larbi £10 each in Englis money. He was scared to death of accepting the gift off us but David insisted, so he took the money saying it was for his family. He said it was too much but considering the things he did for us and the places he took us to it was well worth the money. Another stop we made en route was to refuel at Beijing in China. None of us were allowed to leave the aircraft and after about an hour we were on the last lap of our journey, bound for Narita Airport, Tokyo.

We arrived at Tokyo International Airport at 3 p.m., on 29th November, which was a Monday. All together it had taken us twenty-one hours' flying time on a Jumbo Jet. I said to David "I hope it's worth it!" There was a taxi rank outside the airport, so we caught a taxi to Tommy's hotel which was called the Shiba Park. On our arrival I enquired if a Tommy Price had checked in and was told yes. They gave me his room and phone number. When I spoke to Tommy he told us to take our holdalls up to his room, number 204 on the second floor. Tommy had arrived earlier that morning and when we told him about our escapades he could not believe it. "Get changed" he said. "We are going out in the town." He was sharing with Derek Howarth, his brother Simon had decided to travel at the last moment, and he too was sneaking in the room. They had a twin room but now there was five of us sharing it. Both David and myself had a quick shower. Within half an hour we were both changed and drinking in the hotel bar. There was another crowd of people from Ashton-under-Lyne who had booked accommodation in the hotel. Their names were Nipper Royale, Nigel Barret, Cockney Mick Davies and Sammy Gilbey. Sammy had made this event his main holiday. He had booked two weeks off work to see the World Golf Championships in Kuala Lumpur and on his return journey had arranged a three-day stopover to see the game. So the Ashton mob had somehow got to Tokyo for the big game. Altogether there were about ten of us. We were all amazed at how many reds had made the trip from Manchester. My estimation was about a thousand people had made it. Tokyo is another beautiful place, it is very modern and clean as well as the people being very polite and honourable; they always bow their heads to you as a mark of respect.

As we were walking around Tokyo sightseeing, I noticed that they had their own Disney World and also that if the Japanese had a cold they would wear facemasks to prevent infection. The weather in Tokyo for that time of year was very similar to England. I am glad that we were prepared for this, by taking a couple of sweatshirts with us. The only problem I found with Tokyo was how expensive it was. We were paying £8 for a bottle of Heineken in the bars on the main street. The town is called Rogpongi, there are over one thousand bars in one street; you could get skint before you got drunk! The bars we always ended up in were called the Motown Bars, one and two. On the Monday night we were all drinking together in Motown two when Kevin Moran and Ashley Grimes walked in. They were surprised that we had recognised them. I spoke to Kevin saying to him how could you forget the first man to be sent off in FA Cup Final history. Kevin laughed and they both enjoyed the rest of the night with us. Another bar we used to drink in was an Irish bar called Paddy Maloneys. When I was at the bar getting a drink, met an old footballing friend who was a pipe-fitter/welder called Steve Lunt from Flixton. He had travelled to the game with Coco. Coco has followed the Reds for years; now running trips to United games. I was now beginning to wish I had taken Tommy's advice and paid £800 to go on Coco's trip as the journey back to Manchester was still at the back of my mind.

Next morning, on the day of the match, everyone was counting the cost of last night's session. I estimated that David and myself had spent over £100 each. Like I said we were nowhere near to being drunk. When you compare that to spending £6 in Karachi getting absolutely pissed and with food included, this gives you some idea of how we had gone from one extreme to another. On the day of the match, 30th November, all the lads were wearing their United colours. We were all singing and dancing with the Palmeris supporters, with Sammy Gilbey exchanging his United shirt for a Palmeris one. Three months earlier, Sammy had travelled with Ray Price and Mick Cox to the European Super Cup game against Lazio at Monaco's ground, where United were beaten by the Italians. Unfortunately I had to miss the game as it coincided with my family holiday in America. It is always good fun to be with Sammy on these occasions, the only bad thing I can say about him is that he is very careful with his money; some people are convinced he is a Scotsman! We all arrived at the stadium with plenty of time to spare. The stadium is actually in the city centre and is a wonderful sight. In fact Tokyo at night compares to nothing I have ever seen; no wonder they call Japan the land of the rising sun. The game was a complete sell out with the majority of the support being for United, which shows how far the club has gone from the seventies. Most of the Japanese supporters at the game were girls only interested in Ryan Giggs and David Beckham. I could not believe the boots they were wearing with eight-inch heels, they said they were copying the Spice Girls but they reminded me of the high heels worn in the seventies by ourselves.

The game kicked off at a fantastic pace with both teams going all out for an early goal. United's goalkeeper Mark Bosnich, who was our new signing to replace the great Dane Peter Schmeichel, was having a great game, making quite a number of fine saves. Roy Keane gave the Reds the lead after a great cross from Giggs that totally eluded the keeper. Perhaps it was against the run of play but who cared, the fans were jumping up and down embracing each other. This trophy nearly meant as much to me as winning the European Cup. United held on and we were crowned World Club Champions. Ryan Giggs was named 'man of the match' but my opinion was that Mark Bosnich should have been awarded it. 'What more could United achieve' I thought. That night everyone returned back to Tokyo, where everyone headed straight for the Motown bars. Money was no object, even Sammy Gilbey bought the first round. "It is not everyday your team is called the best in the world" he said. I still remind Sammy of that round today, I think he now has some regrets, as Sammy does not drink a lot. After buying the first round he had to ensure that everyone bought him one back, so he ended the night extremely drunk! At the game I bought my son Robert a Palmeris shirt. It is his prized possession; he never seems to take it off. Robert had pleaded with me to take him on this trip but I had other plans for him that I will explain later.

Our flight back to Manchester with Pakistan International Airlines should have been in the afternoon the day after the match, which was Wednesday 1st December, with Tommy and the rest of the lads leaving the day after. David and myself arrived at Narita Airport Tokyo, then proceeded straight to the check-in desk, but found to our disgust that the authorities would not let us board. The return journey again required the plane to refuel at Beijing in China. We were then asked to produce our visas, so I explained that our tour operator had told us that no visas were required, due to the fact that we were not actually disembarking. I also explained that no visas were asked for on our arrival, so why the problem on the return? All this arguing between the PIA staff and ourselves was to no avail, so I enquired as to what the alternative was? The Pakistan official, who I found to be both rude and untrustworthy, explained that if the Beijing authorities boarded the plane and found two British passengers without visas then the airline would be fined $4,000 each. If David and myself were prepared to hand over the money to him then he would ensure that it was returned to us in Manchester only then would he be prepared to let us board the aircraft. We both had a quick chat, but the plane was due to leave in less than half an hour. The problem was that even if we could get the money, which we couldn't, where can you put your hands on £2,600 each in half an hour when you are in an airport terminal. My mind went back to Simply Red's Mick Hucknall at Amsterdam Airport where Doss had misplaced our tickets. This situation was a lot more serious as places like Japan are not fluent in English like most of Europe and the British Consulate was thirty miles away. We just didn't know what to do. Our last resort was to ring a man we had met who lived and worked in Japan, his name was Gazza, he was a translator and could speak several different languages. He was a Jordanian who had lived in Tokyo for the last thirteen years. Our luck was in, Gazza told us to stay where we were, then came to our rescue. After lengthy discussions with the authorities it was decided that we would still not be allowed to board the aircraft, but due to Gazza's negotiation on our behalf we would be allowed to catch another PIA plane the day after, which did not fly over Chinese air space or refuel in Beijing. The plane we should have flown on took off after a two-hour delay due to two English lads, which gave us some comfort! Another bit of luck was that Tommy Price was not leaving until Thursday 2nd December, so Gazza took us both back to the Hotel Shiba Park. Tommy and the rest of the lads gave us a lot of stick. What more could we do than go out and get pissed.

In the morning Gazza picked us both up, then dropped us off at the airport. This time the same PIA official let us board the plane. At last we were on our way home, or so we thought. To our horror the plane was bound for Manila in the Philippines. It was totally the opposite direction to where we wanted to go. Then on the way back to Karachi we had to refuel in Dubai. This trip was going from bad to worse. Eventually when we arrived back in England, touching down at Heathrow, David and myself had spent more than sixty hours on Jumbo Jets. I was wondering if this was some kind of record to watch a Manchester United game? We arrived at Heathrow on Sunday 5th December. Originally the plan was to get home in time for the Everton game at Old Trafford on Saturday 4th December, which United won 5-. David didn't want to see another aeroplane and I had to agree, so we decided to catch the train back to Manchester courtesy of Richard Branson and Virgin trains.

When we arrived at Manchester Piccadilly I phoned my parents to ask them to get in touch with Adam to see if he could pick us up in my BMW. More bad news I'm afraid, my car had been stolen outside his house, and it had been involved in a bad accident due to joyriders. The garage was estimating the damage at over £6,000, so bang went my no-claims bonus. My renewal was due in December, so the cost of insuring my car had snowballed from £540 fully comprehensive to £1,500 with a £500 excess; it had nearly trebled — as you can see United have a lot to answer for. *The Manchester Evening News* covered our story. No one in Manchester could believe what lengths David and myself would go to watch Manchester United, but now the world knows.

United played Valencia at Old Trafford in the European Cup following our good win over Everton, easily outplaying the

Spaniards winning 3-0. To be perfectly honest they did not impress me at all. The good news was that United had qualified for the later stages, which were not to be played until the next March. The Reds were now playing with confidence, winning our next two games easily, 4-2 at West Ham and 4-0 over Bradford on Boxing Day, but my mind was now on the FIFA World Club Championships to be played in Brazil.

Before I go into more detail about that, the Reds had an important league game to play at Sunderland's Stadium of Light ground on Tuesday night, 28th December. This was my first trip to Sunderland's new ground. The Stalybridge branch had organised a full coach to take us there at £10 per head, plus the cost of the match tickets that were £22 each. I booked two seats for David Ashworth and myself. The coach left early in the morning ,arriving in Hartlepool about lunchtime. Nigel the branch organiser had arranged for the coach to stop off at a local pub near the town centre, where we were to meet some of the other Ashton lads. They made us very welcome. Again the beer was £1 a pint and the landlady even made pie and peas for us all. I wasn't very long before all the old songs were being sung. Next door was a bookmakers, so David and myself picked one horse each, then placed £20 on a double. Both horses came in, giving us a return of £120; the perfect start to the day I thought. By about 6 p.m., everyone was very drunk but no one was out of order. Nigel had asked everyone to be back at the coach park by 6 p.m., which we were, then we were on our way to the Stadium of Light. It was about half an hour before kickoff when we arrive at the new stadium, which was very impressive. Just as we were about to leave the coach the police arrived saying that as we were all so drunk, none of us were going to be allowed entrance to the game. They asked us all to get back in our seats, then we were to be given a police escort all the way back to Manchester. No one could believe what was happening. Yes people were drunk, but not to the state where they could not see the game. Anyway the police were not going to change their minds. One police car in front with two police motor cycles behind, began to escort us away from the ground. I said to Nigel that this was out of order. Nigel said there was nothing he could do about it, so old him that David and myself had not travelled all this way to e locked out and when the coach stops at some traffic lights we vere going to jump off and find our own way back after the ame. Nigel agreed to my request so at the next available red ght the driver reluctantly opened the doors. Both David and nyself made a run for it, jumped over a fence, then headed straight or the stadium without turning round. We could hear the police n their Tannoy system saying that if we did not return they vould set the police dogs on us, but we paid no attention to nem. We kept our heads down and kept on running. When we rrived back at the ground the match had just kicked off. underland took an early lead, then made it 2-0. I thought we ere dead and buried, but Roy Keane scored a great goal to ring us back into the game. United then pressed forward with licky Butt scoring the Reds' equaliser. It was a bit of a miss hit ut who cares, the Reds had made a great come back and the ame ended 2-2, which I thought was a fair result. It had been an ntertaining game, but the problem now was how do we get ome. On the way back to the coach park I spotted Mark dshead with the Stockport lads. Mark has been going to the eds as long as myself. We explained what had happened to the shton coach and he said no problem, giving us both a lift back Ashton.

The next day I called in the Star, which is a Boddingtons' pub a Ashton. I spoke to the landlord Bish who informed me that we vere the only two lads who got to see the game. The police had scorted the coach back as far as Huddersfield not Manchester, ut by then it would have been too late to get to the game. Steve lepburn the Supporters Club Chairman made a complaint to Jnited about the police behaviour. Apparently a coach full of Jnited supporters had caused havoc in a nearby town and they nought it was our coach, when in fact the coach they were poking for was Tony O'Neil's. So for the lads who didn't get ito the game it was a very expensive trip. No one on the coach ven got their money back for the match tickets.

The New Year approached with a lot of controversy. United ad entered the FIFA World Club Championships to be played a Brazil in January at the expense of not entering the FA Cup.

What made matters worse was that we were the holders and would not be able to defend our title as FA Cup winners. To me the FA Cup is the greatest knockout tournament in the world. have had the pleasure of playing in the qualifying rounds in my earlier days for Ashton United, so I was saddened to hear United would not be defending their trophy. It was also the first major trophy manager Alex Ferguson had won going back to 1990 when my friend Lee Martin had scored the winner over Crystal Palace, thus ensuring the Reds could set a platform to go onto better things. Even if United had sent out a virtual reserve side like they did in the League Cup, it would not have bothered me But to withdraw from the competition was something I could no agree with. Having not missed a FA Cup Final since 1963, I feel I am entitled to voice my opinion, which I did, but to no avail a the chairman Martin Edwards and the board of directors had made their minds up and nothing was going to make them change it.

My son Robert had begged me to take him to Tokyo to watc United, but I had promised him I would take him to Brazil instead His mother Carol said it would be ok if the school gave hir permission to go, which they did. Robert had also taken hi inoculations with myself, so even though I know Brazil is dangerous country I could not bring myself to tell him that h couldn't go, so we were now bound for Rio, leaving Mancheste on 3rd January with an eight-hour stopover in New York, bot outward and on our return. There were five of us that made th trip. We were to meet the other Ashton lads out there. The fiv people were my son Robert, Tommy and Dennis Price, Joh Clegg and myself. Dennis and John had been going to Unite matches with Tommy since the sixties, so Tommy had decided pay for them, leaving them only to find their spending money Over the next three weeks we were to have the best holiday of lifetime. We flew from Manchester at 10.15 a.m., arriving at Newar Airport, New York, at 12.30 p.m. lunchtime, giving us a full da to go sightseeing around the Big Apple. Robert could not clos his eyes in amazement at the sights. We took a yellow cab from the airport to the Statue of Liberty, then we were all dropped o

42nd Street where Tommy suggested we go to Madison Square Gardens, which is a wonderful place. We walked in Central Park, then down Broadway, we even went to the top of the Empire State Building and before you knew it the time had gone, it was now 8 p.m. In New York time waits for no one and I can understand why people call it the fastest city in the world. We had to be back for our flights to Rio two hours' before, so we flagged another taxi down who took us back to Newark Airport. The weather in New York was like it was back in England, which was very cold, so I said to Robert that on our return journey we could go to all the major stores like Lacey's to buy some winter clothes.

All the lads boarded the plane, there were no hold ups like, David Ashworth and myself had endured going to Tokyo in November. The plane left for Rio at 10 p.m., arriving at Rio International Airport at 9.30 a.m., on 4th January. My friend Gilles from the Meridian Beach Plaza in Monte Carlo had reserved us three twin rooms at the Meridian Hotel in Rio, which was again a five-star hotel. He had also ensured that we would be charged corporate rates, which saved us £50 a night, a big saving to most United fans. All our rooms had sea views. I can only describe Rio as the eighth wonder of the world, everything you hear about this place is true. The weather was in the hundreds, the women outnumber the men about fifty to one and the food and beer is very cheap, what more could you ask for? The drawback is that if you walk off the front, there is a good chance you will be mugged. We were also told not to go on the beaches after dark and not to wear any jewellery of any description. They also said only to carry enough money on you as you would need that day. These tips were well worth listening to as the crime rate in Rio is very high, there is reputed to be fifty murders a day and we did not want to be one of those statistics. I booked us all in at reception. The lads were very impressed and we also found out that the entire South Melbourne team along with their wives and relatives were staying at the Meridian for the entire duration of the tournament. Tommy Price, Robert and myself shared one twin room with Dennis Price and John Clegg sharing the other. The third room was for Sammy Gilbey and Brian Bundock who were arriving the next day. They had booked their holiday at the last minute. Sammy had got them a good deal, flying direct wit British Airways. I was amazed at how many United fans mad the trip. My estimates were about a thousand. United did n run any trips, as they were concerned for the safety of the supporters which I had to agree with; the Brazilians are fanatic about their team. The tournament was due to commence c Thursday 6th January and the Reds were in a group with Vasc da Gama from Rio and Nexaca from Mexico, along with th Australian champions South Melbourne. All our games were be played at the Maracana Stadium. The winners of each grou would play each other in the final; the runners-up would play f third and fourth place.

We quickly unpacked, changed into our shorts and tee shirt then made our way to the beach which was two minutes' awa Brazil has two beaches with breathtaking views; one beach called the Copacabana the other is called the Ipanema. Bo have a lot of records sang about them, we even had a meal at th restaurant where the lyrics were written for the song 'The g from Ipanema'. Whilst the lads were eating, Robert and I we walking back down the Copacabana beach when I heard a voi shout my name. I looked across and there stood a lad call Clifford Crehan who lived in Denton. I used to play football wi Cliff for Haughton Villa way back in the eighties. He had book his holiday to take in the millennium in Rio, travelling on his ov without any tickets for the games. Cliff had already been in R for one week, so he gave us some valuable advice about whe to go and where not to. I introduced Cliff to all the lads and h hotel was only around the corner from ours. The Brazilian beer only about thirty pence a pint, it is also quite strong so it was long before we were feeling the effects. Over the next day or we met more lads from Ashton. Big Nigel arrived along wi Nipper Royale and Cockney Mick Davies. There were also fo taxi drivers from Ashton who own Radio Cars, their name is Daekins. They travel all over watching the Reds. I seem to s one of them, Damian, wherever I go. We must have the sar taste in hotels. They too were booked in the Meridian, altogether about fifteen of us from Ashton had made the trip

The meeting place for all of us was the bar/restaurant outsi hotel called Mab's. As soon as we were all seated at our tables about fifty girls would arrive from nowhere. They were the most beautiful girls I had ever seen in my life, but as you can guess they were call girls. I was told that the price for a full day with one of these beauties was £20, but because I had Robert with me it never crossed my mind, but I have to admit I was very nearly tempted to at times especially after a few drinks at Mab's. The place was that cheap that no one complained whose round it was. At the end of the night we would share the bill amongst us; it would cost us at the most £10 each. The pricing structure was like it used to be in the seventies, so you can imagine no one complaining. When you walk along the front in Rio anything goes, it is like the rule of the jungle, which is why you have to have your wits about you. The locals are all trying to sell you something from guns, knifes even machetes — you name it in Brazil, you can buy it. We thoroughly enjoyed our first night in Rio but with all the travelling Robert had a bit of jet lag, so I took him up to bed. He slept well and it was lunchtime by the time we woke up.

The plan on Wednesday was to get taxis to the hotel where United were staying, then pick up our tickets. The hotel we were told to go to was the Sheraton Hotel in Rio, which was about three miles from our hotel. When we arrived at the hotel we were met by the club's secretary Ken Merrett, who advised us that due to security problems the United team had been moved to another hotel, one mile away, called the Inter Continental Hotel, but not to worry as United had arranged for minibuses to take us over to the team hotel to pick up our match tickets. Upon our arrival I bumped into Pat Crerand who was commentating for Piccadilly Radio. Paddy had just finished lunch with the team and told me that later on he would introduce me to all the players. Also the Real Madrid team were staying in the same hotel as the Reds, so I then proceeded to the ticket office where I purchased all the tickets for the lads, remembering Cliff, Sammy and Brian, eight in total. The cost of the match tickets will tell you how cheap it is in Brazil, the three group matches and the final, cost £30. Can you tell me one Premiership ground in our country that charges £7.50 admission? Considering this was the World Club

Championships it was hard to believe, but yet again no one w
complaining. Once we had received our tickets, we had a drink
the hotel bar. Paddy kept his word and introduced Robert a
myself to all the United players. Robert had his photogra
taken with all his idols; they also signed his autograph boo
the smile on his face will live with me forever. I was al
introduced to the ex-Liverpool player Steve McMannaman wl
I found to be a decent person. He offered to take Robert over
all the Real Madrid team to get their photos and autograph
Robert's best memory of the trip was meeting David Beckha
followed by meeting the great Brazilian Roberto Carlos. My be
memory was meeting Zico the great Brazilian free kick speciali
who now coaches the children at his ex-club Flamengo. I cou
not resist buying Robert a Brazil shirt, but Robert wanted tl
great Ronaldo number nine on the back of his shirt — he h
never heard of Zico. 'How time flies' I thought. 'Robert is on
eleven years old and Zico was someone famous from tl
seventies.' Our second day in Rio vanished quickly. By the tin
we had spoken to all the players from both teams, then receiv
our tickets, it was getting towards 8 p.m. I must say that Unit
treated the fans who made the trip to Brazil with the utmo
respect — sitting down chatting with the fans. It is somethir
you could only dream about, but for one United fan it was h
dream come true; his name was Robert Nathan MacInne
Tommy Price rang for two taxis to take us back to the hotel whe
we met all the South Melbourne team. I found them to be workin
class lads, as a lot of their squad had only recently turne
professional. They only get crowds of about 8,000, so we
looking forward to playing Manchester United. All their sponso
had paid large amounts of money to have their names on the
shirts for the televised matches that were being shown all ov
the world. The problem they had was that FIFA would onl
allow two names on their shirts, but they eventually relente
and allowed the South Melbourne team to have all the
sponsors' names on their shirts. It wasn't long before Samm
Gilbey was introducing himself to all the FIFA delegates stayir
at the Meridian. He managed to convince them that he was tl
chairman of the Manchester United Supporters Club, and befo

you knew it Sammy had a collection of shirts and badges for everyone free of charge.

Thursday 6th January was our first game at the Maracana Stadium, against the Mexican champions Rayos De Nexaca. Everyone in our party was very excited at the prospect of United playing in the great Maracana Stadium. I remember back in the seventies when a rival semi-professional football team, whose name was Grassmere Rovers, played a match in the great Maracana Stadium. They used to go on tours as Manchester FC — the Brazilians thought they were Manchester United! A local lad called Micky Dewhurst scored for Manchester FC, ironically he is a City supporter. Manchester lost the game 2-1 but the people in Manchester still talk about the trip, as apparently 30,000 watched the game. The Meridian Hotel organised a coach to take us to the game. Everyone was wearing their United colours. The atmosphere on the way to the game was truly amazing. I instructed Robert to stay at my side no matter what. Our coach approached some traffic lights near to the Maracana, when the United team coach pulled up alongside us. The players could not believe what they were seeing — a full coach of Manchester United supporters who had travelled half way round the world. The players, including the manager Alex Ferguson, were taking photographs of us. Can you believe that the likes of Yorke, Becks and Giggs were taking photos of Tommy Price and Bruce MacInnes? "Fame at last" I said to Tommy! The coach dropped us off at the ground and we arranged for the driver to pick us up at half-time in the second game. The first two games were United against Nexaca at 18.15, then Vasco da Gama against South Melbourne at 20.45. Tommy led us to the first bar outside the ground where we started to sing all the old songs. The Vasco da Gama fans were joining in with all the festivities, they were even buying us drinks and encouraging us to sing more songs. Tommy had a bright white hanky on his head and was wearing his United shirt. We were told later on by Pat Crerand that Tommy's face was shown all over the world! We left the bar a little worse for wear, then entered the Maracana Stadium, which was about half full but even so the atmosphere is something to be witnessed. I have been to some of the great stadiums in

Europe, but all I can say is the Maracana, although a bit dated must have opened a few eyes in its day. It is a magnificent stadium, built for supporters whose passion for their team has to be seen to be believed. The game against the Mexicans was played at a tremendous pace but ended a 1-1 draw; Dwight Yorke scoring United's goal. We watched the first half of the Vasco da Gama game, which they won easily and we knew then that the game we had to win was against the Brazilians. One thing that surprised me about the Maracana is that they do not have turnstile operators to let you in. Instead they use swipe cards which they click when you are in the ground. Fifty yards further on you are searched for knives, guns, etc. Anything they find on you will be returned at a price. After the game we saw piles of knives and machetes all piled up against a wall. They take their football very seriously indeed and I now know why United did not take any of their own trips to the games.

No one wanted to hang around the ground after the game, so the coach driver took us back to Mab's restaurant, where by now word had spread round that the United supporters were there. The waiting time for a table outside was about thirty minutes. The place was full of Brazilian girls. The place is hard to describe; the food is very good; you eat until you are full; the girls outnumber the men ten to one and everyone enjoys the carnival atmosphere. About a mile from Mabs is a nightclub called Help. It is reputed to be one of the biggest clubs in South America as it holds up to 5,000 people. A few of the lads tried it out after United's first game and their stories were amazing. Tommy Price told me that the champagne was only about £4.00 a bottle; the girls outnumbered the men ten to one and all the men in there were United supporters. We also heard stories of United fans having doubles and trebles with the ladies, but the only problem was that you could not tell the women from the men. In Brazil you will find that it is very difficult for a lad to find work so a lot of them have had sex changes, they call them girlie boys and it is very difficult to tell them apart.

The day after the game was spent lounging around the pool area topping up our suntans. My son Robert loves swimming; the pool at the Meridian is on the fourth floor, they even have their own secluded area on the beach, which you can use without being disturbed by the locals. Robert and myself decided to go for a walk along the front. We entered the other hotels without any problem. One hotel that was about 100 yards from the Meridian was very special indeed. It was called the Copacabana Palace Hotel — again it was a five-star hotel. We saw Gary Lineker the ex-England centre forward having a drink of coffee in the restaurant. He was with the Match of the Day team. Mick McCarthey the Irish manager was with him along with Trevor Brooking and David Davies. Robert had his photograph taken with them and they also signed his autograph book, which pleased him. He also wanted me to buy him a Vasco da Gama shirt, who the Reds were playing the next day, so we went along to this shopping centre. The Brazilians are very fashion conscious, we spent hours looking around and I bought Robert his Vasco shirt for about £8.00; we also bumped into the ex-United captain Steve Bruce who had a quick chat with us. When we got back to the Meridian all the lads were talking to the South Melbourne team. They had been using the pool to do their stretching exercises. The players had told Tommy Price that they were not getting paid a lot of money for the tournament. A lot of the players were entitled to get their own sponsors, the club had paid for the rooms at the Meridian but all other expenses had to be paid for by the players. I couldn't believe it but Tommy got the South Melbourne centre forward who was a TV maintenance engineer to make some modifications to our TV, so we could then watch all the latest programmes at no extra cost to ourselves. The food at the Meridian was top class; the Manchester United chairman Martin Edwards was surprised to see how many Reds' supporters were staying there.

I must admit that I was a little concerned at United's interest in the tournament. The Reds never really showed real commitment in the first game against the Mexicans. Vasco da Gama was going to be the real test, as the Maracana is their home ground. The game was played in front of 73,000 fanatical supporters, which was very near to the full capacity, which due to redevelopment was now 90,000. Every time the United supporters tried to sing to encourage their team on, we were drowned out by the hordes of Vasco fans that surrounded us. The game commenced with Vasco straight away attacking the Reds. They had two great forwards in Edmundo and Romario; these two were dragging United's back four all over the place. Poor old Gary Neville was having a nightmare, we faulted him for the first two Vasco goals. It did not help having David Beckham suspended. Becks had to miss the game through suspension as he was sent off late in the Rayos Del Nexaca game for retaliation. Vasco wanted to win more than the Reds, so the game ended 3-1 to the Brazilians. Nicky Butt scored United's goal but results elsewhere ensured that the Reds were out. They could only secure third or fourth place and our last game was against South Melbourne at the Maracana on 11th January.

The Australians kindly let us travel to the game with them on their supporters' coach, so we were with all the players' wives and relatives. I felt very sorry for the Aussies, this was the biggest game in their club's history, the match was being televised all over Australia but unfortunately the game was disappointing. United won 2-0 with Quinton Fortune scoring both goals for the Reds in front of 25,000 fans. United missed a hat full of chances which made me feel that they were not interested in third or fourth place. Alex Ferguson now had one eye on United's next Premier League game, which was against Arsenal at Old Trafford.

The other group's results at the Morumbi Stadium in Sao Paulo ensured that the final was a Brazilian affair between the top two teams, Vasco da Gama from Rio against Corinthians from Sao Paulo, the game was played on 14th January. The Corinthians boast the country's second largest number of supporters and they are currently one of the country's best teams, but nevertheless it strives to overcome the fact that they had never conquered an expressive title in International competitions. The club have made investments to set up a true all-star team, signing goal keeper Dida, full back Carlos and striker Luizao but they lost their coach Wanderley Luxemburgo who took over the National Brazil team; but this does not seem to have affected them. Any team that can beat Real Madrid must be taken seriously. I was a little disappointed in the Reds as would have liked to see them take on the great Real Madrid; little did I know what was in store for us in the European Cup.

It was decided amongst all the lads that even though United were on their way back home, there was no way we were going to miss the final. It was played at the Maracana in front of a full house crowd; nearly 90,000. The Corinthians brought 20,000 fans with them from Sao Paulo; it was a six-hour coach journey but they didn't seem to care. The seats, which were reserved for the United supporters, were filled with Corinthian supporters. Tommy supported the Corinthians whilst Robert and myself wanted Vasco to win. It was a good final with the Corinthians coming out on top winning the first World Club Tournament. The Corinthian supporters were locked in the ground for five hours after the game. When we returned to our coach, we noticed that all the Corinthians supporters' coaches had been damaged. Most of the windows on the coaches had also been smashed. Like I said before, the Brazilians take their football very seriously — it is definitely more important than life and death.

There was still over one week of our holiday left. People can say what they like about United not entering the FA Cup but my opinion is that this tournament was a success. Everyone who came over to Brazil that I spoke to had thoroughly enjoyed themselves and we hope that they continue with the World Club Championships each year. It can only be a good thing for football, to compare yourself with other teams from around the world. It is like a mini World Cup. I know when I say this that all the lads are praying that the tournament is held in Brazil again, myself included, but wherever they decide to play it if Manchester United are invited to compete I will be there. Our last week in Brazil was spent sunbathing. We also went on a full-day boat trip to all the surrounding islands. The cost of this was about 15.00 a head, with all the food and drink included. We all had a great time, with Tommy and Sammy even managing to get a round of golf in, played at a nearby course. They met an Englishman whilst playing, his name was John Stanley Pickston. Tommy was so impressed with some of the stories Johno was telling him that he brought him back to the Meridian to meet me along with all the other lads. I was also very impressed with Johno whom I found to be a wonderful character, who had travelled all around the world. He had now decided to settle in Brazil where he lives with his wife. The apartment they shared was just around the corner from the hotel. Johno was about sixty-seven years old and his best friend was the Great Train Robber, Ronald Biggs. I must say that I found it very hard to believe some of the escapades that he had been involved in. He told me that some people who were involved in the Great Train Robbery had never been caught, and he also asked us if we would like to meet Ronnie Biggs. I said "Of course, the man is a piece of British history" so Johno rang Ronnie who was just recovering from a stroke. His son said it would be no problem to call round at their house the next day for a chat, so Johno stayed with us for the rest of the day; he even came over to Mab's restaurant for a few drinks.

The next morning two taxis picked us all up at the hotel and off we went to visit the Great Train Robber Ronald Biggs. His Rottweiler greeted us at his house, and the entire morning was spent listening to Ronnie's son tell us stories about the robbery. Ronnie's recovery from his stroke had taken a little longer than expected. He is a tall man about six foot two inches, we all had our photographs taken with him. He placed his arms around Robert and asked how England was. He told us all that he would like to return one day and his favourite team was Arsenal. You should have seen all the famous people that had visited him from pop stars like Rod Stewart, to footballers like the great Bobby Moore. No matter how famous these people were, they all had found the time to visit Ronnie. In the afternoon Johno invited us to his apartment for a few drinks and to meet his wife who is a lovely lady. Robert was intrigued by her collection of diamonds and precious stones. Brazil is a place where you can buy diamonds very cheaply. Tommy decided to have a ring made of 22-carat gold with a blue topaz set in the middle of it. It looked like the heart of the ocean from the film Titanic; the ring was ready for Tommy the day before we were due to return home.

Our holiday was coming to an end, we only had two days left and everyone was beginning to feel depressed at the thought of returning to England in the middle of winter. Another great trip we went on was to Sugar Loaf Mountain; this is where the giant statue of Jesus Christ is set high up at the top of the mountain. The views from the top have to be seen to be believed. The cable cars take you right to the peak, when you reach the top you can take a helicopter ride around the mountain and down the sandy beaches of the Copacabana and the lpanema. This was a ride we couldn't refuse. So Robert, Clifford, Dennis and myself paid £25.00 each to do the 25-minute tour. I had never been in a helicopter before; my heart was in my mouth. The helicopter takes you fifty yards from the statue; we went right over our hotel; the views we saw left me breathless and again I could see the excitement in Robert's eyes.

On our last day we spent the morning buying presents for everybody. Our flight was not departing until 22.00 on 21st January. No one wanted to leave, I wished that the tournament went on for four weeks! We all arrived at Rio International Airport bound for New York; everyone said their goodbyes and boarded the plane with no delays, everyone slept for most of the return journey.

We arrived back at Newark Airport, New York, at 06.15. It was 22nd January. No one expected the weather to be like it was — minus six below freezing. We had gone from one extreme to the other. New York was having a terrible winter, one it had not witnessed for many years. Our connecting flight back to Manchester was not until 8 p.m. the same day, so we had two choices, we could either hang around the airport all day or take a taxi into New York, then walk around all the major stores. We decided to walk around the major stores, so we all wrapped up in our winter clothes then caught a taxi. The major stores like Lacey's have everything you can think of at very competitive prices, so I bought Robert some tee shirts and trainers. The Americans really know how to make you spend your money, you are spoilt for choice. We all had some lunch in one of the many restaurants near to Broadway then flagged a taxi back to the airport. Robert and Tommy played computer games all the way back and the plane touched down at Manchester Airport at 08.45 on Sunday 23rd January. The lads had been on tour for nearly three weeks. "Brazil is the nearest thing to heaven I have ever seen" Dennis Price said to me. You are dead right there Dennis. You can stick the FA Cup, who wants to travel to Wimbledon on a cold winter's night in January? 'How my opinions had changed' I thought.

You have to admire our timing, as on Monday night it was United's first game back in the Premiership. Results had gone our way and the mid-season break would do us no harm. In fairness the Reds had used the tournament just for that. Alex Ferguson's team selection for the last game against South Melbourne disappointed everybody, but he obviously knew the Arsenal game was important to us. Arsenal again needed to win to keep their chances alive. The game ended in a dull 1-1 draw, with Teddy Sheringham scoring for the Reds. United then proceeded to win their next three matches. 1-0 at home to Middlesborough, avenging that shock defeat at Old Trafford the season before. United's next away game was to our bogey side Sheffield Wednesday on Wednesday 2nd February. This game coincided with a promotion from Rogersons Brewery at the Top Wok restaurant in Ashton. Rogersons Brewery is situated in Ashton and both Tommy and myself use them for most of our beer orders. They are a very organised firm who give you competitive prices and they had kindly given us a table for ten at the promotion. The promotion was to try out all the latest beers and Alcopops, followed by a Chinese meal; needless to say this was all free of charge. It started at 1 p.m., and by the time we were due to catch the coach at 6 p.m., everyone was extremely drunk. We eventually got to Hillsborough but I cannot remember much of the game. I know we won 1-0 thanks to Teddy Sheringham who scored the winner. I again missed the coach back to Stalybridge along with Ray Price, but luckily I saw a friend of mine who I worked with at the Prudential, his name is Mark Wilson. Mark kindly dropped us off at the Pineapple in Stalybridge where we had a few drinks — the coach bringing back the lads arrived about thirty minutes after us!

This match was followed by a 3-2 home win over Gordon Strachan's Coventry City. Strachan had been upset about remarks made by Alex Ferguson in his recently published autobiography, but had kept his pride by not retaliating. The Reds had a testing time in mid-February losing 3-0 to an Alan

Shearer inspired Newcastle. Every time we play them they raise their game. This tells me why everyone loves to play Manchester United. If Bobby Robson's Newcastle had played like this every week they would be up there with us challenging for the title. I must admit the goal scored by Duncan Ferguson was a fine effort. The Reds now had to travel to our Yorkshire rivals at Elland Road and face an in form Leeds team, but there was trouble in the United camp. Rumours were circulating that Alex Ferguson and David Beckham had fallen out over something trivial. The papers as expected had covered the full story. I must admit that I was surprised when I went to Elland Road to find that David Beckham had been dropped. He was not even named as one of the subs, so there must have been some truth in the rumours. You have to admire a manager like Alex Ferguson who can make decisions like this, as they can so easily go against you, but in this case it went United's way and Andy Cole scored the winner, with the game ending 1-0.

Our next game was away to Wimbledon. David Beckham returned to play central midfield in place of the injured Roy Keane. The Reds came away with a 2-2 draw after going behind twice, and Mark Bosnich was under a lot of pressure in goal. He looked a bit shaky, but goals from Cruyff and Cole kept the Reds at the top of the league. March was now upon us and it was time to restart our European campaign, where the visitors to Old Trafford were the French side FC Girondins Bordeaux. They put up a good fight but lost 2-0. What surprised the United supporters was Alex Ferguson's decision to drop our goalkeeper Mark Bosnich and replace him with Rai Van Der Gouw. The goalkeeper's position had never been the same since the departure of Peter Schmeichel. United's defence had always been the backbone in past Premiership campaigns, but this season our goals against were beginning to make me feel a little nervous.

Saturday 4th March was Robert's birthday and we were playing Liverpool at Old Trafford, so I took Robert to the game as his birthday treat. To be fair to Liverpool they had turned the corner from the bad start to the season they had had, and were now on a bit of a roll, beating some top sides in the process. They were now near the top of the table on merit and we knew this wouldn't be an easy game. Alex Ferguson decided to keep Rai Van De Gouw in goal. Liverpool took the lead only for Ole Gunner Solskjaer to equalise on the stroke of half-time whilst Liverpool had a man off the pitch receiving treatment for an injury. The game ended all square at 1-1. I couldn't have any complaints as a draw was a fair result.

On Tuesday 7th March the Reds were playing our away fixture to FC Girondins Bordeaux. I booked to go with Tommy on the one-day 'in and out' trip with United; the Reds winning the game 2-1 but not without a scare. Our goalkeeper Rai Van De Gouw made a terrible mistake to give them the lead, but Roy Keane equalised for United, then Alex Ferguson produced masterstroke when he brought on Ole Gunner Solskjaer, who with his first touch brought the ball down, eluded three players then coolly slotted the ball home. The Reds held on to win 2-1 our dreams of retaining the European Cup were still alive. Our next game at Old Trafford was the visit of Derby County. All eyes were on Dwight Yorke who was going through a barren patch — his last goal for United was in the World Club Championships back in January. He had a great game, scoring hat trick. The Reds won 3-1; people were already saying that the league title was over.

Wednesday 15th March was Manchester United's last home game in the Champions League. It gave us a great chance to gain revenge over the Italians Fiorentina for the away defeat way back in November when we lost 2-0. The game was a classic. The Argentine Batistuta gave Fiorentina an early lead with thirty yard unstoppable shot, which gave the United keeper Bosnich no chance; Van Der Gouw's error over in Bordeaux had cost him his place. Roy Keane dragged the Reds back into the game with Cole and Yorke scoring further goals to give the Reds a great 3-1 win. United followed this up with a 2-0 win at Leicester City. A gap was beginning to appear in the title race. Arsenal manager Arsene Wenger was moaning as usual, saying that United's January break had helped them. No one took any notice of him. Our main concern now was to progress to the European Cup quarterfinals.

Our last game in the group was away against the Spaniards

lencia. This coincided with Ray Price's fortieth birthday, so
out forty of the lads from the Stalybridge branch booked one
ek's holiday in an all-inclusive hotel in Benidorm, called the
ystal Park. I managed to get four tickets for the game from
ited. Our plan was to fly with Easy Jet from Liverpool to
rcelona, then hire a car to drive through to Benidorm where
would meet the rest of the lads. When we arrived at Barcelona
rport, it was about 1 p.m. their time on Sunday 19th March.
e four lads who came on the trip were Ray Price, Tino who
d never been to an away trip with United before, Ralph Paddy
apburn the Arsenal supporter and myself. I hired a car from
e airport for five days. We were due to fly back to Manchester
Thursday 23rd March. We had made one mistake, Paddy had
d me that Benidorm was only a three-hour drive away, when
fact it is a seven-hour drive. On the plane going over we met
Blackburn fan called Colin who was on his own. His intentions
re to have a week in Barcelona. In our discussions he told us
was a HGV driver who drove all around Europe. Paddy asked
n if he fancied five days in Benidorm instead, so after a bit of
rsuasion Colin agreed to come with us, so now our problems
re over. Colin knew the roads, then proceeded to drive us to
et the rest of the lads arriving in Benidorm at about 8 p.m. We
en asked for directions to the Crystal Park Hotel that was
uated in the old side of Benidorm. It wasn't very hard to find
e hotel as we could hear United songs. Knowing it could only
the Stalybridge branch. We met up with them all. They offered
let us bunk in with them, but I said no thanks. Straight across
e road was another hotel that was not all inclusive. The price
r a room was £15.00 a night, so we booked two twin rooms
th Colin, Ray and myself sharing one and Paddy and Tino the
er. We only used the hotel to get our heads down and for
ving a quick shower. For the full five days we used the Crystal
rk facilities, eating three meals a day. No one challenged us.
ere was about fifty Manchester United fans in the party. The
r in the hotel was open until midnight and each day all your
nks were free. Our lads certainly took advantage of this, there
no way on God's earth that the hotel made any money on this
rty's booking. The lads from Stalybridge, the likes of John

225

Redfearn and Nigel Roberts know how to drink. Then you ha
the Dukinfield lads like Dale Ellis, his brother Shag and Harr
Gill, not to mention the Ashton lads like Michael Walker, Winni
Sid Royale plus many more.

After the hotel bar closed at midnight, we would all hea
down to Benidorm centre where it was packed with Unite
supporters. The first night we went into a bar called Ca
Benidorm which is a massive bar. Most of the bars ha
entertainment on; this bar had a Liverpool comedian on. No o
in the entire place was laughing at any of his jokes; I felt sor
for him as he took terrible abuse. In the end he just stormed o
By the end of the night we were all very drunk, and an incide
nearly occurred with the doormen who all carry batons. Wh
had happened was, we were all having a laugh, Billy Crooks w
with Joe Lee who has a pub in Droylsden, knocked over a f
table of drinks; within seconds the doormen appeared a
escorted them to the door. The bar suddenly emptied; all of
finished our drinks and left with them. The doormen soon realis
we were all together and backed off. It could have got nasty b
thankfully it didn't. The weather in Benidorm was quite nice
that time of year and I was very surprised at how many peo
were on holiday over there; the place was packed. I had n
visited Benidorm since 1976. How it had changed, as there a
hundreds of bars everywhere you turn. All we did was dri
drink, then more drink. Colin had left our car parked outside
hotel on a side street. On Monday morning he walked past
see if everything was still ok, but when he returned he s
"Bruce, you are not going to believe this, but the car has be
towed away." He had left it in a restricted area, so the police h
towed it to a local compound where we had to pay £40 to hav
returned.

United's match against Valencia was on Tuesday night 2
March. Most of the lads had booked to go on a coach from a
called the Stretford Ender. Thousands of United fans must ha
had the same idea, as it seemed like every good Red fr
Manchester was in Benidorm. I bumped into Gary Wright v
was with all the Droylsden lads, as well as Tony O'Neill who
travelled over with Easy Jet like myself. Valencia was a two-h

226

ive away from Benidorm. We had convinced Colin to drive us
ere, by buying him a match ticket for £50 from a Scottish lad in
e Stretford Ender. We loaded up the car with a few cases of
n Miguel, then headed off for Valencia where we had arranged
meet the rest of the gang, Tino was enjoying the trip, he even
anaged to meet up with a friend of his that was working in
neker's bar over there. It was about 4 p.m. when we arrived at
alencia's ground. Colin had done well, getting us all there in
e-piece. Valencia is an industrial town, nothing like Benidorm.
e police were all over the place; they were obviously expecting
ot of Manchester United supporters to be at the game. Both
ams had a good chance to progress to the next round, which
as the quarterfinal. We all entered a wine bar near to the ground.
was only £2.00 for a bottle of wine, needless to say the place
as jam-packed with United supporters. We met up with the
tire Stalybridge branch, they were all pissed and everyone
as enjoying themselves singing and dancing. John Redfearn
as encouraging everyone to sing up for the champions. MUTV
ere filming everyone outside the bar. They saw that I was
earing my Brazil cap with all the club badges of the teams we
d played on the front, so I was interviewed about the World
ub Championships and then Tokyo. They then asked me how
hought the Reds would go on against Valencia without the
spended David Beckham? I replied jokingly "It will be close,
t I think we will win 5-0!" They then asked Paddy Chatburn
w he thought we would do; to which Paddy replied "'I don't
re mate. I'm an Arsenal fan and I'm only here for the beer!"
lin then told them he was a Blackburn Rovers fan and how we
d virtually kidnapped him in Barcelona. MUTV showed the
terviews at 7 p.m. that night. 'Another claim to fame' I thought
myself. It was now time to get into the ground. Valencia's
dium is only small when you compare it to the likes of
rcelona. There was a capacity crowd of nearly 50,000 to cheer
both teams. We were seated up in the gods, which was a bit
e being sat in United's new third tier; so the view was very
sappointing. The first half commenced with both teams playing
me entertaining football. However results elsewhere were going
th teams' way, so if the result stayed 0-0 both teams would

qualify for the quarterfinals. This sequence of events resulted in both teams keeping possession, without any team trying to penetrate the other's defence. Both teams played out a 0-0 draw to the delight of both sets of fans. This could not have happened in the old days, when the games were played over two legs on straight knockout basis, but we were not complaining as the Reds had progressed to yet another European Cup quarterfinal. We were all ecstatic when the draw was made, we had avoided Barcelona and drawn the great Real Madrid whose name is associated with the European Cup. It took me back to 1968 when my older brother Wallace and myself were glued to the radio upstairs in our bedroom. United were playing Real Madrid away in the European Cup semifinal. We had a 1-0 lead from the first leg, thanks to a great goal scored by George Best, but would the slight advantage be enough to take us through, especially as the game was at the San Bernabou a graveyard for most visitors. United were slaughtered in the first half, they went in at the interval 3-1 down. I don't know what Sir Matt Busby said to the team, but in the second half it was a different story. United were all out on the attack and deservedly scored two goals to bring us back into the game against all odds. Even the goal scorer that night could not believe what had happened, our centre half Bill Foulkes who had survived the Munich disaster scored for the Reds along with David Sadler, these two rarely got their names on the score sheet. Now more than thirty years later I have the chance to visit the San Bernabou.

The away leg was to be played on the 4th April, but before that game the Reds had to concentrate on the Premiership where we had built up a good lead over our nearest rivals who were Liverpool. They had moved up to second place in the table. On our return from Valencia we easily defeated Bradford City 4-0 at Old Trafford, then on the following Saturday, 1st April, we destroyed West Ham 7-1, again at Old Trafford, with Paul Scholes scoring a hat trick, but the night belonged to Alex Ferguson as it was his final tribute dinner.

This was the final event of Sir Alex Ferguson's testimonial year at the G-Mex in Manchester. This last year will live in the memories of all Manchester United supporters everywhere thanks to Sir Alex's incredible treble winning achievement with Manchester United. Now Tommy and myself had the opportunity to participate in what promised to be an equally memorable evening of football, food and fun, to pay tribute to the boss. I booked a table for ten people at £155 per person plus VAT. Manchester United players both past and present, along with many people from the world of music, sport and politics attended the event, which was likely to be the biggest Manchester has ever hosted. The G-Mex is one of Manchester's most impressive landmarks. It had been transformed to create the perfect backdrop for a tribute dinner in honour of Sir Alex. The expert hands of the North West's most celebrated chef Paul Heathcote prepared the food; there was also a free bar, which is always useful when there are ten of you, as no one can argue about whose round it is. It was a black tie event so Tommy and I had ordered our dinner suits from a shop in Ashton. Tommy tried to book the Midland Hotel for one night on the day of the dinner, but he was told they only had one room left which was a suite at £460 for a twin room due to the demand. The Midland is situated straight facing the G-Mex centre. Tommy politely refused the suite at £460. I then decided to ring George Best's agent Phil Hughes to see what he could do for us. I remembered him once saying to me that if we ever needed rooms at the Midland to give him a ring. I had not stayed at the Midland since the time I met George Best along with Denis Law and Paddy Crerand the day they opened my nightclub. Phil kept his word ringing me back a little later. To my amazement he had secured us a twin room at £70, what a difference a phone call can make? Tommy checked us in at the hotel reception. He spoke to the same chap who had quoted him £460. "It's not what you know, it's who you know" he said to him. The chap smiled politely then said that the hotel is full now. We had the same suite that Tommy was quoted £460, so we couldn't complain. Some of the lads who came to the dinner with us were David Clay and Simon Howarth, all the others were Tommy's friends from his pub in Denton called the Top House. From start to finish it was pure entertainment, everyone enjoyed the event, which was well worth the money. Our table was two tables away from the players and their wives. We were seated in the World Club Champions section. The whole area was split into four quarters; the FA Cup, the Championship, the European Cup and our section which was by far the best for its views of all the celebrities and the stage. Considering there were over 2,000 people at the event, David Beckham's wife Posh Spice stood out amongst the crowd. We all had our photos taken with our idols from both past and present; people like Martin Buchan, Joe Jordon, Gordon McQueen, Bryan Robson and many more were there along with their partners. At the last count we had our photos taken with sixty celebrities. No matter who they were, they had to walk past our table. No one famous got past our table without having their photo taken alongside Tommy Price or myself. The highlight of the night was Mick Hucknall's appearance to sing a special song for the boss. It was an old Nat King Cole song which brought the house down. I had made security aware to let Mick Hucknall know I was there situated near the team. After his special appearance he came over to our table where he stayed with us for ten minutes; everyone was snapping away with their cameras. Michael had flown in specially for the event, but had to make a quick exit saying "Enjoy the rest of the night. See you soon." Another great sight was Alex Ferguson's speech. He was clearly surprised by the turnout. His voice was full of emotion when he spoke about his time at Manchester United. This night was by far the best tribute dinner I had ever attended. The night ended with an auction, which raised thousands of pounds for the boss. An Eric Cantona shirt went for £20,000 but the top prize was £25,000 that someone paid for a signed pair of David Beckham boots. The evening ended at midnight when there was a disco which played on until the early hours. We all ended up drinking in the hotel residents bar along with the ex-players. I asked Paul Parker to judge who could pick the best United side from the ten of us over the last thirty years. We all gave him £10 each to give to the winner. Paul had played for United as well as England, but I was unhappy with his decision that David Clay's team should win; so he won the money. Just for the record my best United side over the last thirty years is as follows;

1
Peter Schmeichel

2
Arthur Albiston

4
Martin Buchan

3
Dennis Irwin

5
Japp Stam

8
David Beckham

7
Bryan Robson

6
Roy Keane

11
George Best

10
Mark Hughes

9
Eric Cantana

Subs; Bobby Charlton, Denis Law, Ryan Giggs
Manager; Sir Alex Ferguson
Assistant Manager; Sir Matt Busby

My worst United team consists of the following;
1 Paddy Roach 2 Tommy O'Neill 3 Colin Gibson 4 Ian Ure
5 Arnie Sidebottom 6 Ashley Grimes 7 Alan Brazil
8 Alan Foggan 9 Gary Birtles 10 Terry Gibson 11 Ralph Milne

Subs; Massimo Taibi, Steve James, Ron Davies, Tommy Baldwin,
Tommy Jackson
Manager; Frank O'Farrel
Assistant manager; Dave Sexton

Before we knew it it was 5 a.m. Tommy and myself had enjoyed
it that much, we missed breakfast in the morning as usual. The
events from the night before will live with me forever.

April was now upon us and it was time for our Titanic battle
with the Spanish giants Real Madrid. This was my chance to
watch United against one of the best European sides left in the
competition. Tommy Price and myself booked with Manchester
United to go on the one-day trip from Manchester with the club.
We arrived in Madrid at lunch time on Tuesday 4th April,

straightaway we headed for the Grand Via, which I ha
remembered was where all the best bars and restaurants wer
situated from my last visit, but I wanted to forget United's resul
that time, as we got slaughtered 3-0 to Athletico Madrid. All th
Irish bars in the Grand Via were packed with United supporters
What made our day was when Eric Cantona entered the ba
Tommy and I were in. He was accompanied by Ned Kelly th
head of United's security, who is still a close friend of his. Eri
signed autographs for us both; how we wished we had a camer
with us; it was like a dream come true. When it was time to retur
to our coaches to travel to the San Bernabou Stadium, Tomm
had the idea of getting the tube instead. "It will be quicker" h
said. So from Madrid's Grand Via Station we caught the tube t
where Tommy thought was Real Madrid's ground. Can yo
believe it, but he had us going in totally the wrong direction! B
the time we had switched trains and got to the ground it wa
half-time, so through no fault of my own I can only describe th
second half performance. Over 64,000 fans were packed solid i
the San Bernabou Stadium. The Spaniards were pressing forwar
with United creating a couple of good goal scoring opportunitie
which should have given us an important away goal, that woul
have been useful in the second leg to be played in Mancheste
a fortnight later. The game ended in a 0-0 draw, I felt that Unite
had the better chances but had to be content with the resul
Both Tommy and myself felt that we had done enough to go o
to win the return at Old Trafford and left Madrid confident tha
United could secure yet another European Cup semifinal.

The following Saturday United didn't have a game, as ou
match had been rearranged to keep Sky TV happy, so I foun
myself travelling up to the Riverside Stadium to watch the Red
play Middlesborough. My old friend David Dyson, th
Middlesborough fan, arranged for me to stay at his house th
night after the game. He had even got me two tickets for th
match. Not many of the Stalybridge lads managed to get ticke
for this match, as Middlesborough had reduced United'
allocation due to disturbances at last season's fixture, whe
United had won 1-0. The tickets David had for us were i
Middlesborough's main stand. What a cracking match this turne

t to be. I had travelled up with Ralph Paddy Chatburn the rsenal supporter, due to Tommy Price's late decision to stay d watch the game in his pub the Top House. We met David at s house where I left my car. David then took us both on a pub awl around Middlesborough. Every where we went it was £1.00 oint, so none of us were complaining. Like I said before the me was a cracker; United came out on top winning 4-3 and th teams were applauded off the pitch by both sets of fans. I ll always remember seeing Addy Dearnley's flag with his pub me written in huge letters 'The Pineapple Stalybridge'. Another emiership title was now well within our grasp. After the game avid took us to a nightclub where Paddy and myself both got unk. David somehow got us back to his house in a taxi. In the orning, after breakfast, I thanked David for his hospitality and e then made our way back to Manchester nursing terrible ngovers.

Another North East team were the next visitors to Old Trafford. underland came and went home just as quick, after being rashed 4-0. If results went our way, another win in our next me at Southampton would ensure United were yet again emiership Champions, but before that we were to play Real adrid in the second leg of the quarterfinal in the European up. Nothing in over thirty years of watching the Reds could ve prepared me for what was in store for me at Old Trafford. al Madrid attacked from the outset. This surprised United, ey stopped David Beckham from getting his crosses into the anish area; in fact they attacked the Reds with such speed d precision football that we were 3-0 down without knowing hat had hit us. Nearly 60,000 fans were witnessing a fantastic splay by Real Madrid. United fought back by snatching two ick goals, scored by Beckham and Scholes, but it was too late, r dream of retaining the European Cup was over. Real Madrid ent on to win the Cup, easily overcoming another Spanish side alencia in the final in Paris. I watched the final in Tenerife where vas negotiating to purchase my bar Bestie's. Whilst I was over ere I also watched City overcome Blackburn Rovers. The Blues ere back in the Premier League, this match gave me the idea to ll my book *"City till I die"* as that was the song thousands of

Blues were singing when they invaded the pitch at the fin
whistle. 'I'm City till I die, I know I am, I'm sure I am, I'm City t
I die' was all I could hear from the Blues fans. It can't be bad f
the great city of Manchester to have two teams in tl
Premiership. The name became 'United till I die' after Tomn
Price remarked "do not mention the name City anywhere ne
the treble trophies."

Our next game at Southampton surprised everybody, ev
Sky TV. Results went our way and the Reds won 3-0 and we
crowned Champions with four league games still remaining
thought this was bad planning on Sky TV's part. They th
organised for United to be presented with their trophy at t
Tottenham game.

Before that game we drew 1-1 against Chelsea and had a go
result at relegated Watford. I watched the Tottenham game
my friends bar in Tenerife which is called Kormacks. Paul t
Spurs fan was surprised to see me over there. "You always cor
here for the fucking Spurs game!" he said to me. Pa
congratulated us on winning the title, then we both got dru
together and spoke about old times.

Our last match of the season was at Aston Villa, who were
the FA Cup Final the week after against Chelsea. A girl call
Helen who I had met in Benidorm when we played Valencia aw
managed to get us four tickets for the Doug Ellis Stand which
like their main stand. Helen lives in Warwick. Although s
supports Manchester City, her Dad having brainwashed her ir
it as he is a season ticket holder at Maine Road. She wanted
attend the Villa game, so I took Helen to the game along w
Tommy Price and Boss who is about twenty-four stone. V
drank from opening time at the Cap and Gown pub, until t
minutes before kickoff. The place was swarming with Unit
supporters celebrating another Championship. In the seco
half Tommy managed to get both Helen and myself into t
corporate boxes. We were the guests of LDV Aston Villa's m
sponsors. We were given five-star treatment, as much food a
drink as we could manage. We watched the full second half fr
LDV's executive box, which is exactly on the half way line, h
way up the Doug Ellis Stand. The views are superb and Hel

234

as very impressed. After the game we stayed drinking in the ee bar until closing time, which was 7 p.m.

The 1999/2000 Season had finished with Manchester United owned Champions and Manchester City returning back to the remiership, what more could any football fan ask for? Two weeks ter at the home of Ashton United FC a seven-a-side football ournament was arranged; all the monies raised would go to the milies of Eric Mitchell and Tony Braithwaite who I have already entioned earlier. Another Red who has since passed away is a an called Johnny Bent; his nickname was Bentie. John was other mad United supporter who followed the Reds in the arly sixties with the legend Tommy Price. Sadly John died of incer at the age of forty-eight, again he was a great character ho never gave anything less than 100% in everything he did. It with great pleasure that I write this book with all three of them my mind, having had the pleasure of playing football in the me team as the three of them. The trophy is named the Jet rophy after John, Eric and Tony. The competition was played ver a weekend with twenty-four teams entering. Ray Price along ith his brother Carl, Chelley, Gary Wilson, Dean Standring, Mark Loughlin, Kevin Dinsdale, Tony Ryan who is a fanatical lue, Jacko the goalkeeper and myself went through to the final, epresenting the Hare and Hounds pub Ashton, which is owned y Paul Price, Tommy's brother. We were unfortunately beaten y our great rivals from Stalybridge 3-0. It was three days after e game before I found I could walk properly, as my legs were out of condition. Nevertheless there was tremendous support or the event. John Redfern's team from Stalybridge featured ergie, Steve Vance, Dale Ellis, Warren Taylor plus other Reds; ey are now the holders of the trophy, which to me has the me importance as United winning the European Cup.

With that in mind I end this book. My dream for next season is win the European Cup, plus the FIFA World Club hampionships along with the JET Trophy, so if you are reading is book John, Eric and Tony, the lads can't wait to get revenge ext year. God bless our thoughts are always with you.

Bruce MacInnes

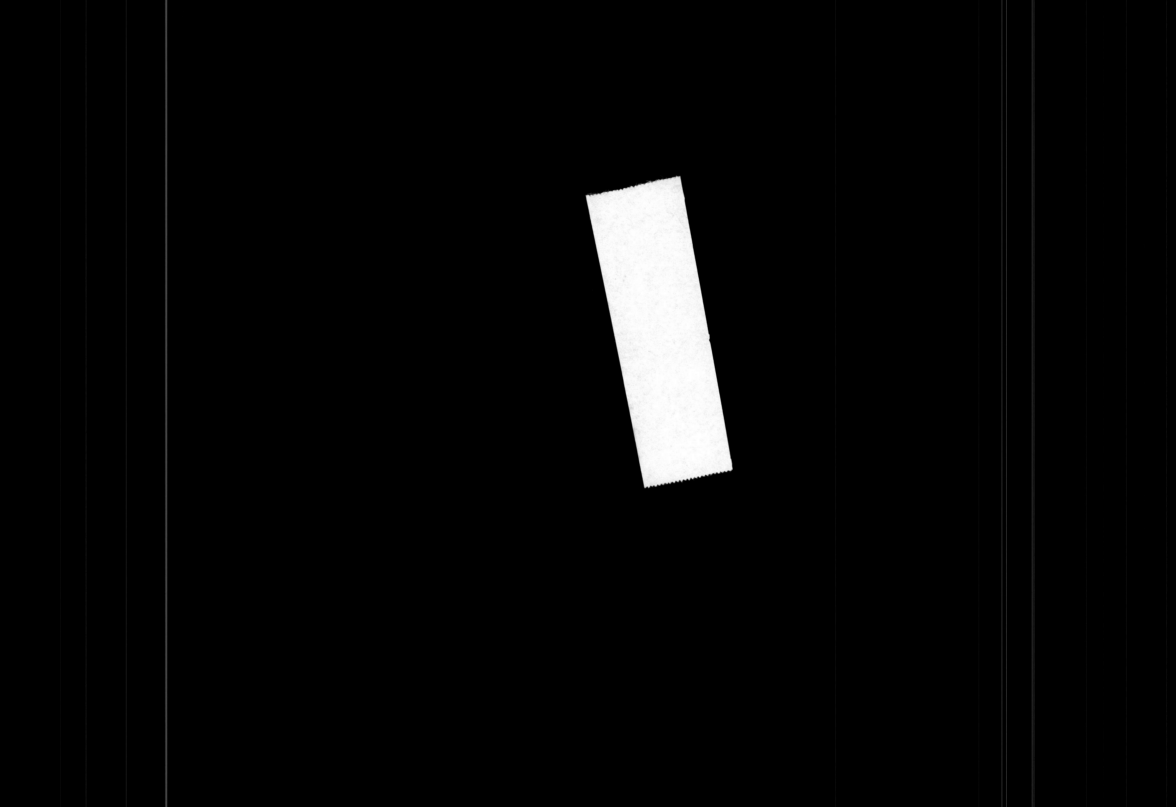

There is a team that reigns supreme,
Their name is Man United;
And when they win the League this year
Their fans will be delighted.
The finest team you will ever know;
So cheer them on their greatest show;
Because onto Europe they will go
To take the cup from Celtic.
We'll never die, we'll never die,
We'll never die, we'll never die.
We'll keep the Red flag flying high,
Because Man United will never die.

There's a placard Man United
Of the famous Busby babes;
Eddie Coleman, Duncan Edwards,
They're the greatest in the land.
They're the boys who died at Munich;
Matt Busby lived to tell the tale
Of the famous Man United,
Never will they show no fear.

Oh it's a grand old team to play for;
Oh it's a grand old team to see;
And if you know their history
It's enough to make your heart go woe, woe, woe, woe.
We don't care what the City fans say
What the hell do we care,
Cause we only know
That there's
Going to be a show
And the Busby aces will be there.

Oh if the Reds shall play
In Rome or Mandalay,
We'll be there,
We'll be there.
Oh if the Reds shall play
In Rome or Mandalay,
Tell the boys that we'll be there.
We'll be there. Where? In Gothenburg Square.
We'll be there, we'll be there,
We'll be there. Where? In Barcelona Square.
Tell the boys that we'll be there,
We'll be there. Where? In Turin Square.
We'll be there, we'll be there,
We'll be there. Where? In Munich Square.
Tell the boys that we'll be there.

Cause it's just one of those teams
That you see now and then.
We often score six,
But we seldom score ten.
We beat them at home,
And we'll beat them away.
We'll kill any bastards
That gets in our way.
We are the pride of all Europe
The Cock of the North
We hate the Scousers,
the Cockneys of course and Leeds.
We are United without any doubt,
We are the Manchester boys.

We are the loyal supporters;
Man United is our team,
And you all know
Into Europe we'll go
In the colours of the team supreme.
Cause we're off to Europe in the Red, in the Red;
Denis Law will dazzle in the sun,
Where the goals are scored,
The crowds will roar
Especially the Stretford End.
Oh, we are the champions
As you all know;
Denis Law and Busby are grand,
We will win the European Cup this year.
We're the best team in the land,
So all you City fans remember this,
We are the greatest side
And when Law goes up
To receive that cup
You're sure to hear us cry,
Bring on the Champions,
Champions of Europe, Europe, Europe.

City Song
In 1962 we went into Division Two,
The Stretford End, cried out again,
That's the end of the Sky Blue.
Joe Mercer came, he played the game;
We went to Rotherham;
We won 1-0, we made history;
We were back in Division One,
Since then we've won the League and Cup,
We've been to Europe too
And when we win the League this year
We'll sing a song to you;
City, City.

Who's that team they call United;
Who's that team they all adore;
They're the boys in red and white
And they fight with all their might
And they're out to show the world the way to score.
Bring on the Sunderland and Arsenal;
Bring on the Spaniards by the score.
Barcelona, Real Madrid,
They will make a gallant bid
But they'll know the reason why we roar.
Who's that knocking on the window?
Who's that knocking on the door?
It's Joe Mercer and his mates,
They've got Turkey on their plates,
Cause they can't get into Europe any more.

Son of a fisherman from Aberdeen;
Played for his country
When only eighteen.
His football magic was a sight to see,
And he'll lead United onto victory.
Who Denis, Denis Law?
The King of the Football League.

Oh we hate Bill Shankly,
And we hate St John,
But most of all we hate Big Ron;
And we'll fight the Kopites one by one,
And throw them in the River Mersey.
So to hell with Liverpool and Everton too;
We will show no mercy,
And we'll fight, fight, fight,
With all our might
For the boys in the red and white jersey,
United, United.

It was on a famous Saturday,
A Saturday afternoon,
A gallant band of Liverpool fans
Were singing Liverpool tunes;
They sang 'You'll Never Walk Alone',
They made a terrible noise.
It was on that same old Saturday
They met the Manchester boys,
We chased them up Piccadilly,
We chased them down Deansgate, Deansgate;
We made them sing,
Denis Law's our king
And fuck Bill Shankly's boys.

We don't carry razors,
We don't carry lead;
We only carry hatchets
To bury in your head.
We are all supporters,
Fanatics every one,
We all hate Man City
And Leeds and Leeds and Leeds and Leeds and Leeds,
We all fucking hate Leeds.
We don't carry arrows,
We don't carry bows;
We only carry crowbars
To break your fucking nose.
We are all supporters,
Fanatics every one,
We all hate Man City
And Leeds and Leeds and Leeds and Leeds,
We all Fucking hate Leeds.

Bertie Mee said to Don Revie
"Have you heard of the North Bank Highbury?"
Don said "No I don't think so,
But I've heard of the Stretford Enders."
With a knock-kneed chicken with two knock-knees,
We hate Arsenal, we hate Leeds.
City fans get on your knees
And bow to the Stretford Enders.
With a knock-kneed chicken and a bow-legged hen,
We haven't lost a fight
Since we don't know when.
We don't give a willie and we don't give a wank,
We are the Stretford Enders.

If I die in the Kippax Street woe, woe,
If I die in the Kippax Street woe, woe,
if I die in the Kippax Street
There will be ten Blue bastards
At my feet woe, woe, woe, woe, woe, woe.
What do you use?
Use your head and use your feet woe, woe.
Use your head and use your feet,
There will be ten Blue bastards at my feet,
Woe, woe, woe, woe, woe,
And if my balls do not mend woe, woe,
If my balls do not mend woe, woe,
If my balls do not mend,
Carry me back To the Stretford End
Woe, woe, woe, woe, woe.

Jingle bells, jingle bells
The circus is in town;
Come and see
Fat Francis Lee
He's our favourite clown;
Oh Alan Oates
Musical jokes,
Glyn Pardoe's too slow,
Colin Bell can go to hell
Along with big fat Joe Corrigan.

I'm forever throwing bottles,
Pretty bottles in the air;
They fly so high,
They reach the sky,
Like West Ham
They fade and die;
Tottenham's always running,
Chelsea's running too,
And we're the Stretford Enders
And we're running after you;
United, United.

Glasgow Rangers Song
Follow, follow, we will follow Rangers;
Everywhere everyone will follow on,
Follow, follow, we will follow Rangers;
And if they play in Dublin, we will follow on.
There's not a team like the Glasgow Rangers,
No not one and there never will be one;
Celtic know all about their troubles;
We will fight
Till the game is won;
There's not a team like the Glasgow Rangers,
No not one and there never will be one.

We hate Nottingham Forest,
We hate Liverpool too and Leicester,
We hate Manchester City,
But United we love you.
Altogether now . . .

We've been to Forest, we've been to Stoke,
We've been to Maine Road, oh what a joke!

We took the Kippax,
We took the Kop,
We took the Trent End,
We've took the fucking lot!

We will fight, fight, fight for United,
Till we win the Football League;
To hell with Liverpool,
To hell with Man City they're shit.
We will fight, fight, fight for United,
Till we win the Football League;
The left side will take the Kippax Street,
The tunnel and the right the Kop,
We will meet them at the River Irwell
And we'll take the fucking lot.
To hell with Liverpool,
To hell with Man City they're shit.
We will fight, fight, fight for United,
Till we win the Football League.

We shall not, we shall not be moved,
We shall not, we shall not be moved,
Just like a team, that's going to win the European Cup again,
We shall not be moved.
Don't go to Elland Road,
You'll get foot and mouth,
Don't go to Elland Road,
You'll get foot and mouth,
Just like a cow that's standing by the waterside,
You'll get foot and mouth.

Aye, aye, ya, aye,
Charlton is better than Pele,
Cause Pele is a no good bum,
And so is Eusebio.

We went down to Wembley
One fine day in May,
With lots of supporters
So happy and gay,
And when it was over and when it was done,
We defeated Benfica, by four goals to one.
The first was by Bobby
He out jumped the rest;
The second was scored by wee Georgie Best.
The crowd were all chanting
Like I never did
The third one was scored by young Brian Kidd.
The crowd were all chanting
Let's please have one more,
So Bobby obliged by making it four.
So the team to remember,
The team to recall,
Is Manchester United
The best team of all.

Six foot two, eyes of blue,
Big Jim Holten's after you.
Na, na, na, na, na, na, na, na, na
Five foot eight, underweight
Gerry Daley's fucking great
Na, na. Na, na, na, na, na, na, na.

United are the greatest
Which no one can deny,
We're here today,
We're here to stay,
We'll be here when City die.
We've won the League,
We've won the Cup,
We've been to Europe too
And when we win the League this year
We'll sing a song to you,
United, United.

My old man
Said be a City fan,
I said bollocks you're a cunt,
I'd rather fuck a bucket with a big hole in it
Than be a City fan for just one minute.

Onward Streford End, onward Stretford End,
E-I-E-I-E-I-0 into the Kippax we will go
And if we catch you wanking
We'll saw your knees right off;
Onward Stretford, onward Stretford, onward Stretford End.
Oh my what a rotten song,
What a rotten song, what a rotten song,
Oh my what a rotten song
And what a rotten singer too.

Hello, hello, we are the Busby boys,
Hello, hello, we are the Busby boys,
And if you are a City fan
Surrender or you'll die
We will follow United.

Oh my lads you're sure to see us coming,
Fastest team in the league,
Just to see us winning,
All my lads and lassies,
With smiles upon our faces,
Walking down the Warwick Road,
To see Matt Busby's aces.